T0097871

The Writings of Frithjof Schuon
Series

World Wisdom
The Library of Perennial Philosophy

The Library of Perennial Philosophy is dedicated to the exposition of the timeless Truth underlying the diverse religions. This Truth, often referred to as the *Sophia Perennis*—or Perennial Wisdom—finds its expression in the revealed Scriptures as well as the writings of the great sages and the artistic creations of the traditional worlds.

In the Face of the Absolute appears as one of our selections in the Writings of Frithjof Schuon series.

The Writings of Frithjof Schuon

The Writings of Frithjof Schuon form the foundation of our library because he is the pre-eminent exponent of the Perennial Philosophy. His work illuminates this perspective in both an essential and comprehensive manner like none other.

English Language Writings of Frithjof Schuon

Original Books
The Transcendent Unity of Religions
Spiritual Perspectives and Human Facts
Gnosis: Divine Wisdom
Language of the Self
Stations of Wisdom
Understanding Islam
Light on the Ancient Worlds
Treasures of Buddhism (In the Tracks of Buddhism)
Logic and Transcendence
Esoterism as Principle and as Way
Castes and Races
Sufism: Veil and Quintessence
From the Divine to the Human
Christianity/Islam: Essays on Esoteric Ecumenicism
Survey of Metaphysics and Esoterism
In the Face of the Absolute
The Feathered Sun: Plains Indians in Art and Philosophy
To Have a Center
Roots of the Human Condition
Images of Primordial and Mystic Beauty: Paintings by Frithjof Schuon
Echoes of Perennial Wisdom
The Play of Masks
Road to the Heart: Poems
The Transfiguration of Man
The Eye of the Heart
Form and Substance in the Religions
Adastra & Stella Maris: Poems by Frithjof Schuon (bilingual edition)
Autumn Leaves & The Ring: Poems by Frithjof Schuon (bilingual edition)
Songs without Names, Volumes I-VI: Poems by Frithjof Schuon
Songs without Names, Volumes VII-XII: Poems by Frithjof Schuon
World Wheel, Volumes I-III: Poems by Frithjof Schuon
World Wheel, Volumes IV-VII: Poems by Frithjof Schuon
Primordial Meditation: Contemplating the Real

Edited Writings
The Essential Frithjof Schuon, ed. Seyyed Hossein Nasr
Songs for a Spiritual Traveler: Selected Poems (bilingual edition)
René Guénon: Some Observations, ed. William Stoddart
The Fullness of God: Frithjof Schuon on Christianity,
ed. James S. Cutsinger
Prayer Fashions Man: Frithjof Schuon on the Spiritual Life,
ed. James S. Cutsinger
Art from the Sacred to the Profane: East and West,
ed. Catherine Schuon
Splendor of the True: A Frithjof Schuon Reader,
ed. James S. Cutsinger

In the Face
of the Absolute

A New Translation with
Selected Letters

by

Frithjof Schuon

Includes Other Previously
Unpublished Writings

Edited by
Harry Oldmeadow

World Wisdom

In the Face of the Absolute:
A New Translation with Selected Letters
© 2014 World Wisdom, Inc.

All rights reserved.
No part of this book may be used or reproduced
in any manner without written permission,
except in critical articles and reviews.

Translated by Mark Perry and Jean-Pierre Lafouge

Published in French as
Approches du Phénomène Religieux
Le Courrier du Livre, 1984

Library of Congress Cataloging-in-Publication Data

Schuon, Frithjof, 1907-1998.
  [Approches du phénomène religieux. English]
  In the face of the absolute : a new translation with selected letters / by
Frithjof Schuon ; edited by Harry Oldmeadow.
    pages cm. -- (The writings of Frithjof Schuon)
  "Includes other previously unpublished writings."
  Includes bibliographical references and index.
  ISBN 978-1-936597-41-3 (pbk. : alk. paper) 1. Religion. 2. Spirituality.
I. Oldmeadow, Harry, 1947- editor. II. Title.
  BL48.S37813 2014
  200--dc23
                                                          2014032935

Cover:
Chomolahari Mountain, Bhutan.
Photo by Joseph A. Fitzgerald

Printed on acid-free paper in the United States of America

For information address World Wisdom, Inc.
P.O. Box 2682, Bloomington, Indiana 47402-2682
www.worldwisdom.com

CONTENTS

EDITOR'S PREFACE

The doyen of American comparative religionists, Huston Smith, has rightly called Frithjof Schuon "the greatest metaphysical and religious thinker" of the twentieth century. The evidence for such a claim is to be found in Schuon's prodigious corpus of writings, including more than two dozen on metaphysical and religious subjects, composed in French, German, and English and appearing over the last five decades of the twentieth century.[1] Schuon's vocation was to reveal and expound the transcendent unity and universality of the great religious traditions while also explaining their necessary diversity and formal divergence. Schuon is the pre-eminent exponent of the perennialist "school", which also includes René Guénon, Ananda Coomaraswamy, and Titus Burckhardt, all of whom explicated the metaphysical and cosmological principles which inform the *philosophia perennis* which, in Schuon's words, is "the totality of the primordial and universal truths—and therefore of the metaphysical axioms—whose formulation does not belong to any particular system".[2] At the same time the perennialists, Schuon especially, have been concerned with preserving the particular religious forms which guarantee the integrity of the various traditions and vouchsafe their spiritual efficacy.

In discussing the spiritual temperament of the nineteenth-century Bengali saint, Sri Ramakrishna, Schuon identifies the Paramahamsa as a *bhakta* rather than a *jnānin*. Schuon explains the distinction this way:

> . . . now a *bhakta* is not a man who "thinks", that is, a man whose individuality actively participates in supra-individual knowledge and who is therefore able "himself" to apply his transcendent knowledge to cosmic and human contingencies;

---

[1] In addition to the more than two dozen books published in English translation during Schuon's lifetime, we now have published translations of his imposing poetic output as well as a series of anthologies which gather together his writings on particular themes.

[2] Frithjof Schuon, "The Perennial Philosophy", in Harry Oldmeadow, *Frithjof Schuon and the Perennial Philosophy* (Bloomington, Indiana: World Wisdom, 2010), p. 312.

on the contrary the *bhakta* attains and possesses knowledge not in an intellectual but in an ontological manner.[3]

This passage not only furnishes a key to the spiritual genius of Ramakrishna, "the living symbol of the inward unity of religions", but also alerts us to the function of the *jnānin*, one who through intellection has realized "transcendent knowledge" and who is able in more or less objective fashion to direct the light of gnosis onto the many riddles of existence. In a quite exceptional manner Frithjof Schuon combined the discriminating wisdom of the *jnānin* with the ontological plasticity of the *bhakta.* Readers can discover more about this sage of our times in Michael Fitzgerald's biography.[4]

In Part I of the present collection the author is concerned with general questions about the nature of tradition, the complementary but sometimes antagonistic relationship of the exoteric and esoteric dimensions of religion, and the metaphysical and cosmological principles germane to such subjects as evil, predestination, and eternity. In Parts II and III he focuses on some distinct aspects of the two traditions to which he so often returns throughout his *oeuvre*, the Christian and the Islamic.

Over the last half-century Schuon's writings have been brought within the purview of English-language readers firstly by Perennial Books and then by World Wisdom. Although World Wisdom has published a wide range of works, drawn from all of the world's major traditions and including books by contemporary spiritual guides and scholars, its primary mission remains the dissemination of Schuon's work. Its commitment to this goal is evident in the on-going re-translation of Schuon's books and their reappearance in fresh editions which include extensive editorial annotations and a full glossary not only of foreign words and phrases but of arcane theological and metaphysical terms—a great many of which must inevitably appear in Schuon's expositions. The recent translations are also embellished with material from the author's letters and other previously unpub-

---

[3] Frithjof Schuon, *Spiritual Perspectives and Human Facts: A New Translation with Selected Letters* (Bloomington, Indiana: World Wisdom, 2007), p. 120.

[4] Michael Fitzgerald, *Frithjof Schuon: Messenger of the Perennial Philosophy* (Bloomington, Indiana: World Wisdom, 2010). See also Jean-Baptiste Aymard & Patrick Laude, *Frithjof Schuon: Life and Teachings* (Albany, New York: SUNY, 2004).

lished sources; these more intimate and informal writings provide us with a glimpse of different facets of his spiritual genius, if one may so express it.

The essays herein first appeared in *Approches du phénomène religieux* (Paris: Le Courrier du Livre, 1984; republished 1993), and then as *In the Face of the Absolute* (Bloomington, Indiana: World Wisdom, 1989, republished 1994), translated by Gustavo Polit. The editions of 1989 and 1994 included two pieces not previously available in English translation. The present fully revised translation by Mark Perry and Jean-Pierre Lafouge follows the French original and does not include the two additional essays; they can be found in *Form and Substance in the Religions* (Bloomington, Indiana: World Wisdom, 2002).

Schuon's opus encompasses all of the world's integral mythological, sapiential, and religious traditions, whether primordial, Occidental, or Oriental. His studies are richly textured with references not only to the Scriptures of various religions but to the other writings which blossom as a tradition unfolds over time—exegeses, commentaries, tracts, spiritual manuals, hagiographies, mystical testaments, and the like. In trying to find their way through Schuon's writings many readers will appreciate some help in understanding the author's myriad references and allusions; the editorial notes at the end of this volume serve such a purpose, as well as occasionally alerting the reader to other material pertinent to the subject at hand. The Authorized Version has been used for Biblical quotations while the author's own French translations from the Koran have been rendered directly into English.

Harry Oldmeadow

FOREWORD

How is the religious phenomenon to be approached? If one wishes to go beyond the mere study of historical and psychological facts, then one will have to concede first of all that this phenomenon represents a positive reality which is simultaneously one and differentiated, in other words it is a phenomenon containing modes that are more or less equivalent as regards their essential content; this is so because "such and such a religion" is one thing and "religion as such" is another. However this axiom will be insufficient if we do not accept at the same time the supernatural character of the religious fact and not just its psychic and social character; this character is the very content and reason for being of religion and the only one rendering it worthy of interest.

To speak of religion is to speak of a meeting between the celestial and the terrestrial, the divine and the human; thus the two poles of a true "science of religions" (*Religionswissenschaft*)—or "of religion"— are metaphysics and anthropology, the science of God and that of man; or we would say "theosophy" and "anthroposophy" had these terms not been annexed by occultist societies which have emptied them of all their meaning. In order to understand what religion is, it is necessary to know not only what the Message is but also what man is—man to whom religion is destined and in whose nature it must be prefigured; if the one and universal metaphysics culminates, quite evidently, in the truth of the Absolute, integral anthropology, for its part, refers essentially to the mystery of the Intellect and thus to intellection; this is the very foundation of the human being.

It is all too well known that metaphysics has become obsolete nowadays and that it has been replaced by a fragmentary and conjectural psychology, whereas anthropology for its part has had to yield to so-called "sociology", which is not a science but a philosophy, the main defect of which is not to know what *homo sapiens* is, namely *homo religiosus*.

To know what man is, is to know what God is, and conversely; the entire science of the religious phenomenon is based on this equation and on this reciprocity.

In the following pages, just as in our previous works, there is a warp and a weft: the weft is the symbolist or traditional language and the warp is the fundamental doctrine; the weft—which is horizontal—consists in applications or in illustrations, and it is diverse like every phenomenal order in which the occasional or the "accidental" play a determinant role; in contrast, the warp—which is vertical—consists in principles or in principial factors; it is the "substance" and therefore possesses a crystalline homogeneity. This is in fact the case with the life of every man: the warp is made up of convictions and of the character, whereas the weft—the play of *Māyā*—makes up the rest; everything in the universe is woven of principles and facts, of geometry and music.

The language of religion is symbolism, and symbolism is what both separates and unites. It is the symbolism that constitutes the particularity, at once enlightening and separative, characterizing the different religions, and it is symbolism yet again that on the contrary, owing to its universal validity and its illimitation in depth, permits one to reach the *religio perennis*, to bring out the oneness of the content, and the reason for being, of the religious phenomenon.

This phenomenon accounts for the double mission of man, of the two dimensions of his *dharma*: to know the Absolute from the standpoint of the contingent, and to manifest the Absolute within the contingent.

I.

GENERAL DOCTRINE

The Decisive Intuition

The content of religions and their reason for being is the relationship between God and man; between Necessary Being and contingent existence. Now the Infinitude of Necessary Being, which is All-Possibility, implies an in principle limitless diversity of modes of this relationship; for to speak of Possibility as such is to speak of diverse, and therefore multiple, possibilities. Consequently, the diversity of religions results from the diversity of the possibilities comprised in the relationship between God and man; and this relationship is both unique and innumerable.

It is this relationship that gives religions all their power and all their legitimacy; and, on the contrary, it is their confessional claim to absoluteness that constitutes their relativity; if they have something absolute, which is indisputable, it is owing to their principle, and not to their particular mode, nor *a fortiori* because of their exclusivism and their formalism. For example, what gives Christianity all its strength is the principial possibility upon which it is founded, namely that the relationship between God and man can take on a sacrificial, redemptive, and sacramental form; by contrast, what constitutes the limitation, and in a certain sense the fragility, of this religion, is that this form presents itself as the only one possible, when in fact the relationship between God and man can, and consequently must, take on other forms; which it does much more often than not, given that the sacrificial and penitential possibility is more particular than the legalistic and obediential possibility, although each one must partake of the other. In other words: the force of absoluteness renders religion compelling because this is a possibility—hence also a necessity—of the relationship Heaven-earth; yet at the same time religion is limited and relative because it is not the very possibility itself of this relationship, but one mode amongst others of this possibility, even though this mode has to present itself nonetheless as the religious possibility as such, on pain of not being able to manifest its reason for being effectively. This paradox entails an exclusivism plainly contrary to total Truth, which alone is capable of satisfying all legitimate needs for logical understanding, and therein lies the entire ambiguity of the different exoterisms, with their disproportions and their divergences.

Hence the *religio*—a "link" that is both natural and supernatural—may manifest the very essence of the relationship Heaven-earth more or less directly, just as it may manifest it more or less indirectly and in an underlying manner by accentuating a particular mode of this relationship; this is what Christianity and Buddhism do, in presenting themselves as spiritual "innovations", whereas Islam, on the contrary, intends to be primordial and normative, universal and not original; it could also be said that the great argument of Christianity as well as of Buddhism is of a phenomenal order, whereas that of Islam is of a doctrinal order, if one may emphasize distinctive features at the risk of seeming to schematize things. Hinduism for its part tends to realize in its midst all the religious modes possible, whence its richness both dazzling and baffling; and the same holds true, in principle, for the other mythological traditions, those anchored in the night of time.

Not everything is to be rejected out of hand in the rationalist critique of dogmatist doctrines, for the inconsistencies—albeit extrinsic—encountered in the different types of religious imagery inevitably provoke doubts and protests in the absence of a sapiential esoterism that could bridge the gaps and bring the accidental dissonances back to the harmony of the substance. Moreover, the disdain dogmatist doctrines have for intelligence, which they wish to reduce to "reason", given their appeal to belief alone, is not unrelated to the fatal limitation besetting them; this being the case, it goes without saying that one is hard pressed to blame those who cannot help noticing the damages resulting from a pious unintelligence, of which the fideist camp offers only too many examples; however, that some people will draw from these observations the falsest conclusions and delight in the most abusive generalizations is another question altogether. Be that as it may, the fact that the reactions of the unbeliever and the esoterist may coincide, does not excuse the errors of unbelief, any more than it invalidates the theses of the metaphysician.

The man who rejects religion because, when taken literally, it sometimes seems absurd—since truths have to be selectively chosen and parceled out in a manner required by the formal crystallization and by the adaptation to an intellectually minimal collective mentality—such a man overlooks one essential thing, despite the logic of his reaction: namely, that the imagery, contradictory though it may be at first sight, nonetheless conveys information that in the final analysis is coherent and even dazzlingly evident for those who are capable of having a presentiment of them or of grasping them. It is true that there is, *a priori*, a contradiction between an omniscient, omnipotent, and infinitely good God who created man without foreseeing the fall; who grants him too great a freedom with respect to his intelligence, or too small an intelligence in proportion to his freedom; who finds no other means of saving man than to sacrifice His own Son, and doing so without the immense majority of men being informed of this—or being able to be informed of it in time—when in fact this information is the *conditio sine qua non* of salvation; who after having powerfully revealed that He is One, waits for centuries long before revealing that He is Three; who condemns man to an eternal hell for temporal faults; a God who on the one hand "wants" man not to sin, and on the other "wills" that a particular sin be done,[1] or who predestines man to a particular sin, on the one hand, and, on the other, punishes him for having committed it; or again, a God who gives us intelligence and then forbids us to use it, as practically every fideism would have it; and so on and so forth. But whatever may be the contradiction between an omniscient and omnipotent God and the actions attributed to Him by scriptural symbolism and anthropomorphist, voluntaristic, and sentimental theology, there is, beyond all this imagery—whose contradictions are perfectly resolvable in metaphysics[2]—an Intelligence, or a Power, which is fundamentally good and which—with or without predestination—is disposed to saving us from a *de facto* distress, on the sole condition that we resign ourselves to following its call; and this reality is a "categorical imperative" which is so to speak in the air that we breathe and which is independent of all requirements of logic and

---

[1] This is the Asharite thesis, determined as it is by the obsession to safeguard the oneness of God at all costs, as if this oneness had need of a zeal that exceeds normal limits. More prudently, the Christians—who do not have this preoccupation—consider that God "permits" sin.

[2] By means of the doctrine *Ātmā-Māyā* that explains All-Possibility, and therefore the hypostatic complexity of the Principle; all this we have treated with sufficient breadth, it seems to us, in our books.

all need for coherence.[3] No doubt this assertion of ours comprises no rational proof, but it nonetheless has the meaning and the value of a concrete vision, as we shall make clearer in what follows.

To reply to the difficulties enumerated above, it will be necessary first to agree on principial notions; hence, to begin with, what must be understood by the term "God"? From the strictly human point of view, which alone is what religions as such have in view, "God" could not be the Absolute in itself, for the Absolute has no interlocutor; we may, however, say that God is the hypostatic Face turned towards the human world, or towards a particular human world; in other words, God is Divinity that personalizes itself in view of man and insofar as it takes on, to a greater or lesser extent, the countenance of a particular humanity. Another question: what does this personalized Divinity, this God become a partner or interlocutor, or this divine Face turned towards man, what does this God "want" or "desire"? The most concise answer possible seems to us to be the following: if the divine Essence, being infinite, tends to manifest itself—so as to project its innumerable potentialities into the finite—the divine Face, for its part, brings about this projection and then—at a more relative level—projects within this first projection a principle of coordination, namely, among other things, a Law intended to regulate the human world and above all to regulate this miniature world that is the individual. This Face is thus like a sheaf of rays with various functions, but it is a Face that, while pertaining to the same divine order, does not however constitute a single subjectivity with a moral intention; thus it is vain to seek behind the infinitely diverse combinations of the veil of *Māyā* an anthropomorphic and humanly graspable personality.[4]

Religious formulations confine themselves to enunciating points of reference without being overly concerned with outward coherence, even though, from another point of view, the mythic and symbolical

---

[3] It is upon this imperative fact—"logical" or not—that Pascal's wager is based, a fact which finds further confirmation in the universal and immemorial experience of men.

[4] This is what the various "polytheisms", and no less so Mazdean dualism, are fundamentally aware of.

image always evokes a profound and living reality: the story of Adam and Eve may clash with a certain need for logic, but we bear it deeply within ourselves, and it is this inherence of the sacred image that justifies it, on the one hand, and, on the other, accounts for a relatively easy adherence to it. Aside from this, it is precisely the surface contradictions, the fissures so to speak which, by a crowning paradox, offer the decisive points of reference for the discovery of the metaphysical homogeneity of doctrines or symbols that seem at first sight to be completely dissimilar.

A few lines above, we expressed a crucial truth that answers the following question: why is it that the Revelations, by accepting the inconvenience of certain contradictions in their postulates and symbols, accepted the risk of scandal and did not deem it necessary to forestall the danger of unbelief? There are two reasons for this: firstly—and this is the main reason—the sacred truth is part of our soul; hence the archetypal symbol is to be found in the deepest layer of our consciousness or of our being; secondly, in disdaining a certain logical plausibility, Revelation subjects us to a quasi-initiatic trial, which shows that faith coincides in the final analysis with virtue—not with a superficial moral quality, but with the virtue of our substance,[5] and this second reason is obviously premised on the first. Man realizes or actualizes virtue of substance by practicing the virtues that are accessible to his immediate will, and he does so in and through faith, precisely; and it is this underlying virtue, joined to immanent and archetypal truth, that produces in the consciousness what we may term the "decisive intuition"; that is to say, our mental and volitive behavior actualizes the values of our substance, just as these values determine our behavior. Of course, the object of the decisive intuition is not the extrinsic limitations of the religions—not the over-accentuations, narrownesses, and ostracisms—but their intrinsic and therefore universal truths, for

---

[5] Before the fall man identified with this substance, but has been separated from it ever since, which precisely requires a methodic effort of realization; all of this is at the antipodes of Rousseau's simplifications. It is this initial separation that the anthropological pessimism of Saint Augustine wishes to explain.

an error could not be an archetype, nor could it stem from a virtue; nevertheless, the exoterist acceptance of these "providential errors" cannot hinder either the intuition in question, nor, quite obviously, virtue, otherwise exoterism would not exist.

The inherence of Truth in our spirit is, in principle, of a nature capable of conferring direct and plenary certitude, without an element of "meritorious obscurity"; if *a priori* it offers only enough of a minimal intuition—but in any case decisive—it is because in "fallen"—hence exteriorized—man there is a veil separating him from the inner light while nonetheless allowing a glimmer to filter through; unless the veil—or series of veils—is rent and gives rise to the Platonic anamnesis, which the religions situate in the next world—in that case it is the "beatific vision"—but which plenary esoterism aims at rendering possible in this very life, if only to a degree which, if it is not unitive, at least pertains already to a supernatural participation.[6]

An important factor to note, which results in fact from our previous considerations, is that the absence of religious intuition derives all too often, and even necessarily so, from a fault of character, of pride above all; and it is known that pride is able to accommodate all the virtues so long as it can poison them, thus emptying them of their substance. Unbelief is excluded, or almost so, in the midst of a traditional society owing to the pressure coming from the surroundings; but in a world where this pressure scarcely exists or even no longer exists at all, it is much easier for moral defects to have an effect on thought, to the point of influencing it in a decisive manner. Under normal psychological and social conditions, to have virtue is practically speaking to have faith, not necessarily a particular faith, but certainly faith as such. It is true that in a milieu determined by unbelief one often, or almost always, professes to have certain moral qualities, but at bottom it is to prove to oneself that one has no need of religion and that man is good by nature.

— ⸖ —

---

[6] As Virgil said: "Happy is he who has been able to know the profound reasons of things". This association between happiness and knowledge is far from being fortuitous, on the contrary it indicates the profound—and moreover evident—identity between wisdom and beatitude. *Sat, Chit, Ānanda.*

The virtues that on the one hand ennoble the individual and on the other enable collective life, result fundamentally, whether one is conscious of it or not, from the conviction in a transcendent Absolute and in the immortality of the soul;[7] these two convictions, to the degree they are sincere and concrete, necessarily produce the essential moral qualities in man, and if these convictions come to be lacking, the qualities disappear *ipso facto*, slowly perhaps, but inexorably. Doubtless, it is possible to conceive of a virtue existing outside of all doctrinal rootedness, but even in this case it is, by its very nature, predisposed to having the two convictions in question, which is to say that virtue pertains to man in the same way as does religion. Consequently, their disassociation can be only artificial and accidental. In this sense virtue is a proof of God, as is intelligence: virtue which permits man to surpass himself, and intelligence which is capable of conceiving the Absolute. And, it is in fact moral liberty and intellectual objectivity that constitute *a priori* man's deiformity.

Another point that we wish to raise is the following: two indisputable proofs in favor of religion and consequently of the decisive intuition that is faith—indisputable for he who has grasped the language of phenomena and who for that reason possesses both the sense of the sacred and the sense of proportions—these two proofs are the phenomenon of sanctity and that of art, because the saints and sacred art are theophanies before being human glories; these two phenomena greatly surpass the capacity of the ordinary man, and even infinitely so in a certain sense, which obviously is not the case for natural virtues nor for specifically profane works.[8] Sanctity is diverse just as art is diverse, but each attests to one and the same spiritual reality; it is thus that the divine Face turned towards man makes itself diverse, because God is infinite, and that this Face remains fundamentally one, because He is absolute.

---

[7] We say "transcendent Absolute" and not "God" in order to forestall the objection that the Buddhists are "atheists", which is the case neither from the point of view of metaphysical reality nor from that of the human attitude, whether mystical or simply moral. The same remark holds true, *mutatis mutandis*, for the immortality of the soul, the reality of which is not negated by the insistence upon our relativity.

[8] As regards art, the comparison between the styles before and after the Renaissance is particularly eloquent with respect to the point being made here. It should not be overlooked that traditional craftsmanship always keeps a certain contact with the sacred and the spiritual.

Were sanctity and sacred art to prove nothing as regards religion, hence as regards the immortal soul and the metaphysical capacity of man, sanctity and sacred art would be nothing, and man himself would be nothing. For man's theomorphic nature does not allow him to be, in his capacity as man and in God's creative intention, something fragmentary or incomplete—which cuts short the absurdities of transformist evolution[9]—but, on the contrary, requires that he be something that is everything, and that would be nothing if it were not everything; and it is in this sense that it has been said that man's fundamental vocation is to "become what he is".

[9] This theory amounts to saying that the center of a circumference is as relative as any other point on the surface.

The Ambiguity of Exoterism

Cathedrals often, and perhaps even always, contain intentional irregularities meant to signify that God alone is perfect and capable of perfection; or, that human works, like man himself, are necessarily imperfect. And this applies to the entire universe, hence to all that is not God; "Why callest thou me good?" said Christ. It is not surprising, therefore, that this principle will also include the domain of the sacred—we have just mentioned cathedrals—and above all religions themselves; thus humility as well as the sense of reality demand that we not be overly shocked by the dissonances we may encounter in celestial ambiences on earth; that we not be annoyed, for example, by certain "providential excesses". The natural shadows, in a particular earthly beauty, do not prevent us from seeing that it is still beauty; they do not prevent us from beholding it with gratitude and to sense that the earthly reflection transmits an archetype that is flawless. Given that he who judges is himself not exempt from imperfection and must be aware of this, by what right then and with what logic would he require that other cosmic phenomena be exempt from it? "God alone is good."

— ⋅⋮⋅ —

The term "exoterism" designates three different orders: firstly, a system of symbols and means; secondly, a way; and thirdly, a mentality. The first category embraces dogmas and rites, and then legal, moral, and other prescriptions, and liturgy in the widest sense; the second embraces the general religious practices, those that are incumbent upon everyone; and the third category comprises the psychism corresponding to a particular religious climate, thus all the manifestations of sentimentality and imagination determined by a particular religion, a particular piety, and particular social conventions.

In other words, it is important to distinguish the following aspects in exoterism: the formal system, that offers symbols and means; the exoteric way, that is based exclusively upon this system; and the exoteric mentality, that is formalistic, voluntaristic, and individualistic, and that adds all kinds of restrictive sentimentalities to simple forms. These are three altogether different meanings of the term "exoterism": according to the first, the religious Law is necessary and venerable, and it becomes a constitutive element of esoterism; according to the second meaning, the Law is different from esoterism without necessarily excluding certain elements of the latter; according to the third meaning, there is an antinomy between the "outward" and the "inward", or between the "letter" and the "spirit".

It is of the highest importance not to confuse these three levels; in particular, not to lose sight of the fact that the first—Dogma and Law—is available to esoterism as regards both interpretation and practice. In order to determine whether a spiritual support is exoteric or esoteric, the question is to know not only what doctrinal and legal forms are involved, but also "who" accepts and practices them, and thus "how" they are accepted and practiced. In Dogma and Law, only those aspects are exoteric that are restrictive if taken literally, but not the aspects of pure symbolism and thus of universality.

When, on the contrary, there is an exclusively literal interpretation of the ideas and symbols on the one hand, and a voluntaristic and sentimental practice of the rites and prescriptions on the other—and this individualism corresponds to an anthropomorphic conception of the Divinity—then the way itself pertains to exoterism; the "believer" accomplishes what the divine Person has ordained, and abstains from what He has forbidden; he does so in view of salvation and without necessarily concerning himself directly with the nature of things as regards human attitudes and divine intentions.

What we have just said shows that the exoteric way cannot be entirely disassociated from the exoterist mentality; nevertheless, extremes—notably pedantry and fanaticism—are independent of religious practice as such; religious practice can inspire human temperaments and comportments, but it is not inseparably linked to them by definition, this is only too obvious. Dogmatic and legal exoterism is of divine institution; the exoterist mentality has a right to exist so long as piety compensates for the abuses, but it has nothing supernatural about it; its rights coincide more or less with those of human nature.

Dogmatic exoterism, as we have mentioned more than once, exhibits providential limitations determined by its mission and thus by its reason for being; to begin with, it excludes the idea of universal relativity—of *Māyā*—and therefore is unaware of the diverse and at times antinomic "aspects" of things, as well as of the "points of view" expressing them; this amounts to saying that it identifies itself with a particular point of view determined by a particular aspect. By excluding the notion of *Māyā*, exoterism situates itself entirely within *Māyā*, the summit of which is the personal God who creates and legislates; *Paramātmā*, the supreme Self—Boehme's *Ungrund*—could not produce a world or found a religion. But religion could not be closed to the total truth, for God is one, and there where the divine Person is, there also is the divine Essence;[1] this Essence is accessible through esoterism, precisely, by full right and despite a certain inevitable opposition on the part of the exoteric framework.

One has to realize that outward religion is not disinterested; it wants to save souls, no more no less, and at the cost of the truths that do not serve its holy strategy. Wisdom, by contrast, wants only the truth, and the truth necessarily coincides with our final interests because it coincides with the Sovereign Good.

In Hinduism, as in other archaic traditions—to the extent that they have kept a sufficient vitality—the relationship between exoterism and esoterism presents itself in another way than in the Semitic religions: the exoteric is that which is merely of social relevance, or what is taken literally; whereas the esoteric is not what of itself pertains to pure metaphysics—*Advaita Vedānta* is not technically an "esoterism"—but what for some reason or other, social especially, must be kept secret.

Hinduism—like the religions of ancient Europe moreover—is not exclusively interested in the salvation of souls; it is true that it tries to prevent men from falling into hell, but it abandons them to transmigration, which in monotheistic language amounts to the same thing. Among the ancient Europeans—Greeks, Romans, Celts, Germans—

---

[1] When it is said that the personal God is situated in *Māyā*, which runs the risk of being ill-sounding, one must be careful to make it clear that this God is the Supreme Principle "entering" into universal Relativity, hence still "Supreme" despite the "entering"; this enables one to affirm that God the Creator and Legislator is at one and the same time *Ātmā* and *Māyā*, or *Ātmā* in *Māyā*, but never simply *Māyā*.

only the initiates go to Paradise, and possibly also the heroes, who then are likened to the initiates; the others remain in the darkness, in some underworld Hades, which practically speaking combines the state of the perishable psychic elements along with the great unknown that the transmigration through non-human and extraterrestrial states represents. Thus the reproach of "paganism" on the part of the Semitic religions is not altogether unjustified, except of course as regards initiates, Platonists, and Vedantists.

But it is not enough to notice the difference—or even the divergences—between religious perspectives and their exo-esoteric structures; our need for logic requires essentially a knowledge of the causes, which result *a priori* from the refraction of the divine Light in the cosmic darkness. The "descent" (*tanzīl*) of the Koran signifies that the organizing Will of the personal God—namely the Principle that upon contact with *Māyā* becomes personalized, and thus limits itself by virtue of the universal radiation required by the very nature of the Sovereign Good—enters into a collective soul determined by particular racial and ethnic factors; that this organizing Will of God enters therein with "temporal" as well as "spatial" purposes, that is to say that it has in view eschatological destinies as well as immediate social situations; succession and the afterlife as well as simultaneity and the earthly city. In descending into a collective soul, the divine Word becomes refracted into the possibilities of this soul: it becomes Judaized, Arabized, Hinduized, or Mongolized, according to each situation; and in making itself human it cannot maintain its original majesty and beauty in every respect or modality; the human state requires the small and the ambiguous and cannot live without it; however, unalloyed greatness, transcendence, and harmony subsist always in the supernatural substance of the revealed Word. Christ is "true man and true God"; the same is true for every Revelation; this is what must never be forgotten when one encounters elements that seem at first sight too human—to the point of seeming implausible—in the ever-varied stream of the divine Messages.

To understand, at least morally, certain apparent contradictions in the Scriptures, the following principial situation must be borne in mind: divine All-Possibility is ontologically "prior" to the divine Personification; hence, divine All-Possibility pours into creation what is ontologically possible; It is a manifestation of Infinitude, inevitably contrasting and amoral because it includes in a certain manner the impossible owing to the limitlessness of Possibility itself. By contrast, the divine Personification, which hypostatically reflects the essential Goodness of the Essence, coordinates the chaos of possibilities and "desires" the good, whence precisely the half-divine, half-human phenomenon that is Revelation.[2]

The ambiguity of exoterism is largely a consequence of the complexity of the divine Order; we say "divine Order" to indicate that we have in mind here not the Principle in itself, but its "extension" within universal Relativity.[3] Now exoterism, which must restrict itself to being a minimal doctrine, so to speak—whatever the mode of its emphasis—cannot render an account of this divine Order, both transcendent and relative,[4] without allowing enigmas and pitfalls to remain, or rather, without creating them.

A typical feature of the monotheistic exoterisms is their dogmatization of theological speculations; it is the position not only of wishing to "dot all the i's", but to do so at the level of "faith", and hence of dogmatic constraint—this being the role of the councils and of promulgations *ex cathedra*—whereas it would suffice in many a case to let scriptural enunciations stand as they are, in a holy indetermination that excludes no aspect of truth and does not crystallize one aspect to the detriment of the others. In fact, the problem here lies less in the existence of speculations and specifications—for men cannot be

---

[2] This precisely is the Muslim *distinguo* between the ontological "Will" of God and His moral "Desire"; the weak point in the theory is that it attributes two hypostatic degrees to one and the same anthropomorphic subjectivity, as we have noted more than once. According to Ibn Arabi, God confines Himself to "bringing into existence" that which "wants to exist"; He is not "personally" responsible for the possibilities as such.

[3] See our book *Sur les traces de la Religion pérenne*, chapter "Dimensions, modes et degrés de l'Ordre divin".

[4] A divine Order purely transcendent at its summit, relative in its reverberation as *Māyā* and yet transcendent in this aspect as well, at least in relation to the world. The mystery of mysteries—noted in the West by Meister Eckhart—is that there is in our Intellect a "divine point" which rejoins pure Transcendence, of which we would otherwise have no notion; and moreover it is this point that explains the possibility of the "central" phenomenon which is man.

prevented from thinking—than in wanting to settle matters dogmatically once for all; one brandishes the threat of hell not only for those who doubt in God and immortality, but also for those who dare to harbor doubts about some exorbitant theological conclusion; and this threat is all the less plausible given that in any case one postulates the incomprehensibility of God while preserving the idea of "mystery" as a safety measure allowing one to avoid the question if necessary. The more one specifies things *ex cathedra*, the more one increases the chances of scission and the risks of persecution, which would not be the case were one to remain content with a level of "admissible" or "probable opinions" to one degree or another.[5] There is no point in objecting that pure metaphysicians do as much, for it is not the action of explaining or specifying which is at issue here, but the formalistic and therefore restrictive character of the specification, and above all the binding dogmatization that is added to it, for this in no way fits into the intentions and functions of pure and disinterested knowledge.[6]

Given its mission, exoterism has to take into account the weaknesses of men, and thus also, be it said without euphemism, their stupidity; like it or not, exoterism must itself take on something of these shortcomings, or at least it must allow them some room, on pain of not being able to survive in human surroundings. Thus one must not be too surprised, nor above all scandalized, at the paradoxical phenomenon of pious stupidity; in truth, this phenomenon is far from being harmless, for it sometimes affects the canonical domain, but it cannot not exist since religion addresses itself to everyone and everyone must be able to recognize themselves in it, if matters may

---

[5] One example of ostracism by exoterists is the case of the Pope Honorius I, accused of "heresy" in a disproportionate manner, to say the least; for the idea that Christ has only one will, the divine—this is the Monothelite thesis—takes nothing away from the glory of Christ, quite the contrary, since it is based upon the axiom that there is nothing in the nature of Christ that could be opposed to the divine Will. All in all, it is a simplistic and "implausible" theological opinion—since the human will certainly exists in the soul of Jesus—but this does not render the opinion subversive; it is an ellipsis, and it would have sufficed to take note of its intention, or to leave it unspecified.

[6] In contra argumentative confessionalism, those among the American Indians who retain a traditional outlook point out that one can always have a discussion about concepts, but not about the immutable symbols of virgin nature; and that books are perishable, whereas the symbols of the Great Spirit abide; what matters is to understand them. This argument is far from simplistic when one considers things in depth, and it even coincides with the Koranic doctrine of the divine "signs" ($\bar{a}y\bar{a}t$) in the world.

be so expressed. A climate of religious belief appeals to emotivity, and emotivity is obviously opposed to perfect objectivity, at least when it goes beyond its rightful limits; when it does so, excessive emotivity damages the power of reflection or even—with all due reservations—intelligence itself, while plainly favoring a fundamental sentimentalism, extending from an initial biased attitude to harmless prejudices.[7] However: remove emotivity from religion and you kill it; moreover, a stream has need of banks in order to flow, and likewise exoterism, or the religious form, has need of limitations in order to be a living influence; "grasp all, lose all", as a proverb has it.

The exoterist mentality is largely nurtured by associations of ideas inspired by religious imagery: for example, in Islam, the sun does not enjoy an unmixed prestige—as is shown by certain symbolisms very unflattering to it—because of the danger of becoming a rival with God and because of the sun-worship cults that existed in the Near East. Aside from this imagery, and prior to it, the Koran speaks of the sun, moon, and stars as slaves upon whom God has imposed forced labor (*sakhara*) in the service of men, and then it enjoins men not to bow down to the heavenly bodies; thus it is considered advisable, whenever one looks upon the sun or the moon, to say that "God is greater" (*Allāhu akbar*). Analogous remarks apply to fire: whereas for the Indo-Iranian, or simply Aryan traditions, fire is sacred like the sun—Agni and Surya being theophanies—in the monotheism of the Semites it takes on a malefic coloration because of its association with hell.[8] Christianity, which is not based upon the jealousness of Unity, does not have such worries regarding the sun, as is proved by the "Canticle to the Sun" of Saint Francis of Assisi; for the Christian, it

---

[7] Very typical of the sentimental, and paradoxically individualistic humilitarianism, is the following opinion of a Hesychast: to remember God constantly is not a great thing; on the contrary, what is great is to believe oneself lower than all other creatures. A surprising ignorance of the sacramental quality of the Name of God is combined here with a strange misappreciation of the qualities and merits of holy perseverance, and with a no less strange abdication of intelligence in the name of virtue. "He that raiseth up himself shall be brought low": which could not mean that humility is incompatible with that prerogative of man which is discernment, hence objectivity; besides, one may well wonder whether "to make oneself low in order to be raised up" is really humility. Such inconsistencies, it is true, are not the sorry privilege of any one religion.

[8] How far we are here from Heraclitus, for whom fire—or rather its divine proto-type—is at the origin of everything.

17

is all too evident that the sun is not God or that it is not Christ; thus he can love the sun in all innocence and without the least complex of guilt. An ancillary question that might arise here is the following: should a Westerner who has serious motives for following the Sufic path be obliged to adopt the Muslim attitude towards the royal luminary—we have chosen this example among others—that is, should he feel obliged to experience an imaginative and sentimental reaction that he does not have and cannot have? Clearly not, and all the more so since essential Sufism could never require it; for the confessional mentality is one thing, and spiritual realization another.

But let us return to the Arabs: in a curious departure from the sensibility we have described above, the expressions "Sun of Princes" (*Shams al-Umarā*), "Sun of the Learned" (*Shams al-ʿUlamā*), "Sun of (spiritual) Guidance" (*Shams al-Hudā*), and others are honorific titles; and "Sun of the Religion" (*Shams ad-Dīn*) is a man's name, whereas "Like unto the Sun" (*Shamsī* or *Shamsiyyah*) and "Sun of Daytime" (*Shams an-Nahār*) are women's names—all of which evoke the unanimous sentiment of primordial man, or of man as such, and thus of esoterism. Moreover, when the Koran declares that "God is the Light of the heavens and the earth" (*Sūrah* "Light"), it is impossible, by the very nature of things, for the sun to be completely excluded from this hierarchy, even though no Muslim could acknowledge this, except perhaps in an esoteric setting. Be that as it may, all these considerations on the solar luminary also apply, to one degree or other and in an appropriate manner, to the moon and even to the stars: "Full Moon of the Religion" (*Badr ad-Dīn*) and "Star of the Religion" (*Najm ad-Dīn*) are masculine names; "Like unto the Full Moon" (*Badrī* or *Badriyyah*), "Star" (*Najmah*), and other images of the kind are feminine names.

In the Koran, the sun is described three times as a "lamp" (*sirāj*), and this word is also applied to the Prophet, whence his name *Sirāj*, which—we have been told—establishes a scriptural and liturgical connection between Muhammad and the sun.[9] This "rehabilitation" of the sun, and above all its indirect glorification by proper names and

---

[9] It should be noted, however, that the image of the lamp is less disturbing to Muslim sentiment than that of the sun, for no one is tempted to worship a handmade object, even if it is a symbol of light. When praying in a mosque, the believer necessarily bows down in the direction of the lamp in the *mihrāb*; he would not do so in the direction of the sun.

other metaphors, seems to indicate that the sensitivity of Muslims is not overly affected by the pejorative symbolism in question nor by the sacred ostracism of the theologians;[10] all of which has to be granted with some reservations, for the "incriminating evidence", in the form of certain classical formulations, cannot be brushed aside entirely. A further remark while we are on the subject: in Muslim imagery, rain holds a privileged rank, as is easily understood in a desert country; the Koran misses no opportunity to mention it with praise, and the Prophet loved to uncover his head in the rain because of the blessing it brings.

In passing, and before going further, we would like to say a few words concerning the integration of a foreign element into a particular traditional formalism; this problem places us between syncretism, which is intrinsically heterodox, and esoterism, which in certain cases can admit such coincidences. This is because, in principle, esoterism is "open to all forms", as Ibn Arabi expressed himself in speaking of his heart; but in fact, such exceptions depend upon certain subjective as well as objective conditions; therefore we must ask, not only what has been done, but also by whom and for what reason.

In esoterism there are two principles which may be actualized sporadically and at different levels, but always in a partial and restrained manner: the first is that fundamentally there is only one religion with various forms, for humanity is one and the spirit is one; the second principle is that man bears everything within himself, potentially at least, by reason of the immanence of the one Truth.

The only plausible explanation for the theological excesses of an Ashari, aside from religious zeal, is the principle of "functional" truth—not "informative" truth—of which we have spoken above; what is "true" is not necessarily what gives an adequate account of a reality, but what serves a particular psychological purpose in view of salvation and in relation to a particular mentality. From this stand-

[10] The same is true for the question of secondary causes: the average Muslim does not doubt that fire has the attribute of burning, notwithstanding the Hanbalite or Asharite hairsplitting regarding this.

point, heresy is not objective error, it is subjective inopportuneness: it is better to reach Paradise with a limb missing than to be thrown into hell with all of one's limbs; this principle, purely moral and mystical in the intention of Christ, becomes intellectual or doctrinal in the domain of certain theological speculations. If Ashari maintains that fire does not burn by its own nature, that it burns only because God decides to bring about the burning, this is because the faithful have to be convinced that "God is without associate", despite the evidence that He surrounds Himself with Angels and Prophets;[11] and if this same doctrine goes so far as to affirm that evil comes from God, otherwise it could not occur, or that God can impose obligations that man is incapable of accomplishing, or that God can make a creature suffer—or even punish it—for no reason and without compensation, or that, being free from all obligation, He can do "what He wills" with man, and that consequently it would not be unjust for Him to send the good to hell and the bad to Paradise[12]—if the Asharite doctrine upholds such preposterous affirmations, this is finally for the sake, rightly or wrongly, of waging preemptive warfare against certain vicious predispositions in man and in the context of a particular mentality—doubtless heroic, but prone to heedlessness and insubordination.[13]

[11] And despite the idea that every single drop of rain is sent down by an angel, and other inconsistencies of the kind.

[12] Asharite atomism is just as absurd, for it stems from a defective conception of causality: from the inability to see —or refusal to understand—that physical causes, far from being excluded by metaphysical causes, on the contrary manifest or reflect them and are relatively real precisely by virtue of the absolute reality of their prototypes *in divinis*.

[13] All these excesses are contradicted by the Hanafite theologian Maturidi, who considers that man's freedom is relatively real and not imaginary, and that God "desires" (*ridā*, "being pleased") only good actions; that when He demands something of the creature, God confers upon it *ipso facto* the capacity to do it; that injustice is incompatible with the divine nature, and not that injustice is justice when the doer is God. Let us add that prior to Maturidi, the Mutazilites had the merit of teaching unambiguously that God is obliged to be just to men; an obligation freely assumed and resulting on the one hand from the divine Perfection itself, and on the other from the intelligent and responsible nature bestowed by God upon the human creature. It might be paradoxically said: if divine nature were to allow God to claim all rights in all circumstances, He would not have created man; a formulation worthy of Zeno of Elea, yet not devoid of meaning.

Different opinions may be held as to the legitimacy or efficacy of such strategems, but what matters here is not their quality, but their purpose, namely the guiding principle of "functional truth", which is indirect and conditional and not direct, informative, and categorical.[14] The "laissez-faire" of the Holy Spirit in theological matters—if one may so express it—can be explained, in short, by the necessity of having to take into account the limited capacities of the majority and consequently of having to renounce the intellectual element to a greater or lesser extent, and to emphasize all the more the moral and emotional element as well as eschatological interests. Muhammad knew whereof he spoke when he asserted that "disagreements (*ikhtilāf*) between the doctors of the Law are a Mercy": differences of opinion are all the more useful in that it is impossible to satisfy the needs of a collectivity of believers by presenting a homogeneous metaphysical doctrine; something more is needed, even in religion, for "it takes all kinds to make a world".

There is room neither for polytheism nor idolatry in Islam; and yet they are to be found in it, insofar as they can have a positive and thus legitimate meaning: "Muslim polytheism" is represented by the ninety-nine Names of God, and "Muslim idolatry" by the Kaaba and the Black Stone, the Kaaba being prolonged by the prayer niche in mosques. One could object that these are not images; true enough, but they are nonetheless material objects, objects situated in space; a tree is not an image either, and yet if one were intentionally to pray towards a particular tree, while disregarding the canonical direction—the *qiblah*—Islam would term it an idol. Logically, and strictly speaking, Muslims ought to pray with their eyes closed—which they do not—and without regard to a ritual direction; abstraction would then be complete; but in fact, they pray before something visible—the *mihrāb*—and in the direction of another visible thing, the Kaaba. Thus it can be seen that the purism of a religion is necessarily relative when it is a question of things that have their justification in themselves and, moreover, are opportune.

---

[14] Despite the support given by Ghazzali to the extreme opinions we have quoted above, Sunnite theology has hardly retained them; the great majority of Sunnites, despite being Asharites, side in practice with the ideas of Maturidi, which can be considered as "reasonable".

Iranian and Indian Muslims,[15] and even certain Arabs, are not afraid to practice the art of painting, even though the *Sunnah* forbids it; it is true that there are differences of opinion as to whether the prohibition of images refers simply to statues, which "cast a shadow"; but the predominant attitude of the *'ulamā* is plainly hostile towards figurative art, and allows for no exceptions. Here again, one has to take into consideration the motive of the Law, namely the tendency of the Semites towards idolatry; the Aryans do not have this tendency, which means that they are not idolaters when they worship images; the Hindus—except in cases of popular deviation—are in the end no more idolaters than the Christians, who certainly are not. Logically, Christians should be as iconoclastic as Jews since they base themselves on the Bible, but in this case as in others, it is the instinct for the "nature of things" that has prevailed and that has even given rise to certain modes of spirituality; the sacramental icon conveys graces and works miracles.

Let us add that music and above all dancing fall into the same category of traditional ambiguities; disapproved of in Islam, they are nonetheless practiced in Sufism, always by reason of the profound justification conferred upon them by that universal criterion which is the nature of things. Inopportuneness is neither error nor wickedness, and there can always be cases wherein opportuneness changes sides, not only because men differ, but also—and above all—because man is one.

An example of excessive formalism—and of a conventionalism which is definitely superstitious—is provided by certain garments of Muslim women: in Islamic India there are certain ways of veiling women that have something truly sinister about them—they are like walking prisons or phantoms—which is contrary to nature to say the least, and which demonstrates to what extent the exoteric spirit can be pedantic, blind, and cramped; by contrast, the veil of Moroccan women is morally and aesthetically plausible, being so to speak "one point of view among others". In the Maghreb, Berber women go unveiled—this should be recalled here—and the same is true for many

---

[15] We mean the Iranians in the proper sense of the term, and not the Persians alone. It is moreover curious to note that the heads of government of foreign countries involve themselves with issues that are strictly the business of the French Academy—a frequent occurrence nowadays; and yet this Academy is not concerned with the question of knowing what France is called in Siamese or in Singhalese.

Muslim women in the black and yellow races, not to mention other examples difficult to classify; which shows that there is nothing essential about this convention of dress from the point of view of the Law.[16]

In all climates of formalistic over-saturation, the instinct for the "nature of things" or for the archetypal and primordial norm regains the upper hand sporadically; while this is not technically an expression of esoterism, it is nonetheless in keeping with its spirit, namely with the disinterested and universal vision of good and evil, of what is useful and useless, beautiful and ugly, and also, it must be said, of what is serious and ridiculous, or human and monstrous, as the case may be.[17] And it is normally one of the functions of esoterism, not to play the *muftī* or the *pandit*, but to bring visible forms as well as moral behaviors back, as far as possible, to the serenity of a Paradise lost, but still accessible in the depth of our hearts.

From the standpoint of pure or total truth, the unavoidable drawback of the Semitic or monotheistic religions is that they reduce man to a privative or negative aspect of the average man, to a "minimal aspect" if one will: Christianity defines man as a "sinner" who must do penance, whereas Islam defines him as a "slave" who must simply obey and whose intelligence exists merely to register orders; it is true that this is not all of religion, and also that it is not without justification at a certain level or given a certain end in view, but this reduction nonetheless suffices to create misunderstandings and uneasiness on a higher level and, above all, to open the door to the abuses of sentimentalism. Moreover, if it lies within human possibility to present the most stupid ideas in the most intelligent manner—which is the case of modern philosophers—the converse must be possible too, namely

---

[16] The prescription to "hide one's charms" allows for many an interpretation, including the most paradoxical since modesty can sometimes be focused on the face alone.

[17] As for the gratuitous hyperbolism of certain kinds of religious language, it is important not to confuse it with symbolism in the proper sense of the term, which in any case is not a matter of style. Let us note in this connection that for the Westerner it is difficult to conceive that exaggeration pure and simple can form part of eloquence, although this should have occurred to someone; this is the same as with Columbus' egg.

that the most intelligent ideas be presented in the most stupid manner, as happens precisely in religions.

Regarding the general question of the balance between faith and intellection, or between their respective rights, this question cannot be solved juridically, for it depends upon personal imponderables; the imbalance between the two points of view or domains is consequently a kind of natural calamity, but man is what he is.

And yet it is in the nature of things that there be means of regulating this balance, by taking into account the factors of harmony in the world and in our spirit. We have in mind here the complementarity between the sense of the true and the sense of the beautiful; the sense of what is evident and the sense of the sacred; now the second intuitive capacity contributes towards regulating the demands of the first. The wise man sometimes abstains from asking himself questions, not because he despairs of his intelligence, but because his sense of beauty imposes upon him a limit, not of darkness, but of light; moreover, there is no sacred science without some modes of holy ignorance. Otherwise the Absolute would enter *tale quale* into the relative, and the Infinite into the finite; Necessary Being would cause contingency to burst and there would no longer be either relativity or, consequently, existence and existing wisdom.[18] To speak of manifestation is to speak of limitation.

When two religions have to exist side by side, as in India, or in Palestine at the time of the Crusades, two things happen: on the one hand a stiffening on the part of the formal religion, and on the other a greater flexibility and a certain interpenetration in the domain of spirituality; it is true that religions exist side by side everywhere, but what we have in mind here are those cases where there is virulent antagonism,

[18] The Koran expresses this as follows: "(O man), follow not that whereof thou hast no knowledge. Lo! the hearing and the sight and the heart—of each of these reckoning will be asked. . . . They will ask thee concerning the [universal] Spirit (*Rūh*). Say: The Spirit is by command of my Lord [by radiation or hypostatic prolongation], and of knowledge [of divine mysteries] ye have been vouchsafed but little. And if We [God] willed We could withdraw that which We have revealed unto thee. . ." (*Sūrah* "The Night Journey" [17]:36, 85-86).

unmitigated by habit and indifference. A crucial truth emerges from such confrontations and reciprocities: from the moment a man has grasped the validity of a religion other than his own—the comprehension of which results from concrete experience as much as from intellectual intuition—God cannot but take into account the widening of this man's spiritual perspective as well as the awareness he will have of the relativity of forms as such; God, therefore, will absolutely not demand of him what he asks of believers who are totally enclosed in the formal system of their religion, yet at the same time He will make new demands. Knowledge is not a gift that entails no obligations, for all knowledge has its price; the "minus" on the side of formal religion will have to be compensated by a "plus" on the side of non-formal religion, which coincides with the *sophia perennis*.

Esoterism, with its three dimensions of metaphysical discernment, mystical concentration, and moral conformity, contains in the final analysis the only things that Heaven demands in an absolute fashion, all other demands being relative and therefore more or less conditional. The proof of this is that a man who would have no more than a few moments left to live could do nothing more than: firstly, look towards God with his intelligence; secondly, call upon God with his will; thirdly, love God with all his soul, and in loving Him realize every possible virtue. One may be surprised at this coincidence between what is most elementarily human and what pertains quintessentially to the highest wisdom, but what is most simple retraces precisely what is highest; *extremitates aequalitates*, "extremes meet".

The Two Problems

From the standpoint of a piety nourished by anthropomorphism, the question of predestination and the question of evil are the two great problems. But from the standpoint of metaphysical knowledge, the only problem is that of expression through language; the difficulty therefore lies in the fact that the cumbersomeness of language requires almost endless prolixities.[1] Be that as it may: on the principial plane, there are no unsolvable questions, for all that "is" can in principle be known, the human spirit being total—not partial as is animal intelligence. The real and the knowable coincide, not for the rational faculty no doubt, but for the Intellect, whose presence—actual or purely potential—constitutes the reason for being of the human condition.

If the questions of evil and predestination appear as unsolvable problems to the average believer, it is because theology, owing to its anthropomorphism, cannot get past a halfway point; it personalizes the Supreme Principle excessively, and this shows that it has an insufficient idea of what we term the "divine Order". Doubtless there is no impenetrable partition between reason and intellection, but intellection cannot enter fully and decisively into a thinking that is beholden to dogmatic crystallizations and their corresponding sentimentalities.

The Absolute by definition includes the Infinite—their common content being Perfection or the Good—and the Infinite in its turn gives rise, at the degree of that "lesser Absolute" which is Being, to All-Possibility. Being cannot not include efficient Possibility, because it cannot prevent the Absolute from including the Infinite.

Possibility has so to speak two dimensions, one "horizontal" and one "descending", or one "qualitative" and one "quantitative", ana-

---

[1] At the opposite pole of the unavoidable complication of abstract dialectics stands visual symbolism, or simply symbolism as such, which presents all the aspects of a problem at once, but without thereby furnishing the keys that would allow everything to be deciphered.

logically or metaphorically speaking. The first contains the indefinitely diverse qualities and archetypes, whereas the second projects them in the direction of "nothingness" or impossibility; in moving away from its source—namely pure Being—the second dimension coagulates the qualities and archetypes on the one hand and on the other manifests their contraries; whence ultimately the phenomenon of contrastive manifestation, and consequently of evil. Being, which coincides with the personal God, cannot prevent evil because, as we have said, it cannot abolish—and could not wish to abolish—the Infinitude of the pure Absolute.

And this resolves the following difficulty: if God is both good and omnipotent, why does He not abolish evil? Does He not wish to, or can He not do so? For the reasons we have just indicated, He cannot abolish evil as such—and He could not wish to abolish it because He knows its metaphysical necessity—but He is able to and wishes to abolish particular evils, and in fact, all particular evils are transient;[2] the cosmogonic unfolding itself is transient since universal Manifestation is subject to phases and becomes reabsorbed "periodically" into the Apocatastasis or the "Night of Brahmā".

In one sense, the Absolute is beyond good and evil, but in another sense it is the very essence of goodness, which is to say that It is the Good as such. The Absolute is neither good nor evil insofar as It determines, by the radiation of Its Infinitude, the genesis of what we term evil, but It is good in the sense that every conceivable good testifies to Its essential nature; evil as such could not have its root in the pure Absolute, nor in that "lesser Absolute" which is Being, the personal God. Moreover, evil ceases to be evil when it is seen as a metaphysical necessity contributing to that "greater good" which is, on the one hand, the contrasting manifestation of the good and, on the other, the reabsorption that transforms every evil into the Good which is both initial and final; *ad majorem Dei gloriam.* As regards the root of the problem, we could also express ourselves as follows: the absolute Good has no opposite; a good that has an opposite is not the absolute good; "God alone is good".

---

[2] Even hell; something that theology, for reasons of moral opportuneness—and in this respect rightly so—could never acknowledge explicitly. We shall return to this topic in another chapter.

If one were to say that supra-ontological Infinitude—or onto-logical Possibility that projects It—is "good" in the contrastive sense normally meant by this word, then the objection that evil does indeed exist could be raised; but, in relation to this indirect causation of evil—whether of privation or excess—one has to say that Possibility is beyond this opposition; it is "amoral", one might say. In another respect however, that of the intrinsic and positive nature of the Supreme Principle, it must be recognized that efficient Possibility or the personal God, as well as *a fortiori* the Infinitude of the impersonal or supra-personal Divinity, has to be defined as the "Sovereign Good".

Parallel to the problem of evil—which calls into question both the Omnipotence and the Goodness of God, and which exists only due to the anthropomorphist confusion between the impersonal Divinity and the personal God—there is the problem of predestination, which calls into question man's freedom on the one hand, and therefore his responsibility, and on the other hand both the Goodness and Justice of God. Here too the solution of the difficulty lies in the distinction between Being and Beyond-Being, or between the "lesser Absolute" and the "pure Absolute": predestination could not derive from a "will"—which in that case would necessarily be arbitrary—of the personal God; it derives from pure Possibility, whose source, as we have said, lies in the Infinitude of the Absolute. From this standpoint it can be said that a creature is a possibility, and a possibility is what it is, hence, in a sense it is what it "wants to be"; destiny is one of its aspects among others. The individual "wants" to be what he "is", and it could even be said, more profoundly, that he "is" what he "wants": what his possibility wants—or wanted initially—is the very one he manifests.

Everybody agrees that free will is what distinguishes man from animals; however, no one can deny that compared to a bird in a cage, a bird who escapes is free; the relative character of this freedom takes nothing away from the reality it represents and possesses. Therefore, even the freedom of an animal unquestionably exists, but it goes without saying that the existence of a thing does not mean that it is absolute; to deny absoluteness does not amount to denying existence, as is only too obvious.

When addressing Himself to the individual and to the collec-tivity—which by definition is made up of individuals—the personal God makes Himself an individual: that is to say, He creates a religion which is necessarily particular and formalistic and which for that reason could not be universal as regards its form, any more than an individual as such can represent or realize universality. By contrast, the impersonal Divinity does not create religions: the divine Self confers universal truth and the corresponding sanctity from within by enlightening the Intellect and by penetrating into the Heart; this presupposes that the Heart be without blemish, without passions, and without errors, and thus that it have reintegrated primordial purity.

But God is one, and there is no question of acceding to immanence while going counter to transcendence, or of approaching the impersonal Divinity against the will or requirements of the personal God; for example, by doing so outside of a religious framework.

Assuredly, theologies have the right to use simplifying and moralizing stratagems demanded by their sphere of action, but human intelligence—to the extent that it is capable of rejoining its own substance—has nonetheless the right to know, beyond moral and other interests, the simple nature of things, even within the divine Order. The theological point of view cannot, in practice, refrain from attributing to the personal God—who is within the domain of *Māyā*—the features of the impersonal Divinity, which alone is above *Māyā* or Relativity; but the pure Intellect—hence man in principle—can go beyond *Māyā* since it is essentially capable of conceiving the pure Absolute, which is beyond *Māyā*, Relativity, and Being. Therefore, man is not absolutely subject to God the Person, or to God-*Māyā*; he is subject insofar as he is an individual, but not in every other respect, and that is why the *pneumatikos* is "a Law unto himself", which evokes the whole question of the immanence of the Truth and the Way in principle; we say "in principle", thereby insisting strongly upon this reservation, for not every man is a *jīvan-mukta*.

Plainly, we find ourselves here at the limits of the expressible, where there is only one choice: either to take upon oneself the task of furnishing points of reference that cannot exclude paradoxes, complications, ellipses, and the other disadvantages of thought and language, or else to abstain from satisfying certain needs for logical understanding, pressing as they are, and confine oneself to asserting that "God doeth what He will", and that the "potter" need not render account to the "pots" he has fashioned according to his good pleasure. However, by refusing to take into account the needs for logical understanding to which man has a right in principle—since these needs stem from the total intelligence that characterizes the human species—one opens the door to luciferian usurpations and thereby to the most pernicious errors and denials, those which affect all that constitutes man's reason for being.

Therefore, man essentially has the right to ask certain questions: "in principle", we said, for in fact there is the original fall, which obliges religions—and thus theologies—to treat man like a child or like an invalid; yet fallen man is not all of man, and as a result there are problems—or rights and duties—against which it would be vain to legislate according to the "letter" of the Law.

Be that as it may, metaphysical explanations have two functions, one *de jure* and the other *de facto*: to furnish information—and thereby keys—to those who are qualified to receive it, and to free from errors those who have contracted them upon contact with false ideologies; in the latter case, the role of wisdom will be *a priori* to allow those who have lost their faith to recover the capacity to believe in God, and all the graces resulting therefrom.

The Notion of Eternity

If one conceives of Eternity according to the proper sense of the word, as that which is beyond duration and therefore having neither beginning nor end, one then understands that this quality could not be attributed to created things. Yet this is what the eschatological dogmas of Monotheism do, or appear to do, when they teach us on the one hand that hell exists and, on the other, that it is eternal; we start with this example because, in practical terms, it is by far the most paradoxical and the most problematical. In other words, if religion sets out in part to inform, it also heeds a concern for moral efficacy, and this to the detriment of the metaphysical exactness of the message; but such exactness is not a pressing concern from the standpoint where exoterism places itself. We readily agree that the notion of a hell situated in time, and that would therefore be transitory, would lose its exacting power over many men, at least in a certain ethnic sector; however, attributing eternity to the infernal fire is nonetheless a two-edged sword in the final analysis, as the history of free-thinking proves.

It is true that in Islam the notion of a hell that is all but absolute is mitigated, or even transcended, by some reservations that are decisive in themselves but that are not necessarily given priority: thus the Koran calls hell "perpetual" (*khālid*), but adds "unless God should will otherwise"; the Prophet even declares explicitly that hell will have an end.[1] Ashari bases this same idea on the essential Mercy (*Rahmah*) of God which, according to the Koran, "reacheth unto all things",[2] and he seems to have had the merit of disseminating this thesis among most Sunni Muslims; according to other information however, the theologians do not agree on this point, despite the *hadīth* just quoted.[3]

---

[1] The same declaration is made by most doctors of the *Torah*, whose authority holds sway in Jewish tradition since antiquity.

[2] Or "encompasseth" (*wasi'at*) every thing (*Sūrah* "The Heights" [7]:156). According to this principle of Mercy, the *Dhyāni-Bodhisattva* Jizo (Kshitigarbha) makes his beneficent appearance even in the hells.

[3] As regards the Koranic reservation, some have interpreted it as meaning simply that God is all-powerful and "doeth what He will".

Some proponents of the Asharite idea maintain that, while neither the Koran nor the *Sunnah* provides any proof of the cessation of chastisement, neither do divine Revelation and prophetic inspiration provide any proof to the contrary—that the Koran would affirm only the perpetuity of hell and not of its torments—and they conclude from this that the question is better not debated in public. However, apart from the fact that their opinion appears hardly defensible to us, it must be realized that the *de facto* contrast between the rigor of the Koran and the mildness of the Prophet—if one may so put it—is a dialectical antinomy and not an inconsistency: each of the traditional sources enunciates an aspect of the Real in an almost absolute fashion, as if it were a closed system, in order to forestall either solutions of convenience or positions of despair.[4] Ibn Arabi's conclusion is, in substance, that it is for the sages to break through this barrier of formal and providential incoherences.

In Christianity the prevailing and quasi-dogmatic view favors the idea of an eternal hell; sin, it is argued, has something infinite about it because of the infinite dignity of God that it offends, and consequently chastisement too has to have something infinite about it. They forget that the sinner for his part has nothing infinite about him and is therefore not even capable of offending God infinitely; they forget above all—and this is the classic objection—that a thing which has a beginning must also have an end, or that a thing created cannot possibly have an attribute of the Uncreated. We could also say that man does not in fact measure up to the divine gift of freedom since he is capable of so misusing it as to damn himself, which proves that he cannot deserve a chastisement that is symmetrical with the dignity of God. Man is not unlimited; to man's limit corresponds the limit of chastisement; hell's limit is man's.

It seems inconceivable that no reservations should have been formulated in the Christian world regarding the "eternity" of the pains of hell, and in fact we recollect having read something of the sort in Saint Thomas Aquinas; however, supposing that no Christian authority has deemed it useful or possible to formulate such reservations, this does not mean that the motive was only moral opportunism or pure and simple ignorance; for the "eternity" of hell, or "damnation", does not

---

[4] A classic example of this type of antinomy is the complementarity—*a priori* unresolved—between predestination and free will.

only mean an endless punishment, it also, and even *a priori*, signifies a definitive exclusion from the human state, this being what Brahmanists and Buddhists understand by "transmigration"; and this exclusion, while not definitively infernal, is definitively non-human—in other worlds than our own—which in the monotheistic perspective amounts to the same thing; he is "damned" who in the end loses the human condition. Therefore the word "eternal" is synonymous here with the word "definitive", not as regards suffering but as regards exclusion from the human Paradise. This interpretation underlies, in principle and as an esoteric possibility, each of the monotheistic eschatologies.[5]

But let us return to the standard notion of an unending chastisement: this notion—which is specifically exoteric, its symbolism notwithstanding—is not unconnected with the temptation of atheism, and we have already alluded to this. In fact the argument concerning the infinite dignity of God which would, if offended against, demand a sanction proportionate to it—hence also infinite in a certain fashion—can only reinforce the position of the atheist who will then contend that a God who is perfect and thus essentially good could not avenge Himself infinitely and needlessly on a creature whose sin, as the case may be, consisted only in forgetting God or in yielding to a passion. Our response will be that the dogmatic image of a God who judges man "from without" is insufficient; in reality this image results from the fact that the sinner judges himself "from within", that is to say, from his own substance and by virtue of the relationship between cause and effect. On the one hand, man does what he is, and, on the other, a particular fault has a psychological consequence entailing particular cosmic consequences, which religious anthropomorphism likens to a "judgment", and rightly so, since the universal Norm judges

---

[5] If, in the canonical prayer of Islam—the *Fātihah*—"those upon whom is Thy Grace" (*an 'amta 'alayhim*) are saved, and "those upon whom is Thine Anger" (*maghdūbi 'alayhim*) are the damned, "those that go astray" (*ad-dāllūn*) could well be they who are cast forth into the endless round of transmigration; cast forth as such, according to an inherent meaning and not to a traditional interpretation, which would be unthinkable in a monotheistic milieu.

phenomena; yet "it is not God that wrongeth them, but they wrong themselves", the Koran says.

When Saint Thomas says that the chosen do not pity the damned, his intention is to stress the identification, in the damned, between the subjectivity and the perversion,[6] whereas Buddhist compassion, on the contrary, is based on the phenomenon of suffering alone; both positions are justified from the standpoints that they respectively emphasize; thus what counts is to know how to put each thing in its place, that is to say, to conceive of the concrete modalities these standpoints entail. Let us add that skeptics who deny the afterlife, because they believe neither in a virtue that could deserve Paradise nor in a vice that could deserve hell, are fundamentally ignorant of human nature, of its substance and its possibilities; their postulate is that of a leveling humanitarianism in whose name the highest human values are denied—those which constitute man's reason for being—in order to be able to declare that the bad man is good; now to claim that he alone is good or "sincere" takes but a single step.

From the viewpoint of Islam, a man is damned because he does not believe that God is One; but what interest, one might wonder, would God have in our believing that He is One rather than manifold? In fact God has no such interest, but the idea of Unity determines and introduces a saving attitude of coherence and interiorization that detaches man from the hypnosis, both dispersive and compressive, of the outward world that is uncertain in all of its modalities; without this unifying attitude man becomes excessively exteriorized and thereby dissipated, hardened, and lost; it is man, not God, who has an interest in believing that God is One. Inwardness, which cannot be imposed straightaway on every man, is anticipated in a framework of Law that makes human life coherent in relation to the universal Norm and in view of the Sovereign Good; every religion takes the measures that are indispensable, but each one with different points of emphasis, for the governing idea is not necessarily that of ontological unity as presented by Islam. Clearly it is not the diversity of points of emphasis that needs

---

[6] His purpose is likewise to suggest that nothing can diminish the beatitude of the chosen, which is nourished on the divine Reality; for in that Reality there can be nothing privative, pure Being coinciding with Plenitude. This, at least, is the essential dimension of beatitude; but, it does not in fact preclude another dimension turned towards contingencies, even those that are extra-paradisiacal, without however leaving the atmosphere of the "beatific vision".

to be highlighted here, it is solely the fact that after the fall—however one may picture this—man is bound to the exteriorizing and imprisoning powers of the lower *māyā*, so that the only means of saving him is *a priori* a key-idea that opposes this *māyā* and that determines and introduces corrective and saving measures. Man damns himself not solely by reason of having committed a mortal sin, but because he remains in the initial state of sin—the state that is precisely the nature of fallen man and from which religion alone can deliver him. Man is not damned for not believing that God is One, or that Christ saves, or that the world is illusory; he becomes lost because, not believing it, he remains at the mercy of the dehumanizing powers of centrifugal *māyā* which appear to be envious of the unique chance that is offered by the human state. When it is said that not to believe in this or that "offends God", this means basically that man courts perdition unless he grasps a particular "lifeline", as a verse of the Koran says.

"Unless God should will otherwise": this basic reservation in the Koran concerns not only the perpetuity of hell, but also that of Paradise which will be transcended—or "absorbed"—in the end by the mystery of *Ridwān*, the divine "Good Pleasure", and this leads us back to the eschatological cosmology of Origen. In this terminal dimension which in reality is "without beginning and without end", there can be no diminishment—quite the contrary: beings are reintegrated into their timeless and uncreated essences, into what they have never ceased to be in their quintessential reality. It follows from this that it is far less incorrect to speak of the eternity of Paradise than of the eternity of hell, and this asymmetry is indeed so obvious—when one takes into account the nature of the Sovereign Good—that we see no point in insisting on it with endless and apologetic arguments. It is consequently the eternity of hell that constitutes a great religious problem; not that of Paradise, which opens out onto pure Being, onto That which is.

Scriptural anthropomorphism does not disturb those who, while not necessarily being metaphysicians, have sufficient perspicacity to grasp intuitively its plausible intentions; but it does disturb those "free-thinkers" who apply a purely mechanical and thereby even an ill-willed logic to the literal meaning of symbolisms; this has nothing to do with the legitimate critical mind—that is, with the awareness we may have of the imperfection of a particular dogmatic or theological manner of speaking—for this awareness comes not from our ignorance but, on the contrary, from our knowledge of what these expressions imply.[7] Whatever the case may be, it is important not to confuse dogmatic expressions with theological explanations; we may accept the apparent contradiction of the former thanks to our intuition, but we are not bound to accept likewise every piece of theological reasoning—such as that of the consequences of the infinite dignity of God—and it is not even possible to do so when the opinion contains a flagrant absurdity, even if not perceptible to the simple believer. It is true that lame arguments are eroded by time, on the one hand because even the fideist is a thinking being and, on the other, because doubt increases with the regression of faith and hence of intuition; what is left is mere rationality with no spiritual background and that is unjustified, not because of its logic as such, quite obviously, but because of its superficial and fragmentary nature. It is then that pure metaphysics, or gnosis if one will—so long maligned by the spokesmen of fideism—should intervene, for it alone offers the necessary information that enables the rights of intelligence to be combined with those of human weakness.

At the risk of repeating ourselves, we should like to insist once more upon the following point: if ancient or medieval man—these designations being approximate—found it easy to accept arguments that were naive and finally provisional, this was not only because he accepted in advance the dogmas that these arguments were meant to illustrate, but also because these arguments themselves had the power to ignite in him intuitions of truth. But worldliness and material progress ended up weakening piety and faith along with it, hence also intuition.

---

[7] A marginal note: the images and accounts of the sacred Scriptures, quite apart from their literal meaning and various symbolical significations of a principial nature, apply equally to an endless series of outward and inward situations; that is to say, they are like archetypes of everything that has a moral or spiritual meaning. Every type of holiness in particular and every saintly destiny is foreshadowed in that iconostasis which is Scripture.

On the one hand there is the man who is philosophically naive but intuitive as regards the supernatural;[8] on the other there is the man gifted with critical sense but insensitive to that which transcends him; the ideal, quite clearly, is a discernment resulting not from the purely outward rationality of the logician and empiricist, but from an intellection that, by its very supernaturalness, also coincides in its dynamic dimension with the "Faith that moves mountains". It follows from all that we have said above that what is needed is a logical explanation that is realistic, intuitive, sober, and thereby legitimate, as opposed to one that is arbitrary, aggressive, skeptical, and thus illegitimate; and it goes without saying that the arguments of metaphysics have to satisfy only the former. When Saint Paul says that the pots must not argue with the potter, his intention is to close the door not so much to wisdom as to a curiosity that is *a priori* insatiable; such an attitude of principle no doubt goes too far—since the dividing line cannot be set in stone—but it has the advantage of putting a firm stop to a thinking that has lost the sense of the sacred and, for that very reason, the sense of proportions.

The temptation to make of Eternity a cosmic attribute would not occur if, through human preoccupations, one did not lose sight of the fact that Eternity is what we could call—for want of a better term—a "dimension of the Infinite". Eternity or Immutability, like Omnipresence or Immeasurability—God as "Time" and as "Space"—result in fact from Infinitude, Eternity referring more to Transcendence and to Rigor, and Omnipresence more to Immanence and to Gentleness; these relationships call to mind the complementarity of Shiva and Vishnu.[9] One might say that Infinitude itself is substantially connected

---

[8] The sense of the supernatural and the sacred was not lacking in the pagan Semites, for they had an irresistible need to worship something, be it the golden calf or the idols of Mecca; therefore the analogy between the pagans of antiquity and modern disbelievers can only be partial.

[9] Too often has it been maintained that space and time are categories pertaining exclusively to the physical universe and that beyond these "limiting conditions" there is nothing of the kind; this is to forget, by overstating transcendence, the relationship of immanence, for which physical—or possibly psychosomatic—categories are no more than a translation of heavenly and divine categories into perceptible terms.

with the Absolute, for the Absolute radiates precisely through its dimension of Infinitude and by virtue of its nature as the Sovereign Good, therefore as a result of its essential tendency to impart itself.

The divine Omnipresence, while constituting a threat to the proud and the evil-doers—and there is no "mortal sin" without pride—has on the contrary something reassuring and consoling for those who are good, and who, moreover, represent the norm; the Omnipresent is the refuge that is accessible everywhere, hence those who love God are nowhere separated from Him. By contrast, the divine Eternity, while nourishing the hope of the man who knows he is in exile here below and who aspires to the heavenly homeland, has something cold and terrifying about it seen from the point of view of earthly dreams, for the Eternal is He who is enthroned immutably above the evanescent things of this world below; He seems to look upon them with the implacability of the stars. Thus the Name "the Eternal" is synonymous with Majesty; while the Omnipresent is near, the Eternal is distant. The two aspects meet and merge in their common Infinitude, hence in Divinity as such.

When the Bible recounts that "the Eternal" speaks and acts, one might object that this sounds contradictory, for that which has the quality of Eternity can no more enter into time than the Absolute can enter into contingency; now this apparent contradiction is in fact the key to ontology: it signifies that without the Eternal, temporal things would not exist; without the Absolute there would be no contingent order; this is tantamount to saying that the Divine must always be able to make itself perceptible to men, either indirectly in its existential traces or directly through its theophanies. "Water takes on the color of its container", a Sufi said, and it is thus that divine Reality, transcendent in itself, enters into the temporal order without departing from its Immutability. "True man and true God": this is the entire mystery of the "manifestation of the Void" (*Shunyāmūrti*); the sun is unaffected by what it shines upon. The phenomenon of the miracle is ontologically indispensable because the meeting between the Eternal and the temporal is possible and necessary; the archetype of the miracle is the eruption of the Absolute into contingency. And this eruption would be inconceivable if contingency were not, precisely, "something of the Absolute".

II.
CHRISTIANITY

The Complexity of Dogmatism

Every religious confession claims the guarantee of perpetual assistance of the Holy Spirit, and rightly so inasmuch as a confession that is valid in itself—hence having the power to save, if not to lead to every mystical summit—could not contain an intrinsically false dogma or a totally inoperative rite; but this assistance is nonetheless always relative, given that Revelation itself is relative in relation to absolute Truth—the *Sophia Perennis*—otherwise there would not be different Revelations;[1] the total assistance of the Holy Spirit is only for the total Truth. One thing that should not be forgotten is that the purpose of religions is the divine wish to save men bound by passion, and not to present an explanation of universal Principles and of the world; in consequence, the Holy Spirit claimed by Christianity is more a savior than it is a metaphysician, at least as regards its manifestation on the religious plane; it is more concerned with warding off that which, for a particular mentality, is detrimental to salvation, than with rectifying doctrinal errors that are more or less a matter of indifference in this respect.[2]

Intrinsically "orthodox" dogmas, that is, those set in view of salvation, differ from one religion to another; hence they cannot all be objectively true. However, all dogmas are symbolically true and subjectively efficacious, which is to say that their purpose is to create human attitudes that contribute in their way to the divine miracle of salvation. This, in practice, is the meaning of the Buddhist term *upāya*, "skillful means" or "spiritual stratagem", and it is thanks to this efficient intention—or this virtually liberating "truth"—that all dogmas are justified and are in the final analysis compatible despite

---

[1] Let us note, however, that archaic traditions do not have exclusivist dogmas; Hinduism in particular, combines a multiform symbolism with one of the best articulated and most explicit of metaphysical doctrines.

[2] Thus it is illogical, to say the least, to wish to contrast the "wisdom of Christ", whose purpose is to save and not to explain, with the "wisdom of this world"—that of Plato for example—whose purpose is to explain and not to save; be that as it may, the fact that the Platonic wisdom is not dictated by an intention to save does not imply that it is of "this world" or "of the flesh", or even that it does not contain any liberating virtue in the methodic context required by it.

43

their antagonisms. Thus the denial of purgatory by Protestants results, not from an exhaustive cosmology, quite clearly, but from a psychological or mystical economy based upon the saving power of faith; now obviously, faith does not save by itself, but does so in connection with the divine Mercy which, in Protestantism, is crystallized in the unique Sacrifice of Christ. In such perspectives, the dogmatic concept does not contain its end within itself, that is, in its capacity to inform; it is merely a means in view of a result, and in this case it can be said without hesitation that "the end justifies the means"; this observation applies to all religious concepts that are objectively contestable, on condition, of course, that they issue from archetypal truths and pertain to intrinsically orthodox systems. The abrupt contrast between the dogmas of Christianity and Islam is, within the context of Semitic monotheism, the most salient example of these formal antinomies; it is obviously impossible for both parties to be right, or for them to be right in the same respect, but it is possible—and necessarily so—for each to be right in its own way, from the point of view of the respective "saving psychology"; and thus by virtue of the results.

In eschatological logic, the Catholic dogma of purgatory results from the idea of justification through works, whereas the Protestant denial of purgatory results from the idea of justification through faith. On the Catholic side, it will be objected that the denial of purgatory leads to lukewarmness and thus compromises salvation; on the Protestant side, it will be thought on the contrary that the idea of purgatory compromises saving trust (the *prapatti* of the Hindus) and leads to the excesses of penitentialism and the abuse of indulgences; in both cases the reproaches are unjust, even though each side contains an element of truth. Be that as it may, if the Protestant denial of purgatory leads to ease and carefreeness, as the Catholics think, and if from the Protestant point of view the idea of purgatory leads to the cult of works to the detriment of faith, Hindus and Buddhists, with no less reason, could express analogous objections against the monotheistic idea of an eternal hell: they could make the point that this concept not only is absurd in itself since it is an abuse of the notion of eternity, but also that it favors despair and in the final analysis unbelief and indifference. The transmigrationists will therefore think that the Protestant rejection of purgatory is neither worse nor better than the monotheistic rejection of transmigration, for this latter concept also has, and necessarily so, its psychological, moral, and mystical virtues.

Thus it is proper to distinguish between "informative" dogmas, that have a direct import, and "functional" dogmas, whose import is indirect: the first serve to communicate metaphysical, cosmological, or eschatological information; the second determine moral and spiritual attitudes. Although purely functional dogmas, if taken literally, may possibly be erroneous, in the final analysis they rejoin truth by their fruits.

It will be understood that all this does not mean that divergent dogmas are equivalent for the simple reason that they have their justification in one way or another, for two contradictory theses cannot be right in one and the same respect; all we wish to point out here is the distinction between informative and functional dogmas, although the dividing line between them is not absolute. If the objection were raised that the denial of purgatory by the Protestants is false since purgatory exists, we would reply firstly that for the true "believer"—and for him alone—this denial means in practice that Paradise is accessible through the merits of Christ; secondly, the Orthodox also reject the idea of a place of expiation because, according to them, souls can no longer gain merit after death, even though they may benefit from the prayers of the Church, which adds an element of compensation; for the Orthodox, as for the Muslims, "purgatory" is the hell from which the divine Mercy has removed particular souls.[3] Next, we would make the point that if the Protestant rejection of purgatory is false—or to the extent that it is false—the Hindu and Buddhist idea of reincarnation, taken literally and not metaphysically, is also false; now the immense majority of Hindus and Buddhists take reincarnation quite literally, not in an arbitrary manner, but in accordance with the literal

[3] To the objection that their dogma is false, the Protestants would reply that they do not deny hell and that God always has the power to save whom He will, which rejoins the opinion of the Orthodox Church and of Islam; however, certain Anglicans accept the idea of purgatory. Let us add that this idea, aside from other motivations, is justified because the sector in hell where the door remains open from above differs, necessarily, by that very fact, from the sector without such an opening, and this for quasi-metaphysical reasons.

meaning of their Scriptures;[4] while this is inadequate as regards cosmic reality, it is not so as regards a specific spiritual psychology.[5] From the point of view of this psychology, the question is not that of knowing what some dogma includes or excludes, but what we draw from it.

Another materially inexact dogma, albeit not functionally pointless, is that of the reduction of animals to dust after the "resurrection of the body": our objection is that the subjectivity of a superior animal is far too personal to be reducible to nothingness: now "nothingness" here is in fact synonymous with "transmigration". Since the notion of transmigration is not admissible in Semitic monotheism, one replaces it by that of "nothingness", and thus extricates oneself from a doctrinal responsibility that a monotheistic theology cannot take on, given that it has to remain centered upon man and the human.

A so to speak classic example of a functional dogma is the denial in the Koran of the crucifixion of Christ; it is true that this denial has been interpreted by some Muslims as meaning simply that Christ was not vanquished, just as Abraham, thrown into the blaze, was not vanquished by the fire,[6] or in the same manner as Daniel, in the lions' den, was not vanquished by the beasts; however, general feeling upholds the literal meaning of the passage.[7] Aside from the fact that the denial of the Cross closes the door to the Christian perspective, which Islam quite evidently was not meant to repeat, this denial contributes indi-

---

[4] Where there is a literal meaning, there is also a legitimate possibility of a literal interpretation: since the Law of Manu teaches that a given sin entails a given rebirth among animals, there are necessarily men who believe it, despite the cosmological transpositions of the symbolism made by others. This gives us an opportunity to insert the following remark: according to certain information, devotional Buddhism is said to teach that women have access to the Paradise of Amitabha only after undergoing a masculine rebirth; this opinion is not only illogical within the framework of Amidism, but is also contrary to numerous accounts issuing from this school.

[5] The idea of reincarnation is equivalent—not by its content but qualitatively—to the conviction that the earth is flat and that the sun circles the earth; in both cases there is "naivety" through lack of experience and also lack of imagination; but this "optical illusion" nonetheless has its use symbolically and psychologically.

[6] "We (*Allāh*) said: O fire, be coolness and peace for Abraham!" (*Sūrah* "The Prophets" [21]:69).

[7] It should be noted that the idea that Christ was not crucified but was taken directly to Heaven existed already at the time of the apostles, which proves that the intentions behind this idea cannot be reduced to an exclusively Islamic function.

rectly to the spiritual attitude pertaining to the Muslim perspective; the function here sanctifies the means, namely the symbolism.

The naivety of certain concepts that for all intents and purposes are dogmatic can be explained on the one hand by the natural symbolism of things and on the other by a wise concern for self-protection; for if the truth has, in the final analysis, the purpose of rendering man divine, it could not at the same time have the purpose of dehumanizing him. For example, it could not have the aim of having us experience the dreads of the infinitely great or the infinitely small, as modern science intends to do; to reach God, we have the right to remain children, and we even have no choice, given the limits of our nature.

A classic example of a naive dogma is the Biblical story of creation, followed by that of the first human couple: if we are skeptical—and therefore atrophied creatures—we balk at the childishness of the literal meaning; but if we are intuitive—as every man ought to be—we will be sensitive to the irrefutable truths of the images; indeed, we feel that we bear these images within ourselves, that they have a universal and timeless validity. The same observation applies to myths and even to fairy tales: in describing principles—or situations—concerning the universe, they describe at the same time psychological and spiritual realities of the soul; and in this sense it can be said that the symbolisms of religion or of popular tradition are a part of our common experience, both on the surface and in depth.

Christian Divergences

On the basis of what has been said in the preceding chapter, we may broach the question of the divergence between Catholicism and Protestantism, by showing firstly that it is improper to apply the logic of one religious confession to another; at least from the standpoint of intrinsic values, but not from the standpoint of a particular symbolism or a particular mode of efficacy.

Religious or confessional phenomena are ruled by two great principles, namely "apostolic succession" and "Mandate from Heaven"; sacramental correctness pertains to the first, and the extra-canonical intervention of Grace to the second. The "mandate from Heaven" is a Confucian term, meaning that investiture, and consequently authority, descend directly from On High, without the intermediary of a sacramental means, by virtue of an archetypal reality that must manifest itself in a given world and in response to earthly conditions that call forth this descent. Such was the case of the emperors of China—it is really the Throne that created the emperor—and also, as Dante observed in his treatise on monarchy, that of the Roman emperors, and later the Christian and Germanic ones; and quite paradoxically, the papacy itself is an example of this kind of investiture, given that what creates a pope is an election and not a sacrament.[1] In the framework of Christianity as a whole, the Reformation, while appearing logically and technically as a heresy—although we cannot forget that Rome and Byzantium anathematize each other reciprocally—possesses in itself a justification and hence an efficacy which it draws from a spiritual archetype that was, if not entirely ignored by Rome, at least certainly "stifled".[2]

In other words, the phenomenon of the Reformation, exactly as other analogous manifestations—notably in Hinduism and Buddhism—results from the principle of the "mandate from Heaven"

---

[1] Let it be noted that baptism—*mutatis mutandis*—pertains partially to the same principle, since it does not necessarily require priesthood; nevertheless it is not unconnected to the initiatic sphere since it brings about the remission of original sin and thus transforms the primordial potentiality into virtuality.

[2] See *Christianisme/Islam: visions d'Œcuménisme ésotérique*, chapter "La question de l'Evangélisme".

hence from the providential intervention of the archetype of a spiritual possibility. In this respect, this phenomenon is altogether independent of the rule of "apostolic succession" and "sacramental technique", and this independence—given the confessional or exoteric mentality—explains precisely the vehemence of the Lutheran denial and others. The sometimes naive character of the formulations plays no part here, for such is the general tone of exoteric ostracism; and it is symbolism, no more, no less.

— ·:· —

Protestants and Amidists—although still other examples could be cited—consider that it is faith that saves, not of itself, but by virtue of a Redemption, historical or mythological depending on the case; and since they can neither admit that works add something to the Grace granted by Heaven, nor contest that moral effort is humanly indispensable, they see the motivation for this effort in our gratitude towards the saving Power. Now one of two things is true: either gratitude is necessary, in which case it is not faith alone that saves; or it is faith that saves, in which case gratitude is not necessary. But if one goes to the root of things, it will be perceived that "gratitude" and "sincerity" are synonymous here: that is, sincerity forms part of faith, thus it is only sincere faith—proven precisely by moral effort and works—that ranks as faith in the eyes of God. In other words, sincerity has to manifest itself through our desire to please Heaven which, having saved us from evil, obviously expects us to practice the good; and this responsiveness can be termed "gratitude".

It is known that the idea of Redemption, whatever its "mythical" expression may be, results from the idea of man's fundamental corruption; now this Augustinian and Lutheran concept, which implies the conclusion that man is totally incapable of righteousness in the eyes of God, is like the theological "caricature" of the very contingency of the human being, by virtue of which we can have no quality or power outside God. In Augustinianism, what cuts the Gordian knot is grace combined with faith; metaphysically, what cuts it is also gnosis which participates in the Sovereign Good, or it is the Sovereign Good that is manifested in and by gnosis. And predestination is what we are, outside all temporal mechanism.

It is true that the anthropological pessimism of Saint Augustine does not apply to the first human couple before the Fall, but to humanity marked by the Fall. Adam and Eve, being creatures, were obviously contingent, not absolute; but the Fall, precisely, derives from contingency and manifests it at an inferior level, that of illusion and sin. It is here that a divergence of perspective intervenes: according to some, fallen man still remains man, and thus there is something inalienable in him, but for which he would cease to be human; according to others, fallen man is defined by the Fall, which necessarily penetrates and corrupts all his initiatives, and this is the point of view of Saint Augustine, but to a less "totalitarian" degree than for Luther, because the Bishop of Hippo admits that under certain conditions we may be deserving of merit, whereas Luther denies this and instead substitutes the as it were impersonal mystery of faith. But aside from this difference in degree, the ancient Churches and the Reformation share in common—and so too Amidism—the idea of using our fundamental helplessness as the springboard of a method founded upon saving faith.

In this vein of thought, one can distinguish between two ways of looking at things. According to the first it will be said: if man does not make efforts to transcend himself, he follows his passions and becomes lost; if he does not advance towards his salvation, he moves away from it, for he who does not advance, falls back; whence the obligation of sacrifice, asceticism, and meritorious works. According to the second way, it will be said on the contrary: man is saved beforehand by religion, that is why religion exists; it suffices therefore to have faith and to observe the rules. In other words, given that every believer is by definition included in saving Grace, it suffices not to step out of it; in other words, it suffices to preserve one's faith while abstaining from vices and crimes—whence the obligation of moral equilibrium on the basis of faith.

The first of these perspectives, which is that of Catholicism for example, is dynamic so to speak: its symbol could be the star whose rays are either centripetal or centrifugal, according to whether man strives towards his salvation or on the contrary retreats from it. This dramatic alternative is addressed firstly to passional men—or to men insofar as they are passional—and then to those whose nature requires a mystical way that is combative and sublime, hence "heroic". The second of these two perspectives, which is among others that of Protestantism, is so to speak static and balanced: its symbol could be the circle which on the one hand includes and on the other excludes, according to whether man remains within the haven of salvation or on the contrary leaves it. This alternative, which in fact is reassuring, is addressed firstly to men predisposed to trust in God, but trusting neither in their capacity to save themselves nor in priestly complications, and then, more particularly, to contemplatives of a calm type, who love simplicity and peace.

The two perspectives have to combine, despite their difference of accentuation; each of them gives rise to characteristic abuses: either to dramatism and to the cult of suffering in the first case, or to complacency and lukewarmness in the second.[3] In any case, an abuse can only serve as an argument in a very relative manner; there are no excesses possible in the archetypes.

In the same vein of thought, we may note the following: the Reformers argue that Redemption suffices to guarantee salvation to those baptized whose faith is sincere and consequently is accompanied by an impeccable morality; this in fact is all that is needed, in Christianity, to satisfy the requirements of the necessary minimum. But when they reject monastic asceticism, which to them seems a useless luxury and even a lack of faith, they lose sight of the fact that asceticism stems not from the dimension of what is indispensable, but from that of love, and sometimes from that of fear; for on the one hand, it is necessary to love God with all our faculties, and on the other hand, it is better to go to Heaven "with fewer members" than to hell "with all our members". The Reformers had in their favor at least two extenuating circumstances, one secondary and one essential,

---

[3] In authentic Protestantism, complacency is excluded by intensity of faith and by the sense of duty, hence by that "categorical imperative" which is virtue and morality. In Catholicism, Thomistic intellectuality is capable of checking the excesses of "baroque sentimentalism"; moreover, medieval art, which is truly celestial, has in principle an analogous function, since it introduces an element of intellectuality and serenity into religious sentiment, for "those who have ears to hear". Mention should be made, however, that it is possible to love "our cathedrals" out of patriotism, hence unintelligently and without understanding their message.

namely: firstly that the Catholics have attitudes which, by their over-accentuations and narrow-mindedness, inevitably provoked reactions,[4] and secondly that, within the economy of the Protestant perspective, love of God coincides with the active joy of gratitude, hence with the happiness that piety and virtue bring. Now this perspective is capable of a deepening that transcends ordinary measures and that pertains to the sphere of holy "peace", not holy "passion".

—— ·⋮· ——

After these general considerations, some points concerning ritual divergences are called for. It is not exact to say that the Lutheran Communion is only a "memorial", that it denies the ontological relation between Calvary and the rite; it is Zwingli and the liberal Protestants, not Luther, who minimize the Eucharistic mystery in this manner; for the German Reformer believed in the real Presence in both species. In denying transubstantiation—not inherence or consubstantiation—he refers moreover to Saint Paul, who speaks of the "bread which we break" (1 Cor. 10:16), and who says: ". . . so let him eat of that bread" (1 Cor. 11:28); that is to say, the Apostle speaks of "bread" and not of "appearance of bread". Even Calvin affirms that "Christ, with the plenitude of his gifts, is no less present, in Communion, than if we were seeing Him with our eyes and touching Him with our hands". What actualizes the ontological relation between the Mass and Calvary is the real Presence, independently of the question of transubstantiation; that one may conceive transubstantiation as a change of substance—an elliptical idea if ever there was one—is an entirely different question.

---

[4] The confusion between the elementary requirements of what is strictly necessary and the possible feats of mystical exorbitance—the first dimension relating to salvation as such, and the second to the degrees of beatitude—is also found in the Muslim world, despite the sober and reassuring realism of the Koran and the *Sunnah*, without which the Revelation would not be "good tidings" (*bushrā*). The confusion in question seems to stem from an overly passional need for absoluteness, which instead of being qualitative becomes quantitative, and which in addition readily confuses legalism with virtue and delights in exaggerations whose sole motive is to please God, as if He could have in His nature some kind of blind partiality, *quod absit.*

The Lutheran Communion pertains in the final analysis to the same ritual economy as the Muslim prayer; it is like a minimal fragment of the Catholic Mass from the point of view of content or grace, but it is something else from the point of view of the container or the form, so that the Catholic objections do not apply to it, except for the self-defense of Catholicism. The Catholic Eucharist offers graces commensurate with the spiritual possibilities of a Saint Bernard; the Lutheran Communion—given that "in my Father's house are many mansions"—offers a viaticum commensurate with ordinary believers of good will—*et in terra pax hominibus bonae voluntatis*—exactly as is the case of the Muslim prayer—the only "sacrament" of exoteric Islam—which proves that it is eschatologically sufficient in its religious context. All Catholics must take Communion, but not all of them are Saint Bernard; and the very transcendence of the Eucharist entails terrible dangers, as Saint Paul attests. No doubt Luther closed a door, but he opened another; if he lessened the Eucharistic Grace, by considerably simplifying and centralizing worship, which was too dispersed in Roman practice, he nonetheless opened the door to a particular spiritual climate which also possesses its mystical virtuality. But this virtuality depends on its being actualized by a Christocentric fervor whose sap is faith, and that results from faith; thus it depends on a comportment that is not "meritorious" or "heroic", but "normal" and "Biblical". Indeed, sanctity does not coincide purely and simply with "heroicalness of virtue", it also comprises modes akin to quietism where moral equilibrium, joined to contemplative union, plays a preponderant role.[5]

What matters in the Lutheran Communion is the fact that the bread transmits Christ's will to save us, or the fact that He has saved us, which here amounts to the same thing; like certain Muslim theologians, Luther aims not at "dotting the i's" everywhere—which is the Roman tendency—but in believing in the literal wording of Scripture[6] and acknowledging that a given enigma is true "without asking oneself how" (*bilā kayfa*);[7] whence his refusal to accept transubstantiation,

---

[5] We were told this by a monk of the Eastern Church.

[6] *Alles geglaubt oder nichts geblaubt*: "To believe all or nothing".

[7] It is interesting to note that the problems of evil and of predestination, which cannot be solved within monotheistic and theological logic, led Luther and others to totally Asharite ways of reasoning, to Gordian knots which they could not cut except by

which in his opinion adds nothing to the real Presence, any more than the Gnostic idea of an immaterial and merely "apparent" body adds anything whatsoever to the divinity of Christ.

Perhaps it is necessary to specify here that for the Lutherans there is only one saving Sacrifice, that of Calvary; Communion does not "renew" it, it is not a new sacrifice; it merely actualizes for believers the unique Sacrifice. For the Catholics however, each Mass is a new sacrifice, "bloodless" no doubt and "relative" in comparison with the blood Sacrifice, but nonetheless having a truly sacrificial character; Protestants see in this conception a multiplication of the Sacrifice— multiple Masses being put in place of the one Sacrifice—whereas for the Catholics these Masses are precisely "relative", as we have just said; which does not satisfy the Protestants, given their archetypist insistence on the unicity of Christ and their abhorrence of "secondary causes", as Muslims would say. On the whole, the Catholic Mass is comparable to the image of the sun reflected in a mirror: without pretending to be the sun, it "repeats" it in a certain fashion, and in practice Catholics readily overemphasize this repetition, despite theological specifications that the religious sensibility does not always remember; whereas the Lutheran Communion is comparable—or aims at being comparable—not to the reflected image of the sun, but simply to its ray. The relentlessness of the Lutheran battle against the Mass can be explained by the idea that the Catholic rite becomes *de facto* too independent of its unique and indivisible prototype, to the point of seeming to substitute itself for it; obviously, the Catholics cannot accept this reproach, any more than the Islamic reproach of tritheism, but they should be able to understand that at the basis of these grievances there lies an intention of method much more than of doctrine, of mystical attitude much more than of theological adequacy.

On the Catholic side—let us insist upon it again—it seems to have been forgotten that the majesty of the Eucharistic sacrifice implies certain practical consequences concerning the handling of the rite. The concrete and demanding character of this majesty has been patently forgotten by submitting the sacrifice to all kinds of intentions, applications, or modalities that are too contingent—we would

---

means of the *deus ex machina* that is "faith", a movement which is *a priori* volitive and sentimental, yet in essence intuitive and, in privileged cases, capable of opening the door to gnosis.

almost say too casual—and thus profaning it in the final analysis;[8] it is as if the sense of the divine dignity of the rite were concentrated upon the Eucharistic species only, particularly the host, which is exposed and worshipped in the monstrance but which is mistreated in being given to anybody and under pathetic conditions. Be that as it may, the Lutherans reject the Masses on account of the historic and sacramental uniqueness of the Sacrifice, as the Asharites reject secondary causes on account of the principial and efficient uniqueness of God; in both cases there is ostracism in virtue of an idea of absoluteness.

Before going further, it may be worth recalling the Eucharistic theses of Catholicism and Orthodoxy; for the Catholics, the Eucharistic presence of Christ is produced, not by "impanation" nor by "consubstantiation", but by "transubstantiation", meaning that the "substance of the bread no longer remains", which they justify—abusively in our view[9]—by the consecrating words of Christ; according to this theory, the "substantial form of the species no longer remains", not even their "raw material". The Orthodox, for their part, either do not admit transubstantiation, or they do not admit that it implies "a substance that changes and accidents that do not change"; their intention is to remain faithful—quite wisely—to the Eucharistic teaching of Saint John Damascene, according to whom "the Holy Spirit intervenes and does what transcends all word and all thought. . . . And if you enquire as to how this happens, let it suffice you to know that it happens through the Holy Spirit, . . . that the word of God is true, effective, and all-powerful, the manner of it remaining unfathomable."[10]

---

[8] Experience proves that the "first communion" of children—obligatory for all and socially conventional—is a double-edged sword, for if on the one hand it benefits children who are really pious, on the other hand it exposes the sacrament to a profanation, which could not be in the interest of unworthy children, even if they are relatively innocent.

[9] As regards the pure doctrine, for we do not deny the possibility of a certain psychological opportuneness for a particular ethnic group. This kind of justification obviously applies also to the Reformation—not in the sense of a profusion of "strategic" specifications in this case, but on the contrary in the name of simplicity and pious inarticulation.

[10] *Exposé précis de la Foi orthodoxe*, 4:13. The Reformers did not think otherwise.

Catholicism is Catholicism, and Protestantism is Protestantism; by this truism we mean to say that a Protestantizing tendency that is merely formal has no organic connection with the archetype that motivated and brought about the Reformation, all the more so in that it is the archetype that chooses the man and not inversely; it is not enough to imitate or improvise gestures in order to be concretely in conformity with a spiritual archetype and consequently in harmony with the divine Will. It is possible that Heaven could will a phenomenon such as the Lutheran Communion; but it is impossible that it could will the Lutheranization of the Catholic Mass, for God cannot contradict Himself on one and the same plane, the very one that would imply an intrinsic contradiction; the fact that God brings about the manifestation of the Islamic possibility in no way means that He wishes Christianity to be Islamized, any more than He desires that Islam be Christianized. The principle of the spiritual economy of archetypes means that one and the same form may be valid in a particular confessional context but not in another, except for an adaptation that stems from the archetype itself and not from a purely human enterprise.

According to Catholic logic, the Lutheran Communion is invalid, not only because the rite has been changed but also because the officiant is not a priest; whereas from the Lutheran—or general Protestant—point of view, the officiant is a priest owing to the sacerdotal virtuality that man as such possesses by his deiform nature; Christ actualized this virtuality through the "Mandate from Heaven" of which we have spoken at the beginning of this chapter; this is to say that Heaven permits this Mandate to descend upon the officiant by virtue of his election by the Community, or by those whom the Community delegates, exactly as is the case—technically speaking—with the Roman pontiff.[11] Tradition—Protestants will reason—may well confirm this Mandate, but it does not create it; the officiant is not a pastor *ex opere operato*. Doubtless, the Western Church never went so far as to deny the laity a kind of indirect sacerdotal function, but it has not granted it the same degree of recognition as the Eastern Church has; on the contrary it overly neglected it, the celibacy of priests

---

[11] And, *mutatis mutandis*, for the 'ulamā', whose authority also derives via delegation, by virtue of the sacerdotal potentiality of man. We have noted above that baptism, inasmuch as it can be conferred by a member of the laity, pertains to the same general principle.

helping to widen the gulf between the tonsured and the laity, which, precisely, was avoided by the Orthodox.

And this leads us to another problem: what is the meaning of the fact that the Reformation rejects Tradition and intends to base itself on Scripture alone? It means that this is a question of a religious possibility that, quite clearly, is marginal and not fundamental: the argument here is that Scripture alone is absolutely reliable and stable, whereas Tradition is not always completely trustworthy, and is often diverse and variable, as is shown by the diversity—and in some cases the doubtful character—of the liturgies.[12] Catholics, Orthodox, and Protestants are in agreement on the subject of Scripture, but not on that of Tradition; in Islam as well, the abrupt divergences between Sunnites and Shiites concern Tradition and not the Book. Quite obviously, the Catholics are right to maintain their point of view, which is fundamental, but that of the Protestants corresponds no less to a possibility within a particular theological, mystical, and moral context, but not outside it. What Christ termed "commandments of men" certainly pertained to the element "Tradition"; the *Talmud* is incontestably "traditional". Yet, the total absence of any tradition is impossible; even Lutheranism, Calvinism, and *a fortiori* High Church Anglicanism, are traditional in certain respects.

In this context, we cannot pass over in silence the following observation: on the Catholic side, there is a certain bureaucratization of the sacred, which goes hand in hand with a kind of militarization of sanctity, if such an expression is permissible; pertinently, there is the cult of the monastic "Rules" and that of the liturgical "rubrics". Protestantism intends to place itself in a more "evangelical" dimension, but it opposes Roman excesses with new excesses; all things considered, only the Eastern Church maintains the Christic message in perfect equilibrium. For the Eastern Church, Protestantism is of a kind with Catholicism, the one does not go without the other; they are the two poles of the Western disequilibrium.[13]

---

[12] Otherwise the Tridentine Mass would not have been necessary.

[13] One example, among others, of "Tradition" as a "commandment of men", is the

In other words: Tradition, when considered in itself and outside any restrictive modality, is comparable to a tree; the root, the trunk, the branches, and the fruits are what they must be, each part comes in its season and none of them wants to be another; this is what the Orthodox have understood perfectly, they who stop at the Seventh Council and wish to hear no talk of an "institutionalized Pentecost", if we may use such an expression out of a desire for clarity. It is not that a patriarch, with the agreement of other patriarchs who are his equals, cannot undertake a secondary adaptation or other required by particular circumstances—the contrary would be opposed to the nature of things—but no patriarch can make a decision regarding a substantial change such as the introduction of the *filioque* or the celibacy of priests, and impose it upon all the patriarchs who are his brothers.[14] As a result of the unstable, adventurous, and innovative mentality of the Roman, German, and Celtic Westerners, the Catholic West has not been able to realize integrally an equilibrium between the principles of growth and conservation, or in other words, it needed an institution that grants pre-eminence to the first principle over the second,[15] and which thus "traditionalizes" a possibility that in itself is problematical. Thus, we accept that the papacy—for that is what is at issue—was a providential although ambiguous necessity,[16] but the

cardinalate: whereas bishops and patriarchs derive from the apostles, there is nothing in the New Testament that prefigures the cardinals. At the beginning of this papal institution, even the laity could obtain this dignity; after the eleventh century, it was attributed only to the bishops, priests, and deacons who surrounded the pope; in the thirteenth century, every cardinal received the rank of bishop and the red hat; finally, in the seventeenth century, the cardinals received the title of "Eminence". All this is more imperial than sacerdotal in character and scarcely accords with the principle "everywhere, always, by everyone" (*quod ubique, quod semper, quod ab omnibus creditum est*); having said this, we do not contest that such an institution may be required by the Roman or Latin mentality any more than we contest what the play of Providence may require.

[14] The *filioque* could have found its place among the possible "theological opinions"; but it was in no wise necessary—history proves this—to impose it tyrannically upon the entire Church.

[15] Let it be noted that the Mass of Pius V was not an innovation, but a restoring of order in things; the abuse lay in a preceding disorder, not in the conservative measure of the pope.

[16] "But be not ye called Rabbi: for one is your Master, even Christ; and all ye are brethren. And call no man your father upon the earth: for one is your Father, which is

Protestant phenomenon benefits from the same justification, at least in a secondary way; in other words, the very ambiguity of the papacy necessarily gave rise to the Protestant reaction and to the denominational scission of the Latin West.

One of the great qualities of the Catholic Church—that it shares with the Orthodox Church—is its sense of the sacred, which is liturgically and aesthetically expressed by its solemn Masses; in Protestantism, this sense is concentrated uniquely on Scripture and prayer, which unquestionably entails a great impoverishment, not necessarily for the individual, but for the collectivity. It is true that the Anglican Church, or at least the High Church, has largely maintained the sense of the sacred, and Luther too was not insensitive to it, he who rejected all iconoclastic fanaticism; it is above all Calvinism that has put a rigid moralism in place of this sense, whereas liberal Protestantism—that typical product of the nineteenth century—has in the final analysis squandered everything; and, as a matter of fact, this is what Catholic modernism does equally and even better than liberal Protestantism. Be that as it may, authentic Protestantism has to a certain extent replaced the sense of the sacred by the sense of inwardness, with analogous psychological consequences; for he who sincerely, "in spirit and in truth", loves to stand before God is not far from the reverential disposition of which we are speaking.

It has been said that the Protestant Reformation brought about an almost total destruction of sacred forms. Unquestionably it produced

in Heaven. Neither be ye called masters: for one is your Master, even Christ" (Matt. 23:8-10). Now the pope is placed in a quasi-absolute fashion above the bishops, his brothers, and requires that he be called "Holy Father", and then there are the "Doctors of the Church"; these facts clash singularly with the passage of the Gospel quoted and offer—to say the least—extenuating circumstances for the Orthodox and Lutheran protestation against the papacy as it presents itself *de facto*. In a certain sense, the papacy is the Trojan horse that introduces the spirit of innovation into the Church.

a certain void—although in Germanic countries there are temples that soberly prolong the Gothic forms—but is this void so much more deadly than the false plenitude of the Renaissance, and in particular the horrible profusion of the Baroque style?[17] In reality, the Protestant "destruction" goes hand in hand with a Catholic "destruction": on the one hand there is negation and impoverishment, and on the other repudiation and falsification.

The Roman, Byzantine, and Gothic styles are not phases in an indefinite "evolution"; they are definitive crystallizations of modes of Christian art.[18] The center of the Western Christian world was the basilica of Constantine in Rome; now one fine day the popes had the disastrous idea of destroying this venerable jewel of sacred art and replacing it with a gigantic, pagan, and glacial imperial palace, as pretentious within as without, and of adorning it with naturalistic works expressing all the sensual and marmoreal megalomania of the time.[19] The art of the Renaissance entails as its consequence the obligation to admire it—no pope has the power to destroy the work of Bramante and Michelangelo—thus it has imposed a lack of discernment that does not stop short at the aesthetic plane, the fruits of which are still being gathered today, indeed today more than ever before; the most general expression of this poisoning is what may be termed "civilizationism", that is, the adulteration of religion resulting from the ideology of total and indefinite progress. Henceforth it is impossible to dissociate the Christian from the "civilized" man, in the narrow and somewhat ridiculous sense of this word; in this respect, the Christians of the East have been the victims of the Christians of the West, notoriously so since Peter the Great. In any case, the Protestants cannot be held solely responsible for the modern deviation, even though it

---

[17] Which was the sentimentalist reaction to the pagan coldness of the Renaissance. The Baroque style has been qualified by some as the "style of joy", whereas it is sad, owing to its pompous but hollow fantasy and unrealism, in short, owing to its falsehood and its stupidity; the dress of the period attests to the same aberration.

[18] There is, of course, "elaboration", but not "evolution": once the "idea" has been fully manifested, the style no longer has to change, in spite of a diversity that is always possible and even necessary. In sacred art, unlimited evolution is as nonexistent as it is in biology: growth stops the moment the idea—the specific type—is fully realized.

[19] And since the price of this monstrous edifice was the sale of indulgences, one should have renounced building it; it is a question of a sense of proportions as well as of moral sense, or a sense of the *barakah*.

has been rightly pointed out that Calvinism favored industrialism; but this takes nothing away from the fact that everything began with the Renaissance, and that the Protestants had no part in that.[20] If we mention these things, it is not to dwell upon a historical question that strictly speaking remains outside our subject matter, but to prevent a possible prejudice on the part of traditionalists who, trusting in their principles—which no one could blame them for—have had neither the idea nor the opportunity to verify some of their seemingly plausible, but in fact inadequate, conclusions. In any case, no Church ever opposed the so-called attainments of "human genius"—whether artistic, literary, scientific, technical, or even political; quite to the contrary, one has sought to attribute them to the "Christian genius" and done so with a baffling lack of discernment and imagination.

Upon further reflection, a few more comments are called for: civilizationism is practically synonymous with industrialism, and the essence of industrialism is the machine; now the machine both produces and kills, at one and the same time: it produces objects and kills the soul,[21] not to mention its practical, and in the long run extremely serious, disadvantages that are only too well known. Religion has accepted and nearly "Christianized" the machine, and it is dying from this—either through absurdity and hypocrisy, as in the past, or through capitulation and suicide, as today. It is as if there were only two sins, unbelief and unchasteness; given that the machine is neither an unbeliever nor is it unchaste, one may then in good conscience sprinkle it with holy water.

It is in the climate of the Renaissance that the Reformation burst forth and spread with the force of a hurricane, to then remain in place to

---

[20] Besides, the French Revolution took place in a Catholic country; and likewise, before it, the enterprise of the Encyclopedists.

[21] What distinguishes the traditional machine—such as the loom—from the modern machine, is that it combines intelligible simplicity and an explicit and spiritually effective symbolism with an aesthetic quality altogether essential for normal man. The modern machine, on the contrary, does not have these qualities, and instead of serving man and contributing to his well-being, it enslaves and dehumanizes him.

this very day, which allows us to apply the argument of Gamaliel to the Protestant phenomenon, namely that a religious movement that does not proceed from God will not last.[22] This argument of course loses all its value when applied to an intrinsically false religious ideology, and *a fortiori* to philosophical or political ideologies, for in these cases their success is due to an entirely different reason: it does not stem from the power of a spiritual archetype, but merely from the seduction of error and the weakness of men.

Protestantism encompasses almost a third of Christianity, consequently its importance in the Western world is immense, and it is impossible to leave it unmentioned when one is considering religions, denominations, and spiritualities. It should be noted that without the Reformation there would have been no Council of Trent nor, consequently, the Catholic Counter-Reformation; now this functional necessity of Protestantism speaks in its favor and indirectly proves the relative—not absolute, but confessionally sufficient—legitimacy of this powerful movement; without it, the Roman Church might not have found the necessary impetus to recover and rebuild.[23] The fact that this scission in the midst of Western Christianity generated at the same time favorable conditions for the final fall of the West, takes nothing away from the positive meaning of the Protestant phenomenon, but shows in any case how the meshing of the positive and the negative are part of the ambiguous and ingenious play of Providence. The same observation applies *a priori* to Catholicism, certain aspects of which have contributed to the origin of the modern world, which does not take away in the least from its quality as a great religious message and traditional civilization, hence from its merits on the plane of intellectuality, sacred art, and sanctity.

---

[22] The ostracism of Calvin—which contrasts with the generosity of Luther—is not an argument against the Reformation, for it is not Calvin who invented the Inquisition; in any case we find ourselves here in an exoterist climate, hence one that is intolerant and formalistic.

[23] It is an interesting fact that the Fathers of the Council of Trent renounced condemning Luther expressly, which would have been required by conciliary customs; they preferred not to "close the door definitively to dialogue", which has a symbolical as well as a practical meaning.

Quite paradoxically, in Lutheranism there is at one and the same time an intention of esoterism and of exoterism, hence of interioriza-tion and of exteriorization; on the one hand Luther aimed at bringing everything back to the inward—"But thou, when thou prayest, enter into thy closet,[24] and when thou hast shut thy door, pray to thy Father which is in secret"—and on the other hand, he aimed at reducing everything to the "supernaturally natural" priesthood of man as such, hence of every man, or more precisely of every baptized man, for "all ye are brethren". With the first intention, the mystic of Wittenberg opens the door to certain esoteric possibilities, by the nature of things; with the second, he closes the door to a certain type of sanctity, founded upon the "chivalric" notion of the "heroism of virtues", a notion which in itself is correct, but which becomes false when the aim is to reduce all possible sanctity to this type, while disparaging everything that relates to quietism and gnosis. Be that as it may: in being inspired by the injunction of Christ to the Samaritan—to wor-ship God neither on Mount Gerizim nor in the Temple, but "in spirit and in truth"—Luther wished to erase as much as possible the outward signs of worship—without being fanatical like Calvin—as if transcendence could not tolerate immanence; but at the same time he actualized a certain desire for esoterism, a paradox also manifested by Amidism and Shiism. The non-formal—or emptiness—is in fact a vehicle of the supra-formal and of plenitude, as Saint Bernard under-stood quite well in emptying his chapels of all images and all adorn-ments, and as the Zen monks understood no less well in making use of an art of bareness, hence of emptiness.

Not unconnected to this question of "esoterizing exoterism" is the fact that the Reformation, which issued from an ascetical religion, "rediscovered" the spiritual potential of sexuality, exactly as was the case in Buddhism—also ascetical—when Shinran, although fully a monk, married and introduced marriage into his sect, the *Jōdo Shin-shu*.[25] The intrinsically sacred character of sexuality was not unknown to Judaism or to Hinduism, from which the two ascetical religions

---

[24] That of the heart, according to the Hesychasts.

[25] Let us not lose sight of the fact that Catholicism witnessed the blossoming of the more or less "erotic" mysticism of the knights, the troubadours, and the *Fedeli d'Amore*; Tantric Buddhism exhibits analogous features, but with a very different em-phasis.

just mentioned issued respectively; however, neither Judaism nor Hinduism overlook the value of asceticism, which obviously keeps all its rights in every religious climate.[26] Man is so made that he naturally tends to slide towards the outward and has need of a wound to bring him closer to "the kingdom of God which is within you", and this notwithstanding the complementary fact that the contemplative—and he alone—perceives the traces of the Divine in outward beauties, which amounts to saying that, given his predisposition, these beauties have the capacity to interiorize him, in conformity with the principle of Platonic anamnesis. This means that man's ambiguity is that of the world: everything manifests God—directly or indirectly or in both ways at the same time—but nothing is God; thus everything can either bring us closer to Him or take us further from Him. Each religion, or each confession, intends to offer its solution to this problem in conformity with a particular psychological, moral, and spiritual economy.

Someone has asked us[27] why Protestantism, since it manifests *grosso modo* the same archetype as Amidism, does not, contrary to Amidism, possess a method of ejaculatory prayer; now this archetype does not of itself imply this mode of prayer any more than this mode of prayer implies that archetype; rather it implies the emphasis upon faith and the assiduous practice of prayer, and in fact we find both of these elements in authentic Protestantism.

Another question that we have been asked concerns the formal homogeneity that every intrinsically orthodox confession possesses; now if Protestantism on the whole does not possess this homogeneity, each of its great branches—Lutheranism, Calvinism, Anglicanism—possesses it. In the same way, each of the ancient Churches is homogeneous, whereas Christianity as a whole is not, any more than are

---

[26] Judaism gave birth to the ascetical sect of the Essenes; as for Hinduism, it is special in that its compartmentalized structure and metaphysical amplitude enable it to fully bring out the value of every spiritual possibility; fully, that is, independently of every antagonistic religious context.

[27] Referring to the chapter "La question de l'Evangélisme" in our book *Christianisme/Islam: visions d'Œcuménisme ésotérique*.

other religions, each of which comprises at least two more or less antagonistic denominations.

"For where two or three are gathered together in my Name, there I am in the midst of them", Christ said. Among all the possible meanings of this saying, there may also be this one: the first two who assemble are Catholicism and Orthodoxy, and the third, which is mentioned apart, is Protestantism. In fact, Christ could have said: "Where three are gathered", thereby placing the three confessions on the same level; but he said "two or three", which indicates a certain inequality, but always within the framework of religious legitimacy; inequality as regards completeness or plenitude, but at the same time legitimacy as regards the love of Christ and spiritual authenticity; hence there is an underlying fraternity despite the differences.

The Seat of Wisdom

The Blessed Virgin is inseparable from the incarnated Word, as the Lotus is inseparable from the Buddha, and as the Heart is the predestined seat of immanent Wisdom. In Buddhism there is a whole mysticism of the Lotus, a mysticism imparting a celestial image of unsurpassable beauty and eloquence; this beauty is analogous to that of the monstrance containing the real Presence, and analogous above all to that incarnation of divine Femininity which is the Virgin Mary. The Virgin, *Rosa mystica*, is like the personification of the celestial Lotus; in a certain respect, she personifies the sense of the sacred, which is the indispensable introduction to the reception of the Sacrament.

One of the names that the Litany of Loreto gives to the Blessed Virgin is *Sedes Sapientiae*, "Throne of Wisdom"; and indeed, as was noted by Saint Peter Damien (eleventh century), the Blessed Virgin "is herself that wondrous throne referred to in the Book of Kings", namely, the Throne of Solomon the Prophet-King who, according to the Bible and rabbinical traditions, was the paragon of a wise man.[1] If Mary is *Sedes Sapientiae*, this is first of all because she is the Mother of Christ who, being the Word, is the "Wisdom of God"; but it is also, quite obviously, because of her own nature, which results from her quality as "Spouse of the Holy Spirit", and "Co-Redemptress";[2] that is to say, Mary is herself an aspect of the Holy Spirit, its feminine counterpart, if one

---

[1] If the Bible condemned his conduct, it was because of a difference of level—the Bible's point of view being *a priori* legalistic, and thus exoteric—and not because of an intrinsic wrong on his part. In Solomon there is the manifestation of the mystery of "wine" and "intoxication", as is indicated on the one hand by his Song of Songs and, on the other, by the actions for which, precisely, he is blamed in the Bible; but Solomon could have said, with his father David: "I have remembered thy Name, O Lord, in the night, and have kept thy Law" (Ps. 119:55).

[2] Not losing sight of the fact that the body and blood of Christ are those of the Virgin-Mother, there being no human father.

will, or its aspect of femininity; whence the feminization of the divine *Pneuma* by the gnostics. Being the Throne of Wisdom—the "Throne quickened by the Almighty", according to a Byzantine hymn—Mary is *ipso facto* identified with the divine *Sophia*, as is attested by the Marian interpretation of some of the eulogies of Wisdom in the Bible.[3] Mary could not have been the locus of the Incarnation did she not bear in her very nature the Wisdom to be incarnated.

The wisdom of Solomon—it is well to recall here—is at once encyclopedic, cosmological, metaphysical, and also simply practical; in this last respect, it is political as well as moral and eschatological. Yet, that it is at the same time much more[4] emerges not only from certain passages of Proverbs and the Book of Wisdom, but also from the Song of Songs, a book particularly revered by the Cabalists.

As for the wisdom of the "divine Mary", it is less diverse than Solomon's, because it does not embrace certain contingent orders; it could never be either encyclopedic or "Aristotelian", if one may put it thus. The Blessed Virgin knows, and wants to know, only that which

---

[3] "The Lord possessed me in the beginning of his way, before his works of old. I was set up from everlasting, from the beginning, or ever the earth was. When there were no depths, I was brought forth; when there were no fountains abounding with water" (Prov. 8:22-24 and following verses).

[4] This is what the majority of modern critics tend to dispute; however, if the wisdom of Solomon had been only practical and encyclopedic, the following sentences would be quite inexplicable: "Neither compared I unto her [unto Wisdom] any precious stone; because all gold in respect of her is as a little sand, and silver shall be counted as clay before her. I loved her above health and beauty, and chose to have her instead of light: for the light that cometh from her never goeth out. . . . All such things as are either secret or manifest, them I know. For wisdom, which is the worker of all things, taught me; for in her is an understanding spirit, holy, one only, manifold, subtle, lively, clear, undefiled, plain, not subject to hurt, loving the thing that is good, quick, which cannot be letted, ready to do good . . . having all power, overseeing all things, and going through all understanding, pure, and most subtle spirits. . . . For she is the breath of the power of God, and a pure influence flowing from the glory of the Almighty; therefore can no defiled thing fall into her. For she is the brightness of the everlasting light. . . . And being but one, she can do all things: and remaining in herself, she maketh all things new: and in all ages entering into holy souls, she maketh them friends of God, and prophets. . . . Being compared with the light, she is found before it. For after this cometh night: but vice shall not prevail against wisdom" (Wisd. of Sol. 7:9-30). If the Wisdom of the Bible were only practical and encyclopedic, there would assuredly be no reason to identify it with the Blessed Virgin, or to identify her with Solomon's Throne.

concerns the nature of God and the condition of man; her science is perforce metaphysical, mystical, and eschatological, and owing to this very fact it contains in virtuality every possible science, as the one and colorless light contains the varied and colored hues of the rainbow.

One observation that should be made at this point is the following: if Mary is seated upon the Throne of Solomon and is even identified with that Throne[5]—with the authority it represents—this is not only by divine right but by human right as well, in the sense that, being descended from David, she is heiress and queen in the same way that Christ, in like respect, is heir and king. One cannot but think of this when one sees the crowned Romanesque Virgins seated with the Child on a royal Throne—those Virgins which all too often are depicted with considerable artistic awkwardness, only a few of them being masterpieces,[6] but which convey then the majesty and gentleness of Virginal Wisdom with all the greater hieratic eloquence. Majesty and gentleness, but also rigor; the *Magnificat* bears witness to this when it affirms, with the accents of a martial Psalm, that *vincit omnia Veritas.*

According to the First Book of Kings (10:18-20) Solomon "made a great throne of ivory, and overlaid it with the best gold. The throne had six steps, and heads of bulls behind,[7] and there were stays on either side on the place of the seat, two lions stood beside the stays. And twelve lions stood there on the one side and the other upon the

---

[5] Theologians, incidentally, do not seem to realize the immense "rehabilitation" that this association with the living *Sedes Sapientiae,* and thereby with the Word, implies for Solomon—an association which is either profound, or else utterly meaningless.

[6] The Germanic peoples knew nothing of the plastic arts, the Greeks and Romans practiced only classical naturalism; Christian art, at least in the Latin world, had great difficulty emerging from this twofold vacuum. In the Byzantine world, the art of icons was able to escape from such pitfalls.

[7] Jewish translations and the Vulgate of Saint Jerome state that "the top of the throne was round behind"; they do not speak of "heads of bulls" as do some Christian translations, whose authors base themselves upon certain semantic factors and the fact that the Second Book of Chronicles (9:18) mentions a "golden lamb", in order—as they see it—to avoid an association of ideas with the pagan cult of the bull. It should be noted that the Jewish historian Josephus (reign of Vespasian) says: "In the place where this prince (Solomon) was seated, there were seen arms in relief which appeared to be receiving him, and at the place where he could support himself, the figure of a bullock was placed as if to support him".

six steps: there was not the like made in any kingdom".[8] First of all, a few observations on the symbolism of the animals: the lions represent, beyond any question, the radiant and victorious power of Truth, whereas the bulls may correlatively represent weighty and defensive power; prospective power, on the one hand, and, on the other, retrospective power, or imagination that creates and memory that conserves; invincibility and inviolability, or again, alchemically speaking, sun and moon. But there is also the symbolism of the materials: ivory is substance and gold is radiation; or ivory, a material associated with life, is the "naked body" of Truth, whereas gold is the "raiment" which on the one hand veils the mystery and, on the other, transmits its glory.

The six steps of the throne refer to the very "texture" of Wisdom, one might say; six is the number of Solomon's seal. It is the number of total unfolding: the creation was completed in six days, and the fundamental metaphysical or mystical perspectives, the *darshana*s, are—and must be—six in number, according to Hindu tradition. This mystery of totality results from the combination of the numbers two and three which, the first being even and the second odd, initially summarize every numerical possibility[9]—in the Pythagorean and not the quantitative sense. Spiritually speaking, the number two expresses the complementarity of "active perfection" and "passive perfection" as the Taoists would say; in its turn the number three indicates in this context the hierarchy of spiritual modes or degrees, namely "fear", "love", and "knowledge", each of these viewpoints containing, in fact, an active or dynamic aspect and a passive or static one.

The cosmic and human significances of the six directions of space—and the subjectivization of space is certainly not arbitrary—reveal the contents of Wisdom, its dimensions or "stations" so to speak. The North is divine Purity and human renunciation, *vacare Deo*; the South is Life, Love, Goodness, and, in human terms, trust in God or hope; the East is Strength, Victory, and, humanly speaking, spiritual combat; the West is Peace, Beatitude, Beauty, and, in human terms, spiritual contentment, holy tranquility. The Zenith is Truth,

---

[8] This last phrase, applied to the Virgin, indicates her incomparability; her "avataric" uniqueness in the universe of the Semites.

[9] This is what space demonstrates: it has three dimensions, but the introduction of a subjective principle of alternative or opposition gives it six directions; this structure retraces the totality of the Universe.

Elevation, Transcendence, and thus also discernment, knowledge; the Nadir is the Heart, Depth, Immanence, and thus also Union and holiness. This complexity brings us back to the cosmological and encyclopedic dimensions of Solomon's wisdom; it permits us to have a glimpse of the ramifications of the various orders of possibilities that unfold between the Nadir and the Zenith, that is to say, between the Alpha and the Omega of universal Possibility.

The foregoing reflections enable us to extend our analysis of the Solomonian number even further, at the risk of becoming involved in a digression that would raise fresh problems; but this does not matter, for it may be useful to specify things in more detail. The axes of North-South, East-West, and Zenith-Nadir correspond respectively to the complementarities "Negative-Positive", "Active-Passive", and "Objective-Subjective", which summarize the principal cosmic relationships and constitute the fundamental symbolism of the three dimensions of space: length, breadth, and height. When looking towards the East, whence comes light, the East will be "in front", the West "behind", the South "on the right", and the North "on the left", whereas the Zenith and the Nadir remain immutable; these last two refer also to the pair Principle-Manifestation, the first term being for us "objective" because of its Transcendence, and the second term "subjective" because when standing before the Absolute the world is ourselves, and we are the world. But the Nadir may also represent "depth" or "inwardness" and thus the divine Self, in which case the Zenith will take on an aspect of "projection", of limitless *Māyā*, and of unfolding and indefinite Possibility; in the same way, the root of a tree manifests and unfolds in and by the crown.

Space is defined likewise, and even *a priori*, by two principial elements, the point—subjectively the center—and extension, which respectively express the two poles "absolute" and "infinite"; time, for its part, also comprises such elements, namely, the instant—subjectively the present—and duration, with the same significance.[10] In

---

[10] From a quite different point of view, it can be pointed out that the number three refers more particularly to space, which has three dimensions, whereas the number

the number six, the implicit number three corresponds to the center or the present, and the number two to extension and duration; if the center-present is expressed by the ternary, and not by unity, it is because unity is here envisaged with respect to its potentialities and thus in relation to its possibility of unfolding; the actualization of that unfolding is expressed precisely by the number two.[11] All this is a way of presenting the "Pythagorean" aspect of the number six and consequently this number's role in integral Wisdom.

"Fear", "love", and "knowledge", or rigor, gentleness, and substance; then "active" and "passive" perfections, or dynamic and static; therein lies, as we have seen, the elementary spiritual message of the principial number six. This scheme expresses not only the modalities of human ascent, but also, and even primarily, the modalities of divine Descent; it is by the six steps of the Throne that saving Grace comes down towards man, just as it is by these six steps that man ascends towards Grace. Wisdom is in practice the "art" of freeing oneself from illusion that seduces and binds us, of freeing oneself firstly through the intelligence and then through the will; it consists firstly in knowledge of the "Sovereign Good" and then, by way of consequence, in the adaptation of the will to this knowledge; the two things being inseparable from Grace.

The divine *Māyā*—Femininity *in divinis*—is not only that which projects and creates, it is also that which attracts and liberates. The Blessed Virgin as *Sedes Sapientiae* personifies this merciful Wisdom that descends towards us and that we also, whether we know it or not, bear in our very essence; and it is precisely by virtue of this potentiality or virtuality that Wisdom comes down upon us. The immanent seat of Wisdom is the heart of man.

---

two applies more to time, whose "dimensions" are the past and the future, without speaking here of the cyclic quaternary contained in duration and which is no more than a development of duality.

[11] The number three in fact evokes not absoluteness itself, as does the number one, but the potentiality or virtuality which the Absolute necessarily comprises.

III.
ISLAM

Islam and Consciousness of the Absolute

In order to introduce our subject, we must once again formulate the following doctrine:[1] the Supreme Principle is both necessary Being and the Sovereign Good; it is Being with respect to its Reality, and Good with respect to its Positivity—or its qualitative Potentiality—for on the one hand, "I am that I am", and on the other, "God alone is good". From "necessary" Being is derived "possible" being—which can be or not—that is to say, existence; and all manifested qualities are derived from the Sovereign Good which is their only cause or essence.

On the one hand the Sovereign Good is the Absolute, and being the Absolute, it is *ipso facto* the Infinite; on the other hand it is hypostasized—if one may put it thus—into three "divine modes": Intelligence, Power, and Goodness; Goodness, for its part, coincides with Beauty and Beatitude. Each of the three modes participates in Absoluteness and Infinitude, for each is linked to the Sovereign Good or necessary Being.

Evil cannot be absolute, it always depends upon some good which it misuses or perverts; the quality of Absoluteness can belong to good alone. To speak of the "good" is therefore to speak of the "absolute", and conversely, for the good results from Being itself, which it reflects and whose potentialities it unfolds.

We have alluded more than once to the Augustinian notion that it is in the nature of the good to impart itself, hence to radiate; to project itself and thereby to become differentiated. This is the Infinitude pertaining to absolute Reality; the Infinite is none other than the Absolute *qua* Possibility, it is both intrinsic and extrinsic since it is first of all divine Life and then cosmic Radiation.

As pure Potentiality or Possibility as such, the Infinite gives rise, in the order of cosmic gradation, to the veil of *Māyā* and hence to the unfolding of universal Manifestation, the content of which is still necessary Being, thus the Sovereign Good, but in relative and differentiated mode, according to the simultaneously exteriorizing and diversifying tendency of Possibility. Moreover, the pole "Infinite", in

---

[1] We have spoken of it in several works, including this one in the chapter "Les deux problèmes".

combining with the pole "Absolute", is mirrored in the space of *Māyā*: if the existential categories[2] and the indefinite diversity of things—in short, all modes of extension—stem from the Infinite, the pure and simple existence of things stems from the Absolute, and the qualities of things testify to the Sovereign Good as such.

The existence of things refers to the Absolute by analogy, and analogy necessarily indicates an ontological link; that is to say the existence of things refers to the Absolute with respect to "abstraction", "contractiveness", and "explosiveness", if these kinds of images are permissible in such a domain; because the incredible miracle of existence—an affirmation of everything in the face of nothingness—is something absolute and consequently must refer to That which is everything and which alone is.

The principle of differentiation does not stem solely from the Infinite insofar as the Infinite unfolds the potentialities of the Good, it results also from the Good itself inasmuch as the Good bears these inexhaustible potentialities within itself—their foundation being the ternary Intelligence, Power, and Goodness-Beauty-Beatitude. All the cosmic qualities, including the faculties of creatures, derive ontologically from these archetypes *in divinis*.

Totality of intelligence, freedom of will, disinterestedness of love, hence capacity for generosity, compassion, and transcending of self, in short, capacity for integral objectivity: these characteristics of man prove that his reason for being is his relationship with the Absolute. This is to say that it is only man's faculties that are commensurate with this relationship, and this moreover is why the posture of his body is vertical and why he possesses the gifts of reason and speech; man is so made that he can conceive, will, and love that which transcends him infinitely. He can be a metaphysician and practice a spiritual method; he can find his happiness therein and prove it by his virtues.

It is this nature of man, thus this fundamental disposition—or specific capacity—to know God and to go towards Him, that every

---

[2] Space, time, form, number, matter. When the meaning of these categories is extended to all the levels of the cosmos the notions then become no more than symbols.

religion necessarily takes for granted; not every religion, however, necessarily bases itself upon the saving power inherent in human nature
by virtue of its deiformity. Whereas Theravadin Buddhism and Zen
have as their starting point this power to the point of excluding from
their perspective all that seems to serve as an objective Divinity, Christianity on the contrary places the entire emphasis upon the humanly
irremediable fall of our nature and thus upon the absolute necessity
of a divine intervention, hence on a power coming from outside the
human being. Islam holds an intermediate position: man is saved both
by virtue of his unalterable deiform characteristics—for fallen man is
still man—and by a divine intervention that actualizes their quality.
What in Islam is human nature fully actualized by Revelation will,
in Christianity, be represented by Christ: it is He, "true man and
true God", who restores man's nature; fallen man—the "sinner"—is
regenerated in and by the Redeemer.[3] This amounts to saying that
Christianity does not refer directly to the Absolute as such, but to the
Good inasmuch as it manifests its reintegrating function of Mercy; this
relativization corresponds to the *de facto* reduction of human nature
to a "historical" or cosmic accident, but it goes without saying that in
Christianity—as in every religion—there is also a key to the Absolute
as such. In Islam, and in analogous perspectives, what corresponds to
the "Christic" principle will be the "heart", sometimes compared to a
tarnished mirror; the purpose of Revelation is to restore to this mirror
its primordial luminosity. Islam, founded on Unity and Transcendence,
necessarily accentuates in its expressions and attitudes the essential
aspects of the One, aspects which we spoke of at the beginning of
this chapter; it is true that the same accentuations may, or even must,
be found everywhere in one form or another, so that our description
allows for appropriate applications to the most diverse perspectives;
but we intend to deal here with the concrete case of Islam.

Infinitude, as we have said, is the radiation, both intrinsic and
extrinsic, of the Absolute: *a priori* it is internal Bliss, if one may say;

---

[3] We have often had occasion to cite this patristic formula: "God became man that
man might become God". In Lutheran mysticism, the relationship between God and
man gives rise to this reciprocity: in making our sin His sin, Christ makes His justice
our justice; that is, Christ takes the chastisement upon Himself and from us requires
faith alone, and also, on the strength of this faith, the accomplishment of our earthly
duty and the sincere intention not to sin; sincerity here being the key to efficacy, and
the support for the justice which Heaven grants us.

in becoming relative *a posteriori*, it becomes hypostatic and creative as well as saving *Māyā;* these two aspects, the Absolute as such and its radiating *Shakti*—Infinitude at once substantial and unfolding—determine the most characteristic manifestations of Islam. They are prefigured phonetically in the very Name of the Divinity, *Allāh;* the first syllable, which is contractive, seems to refer to the rigor of the Absolute, whereas the second syllable, which is expansive, evokes the gentleness of Infinitude.

In conformity with these two poles, the characteristic manifestations of Islam can be divided into two categories: one which evokes implacable Truth (*Haqq*) and the Holy War (*jihād*) associated with it, and one which evokes generous Peace (*Salām*) and moral and spiritual resignation (*islām*). And similarly: the mystery of the Absolute is linked to the idea of the Lord (*Rabb*) before whom there can only be a slave (ʿ*abd*), and the mystery of the Infinite is linked to the idea of the Clement (*Rahmān*) who encompasses everything; Rigor and the Law are related to the Absolute, and Gentleness and Pardon are related to the Infinite; this is the complementarity between "Majesty" (*Jalāl*) and "Beauty" (*Jamāl*).

The objective reality of the Absolute calls for the subjective reality of certitude; certitude gives rise to a characteristic feature of the Muslim mentality, because the entire faith of Muslims is based upon the simple and irrefutable idea of "necessary Being" (*Wujūd wājib*) or "Absolute Being" (*Wujūd mutlaq*); the necessary is that which cannot not be, whereas the possible (*mumkin*) or the contingent is that which can be or not. Not that certitude is lacking in the other forms of religious faith; but in Islam it has a crystalline and implacable quality stemming precisely from the metaphysical self-evidence of its fundamental content; assuredly, not every Muslim is a metaphysician, but the self-evidence of the Absolute is in the very air that he breathes. Thus the Muslim has the reputation for being immune to conversion and this inflexibility is all the more understandable in that, in a certain respect, the simplest truth is the surest.

The sense of the Absolute has produced in Muslim theology a curious over-emphasis on the confrontation "Lord-servant" or

"Master-slave": one piously imagines that God has the right to any-thing, even the right to commit what, for us, is an injustice and an absurdity;[4] thus one forgets that the personal God, being perfect, cannot have the imperfection of laying claim to all possible rights, and that it is only the impersonal divine Essence which, as All-Possibility, has "all rights" in the sense that, given its limitlessness, it manifests the negative as well as the positive possibilities; but this Essence, precisely, asks nothing of man. Being perfect, God cannot be incon-sistent: He could not create a being with the aim of having an inter-locutor without thereby taking upon Himself certain limitations; for reciprocity is not conceivable without certain sacrifices on the part of both partners, intrinsically incommensurable though they may be. Once God turns to man, He situates Himself in *Māyā*, and assumes all the consequences thereof.

One could also say, in this vein of thought, that the notion of right implies that of duty, logically and ontologically; the just man who does not wish to assume a particular duty renounces *ipso facto* a particular right. To say that the pure Absolute[5] has no duty means that it cannot lay claim to any right, for it has no interlocutor.

The Law exists for man, not man for the Law;[6] in other words: the personal God is by definition a moral Person; it is true that the divine Essence is "amoral", if one will, but it does not follow from this that the divine Person is immoral, *quod absit*; to maintain that He is so, even in an indirect way and through the use of pious euphemisms,

---

[4] The Koranic formula "do not impose upon us that which we have not the strength to bear" concerns a relative, not an absolute situation; a factual difficulty, not a principial one, and hence one with some latitude regarding specifications. This formula seems to allude to the ancient Hebrews, whose prescriptions were realizable, but which in fact the Hebrews frequently violated either by reason of shortcomings—obviously relative—in their mentality, or because of the seductiveness of the pagan ambience.

[5] We have alluded more than once to the seemingly contradictory, but metaphysically useful and even indispensable, idea of the "relatively absolute", which is absolute in relation to what it rules, while pertaining to relativity in relation to the "pure Abso-lute".

[6] Exoterically, one submits to the Law in order to please God and escape chastisement, not to mention the practical or moral value of the Commandment, to which every man should be sensitive; esoterically, one submits to the Law taking into account its intentions, and knowing that God does not require anything more, for He sees the nature of things and the "spirit", rather than the "letter".

amounts to confusing the impersonal subjectivity of All-Possibility with the personal subjectivity of God as legislator and savior.[7]

In an altogether general manner, the Muslim tendency to abrupt simplifications, trenchant alternatives, and peremptory gestures—of which the reputedly rough and ready justice meted out by the *qādis* is at least a symbolic example, for in fact Muslim law is not so simple as that—stems, in the final analysis, from a voluntaristic distortion of the sense of the Absolute. Nonetheless, the coarse popularization of the idea of the Absolute in the moral climate of an Imrulqais, of a Tarafa, and of an Antara can lead to a real risk of ending with the logic of the drawn sword.

To repeat, the point to bear in mind here is that the two mental or moral attitudes that typify Islam *de facto*, namely certitude and serenity—which, when exaggerated, become fanaticism and fatalism—derive in the final analysis from the mystery of Unity as polarized in the Absolute and the Infinite. Regarding the consciousness of Infinitude, the importance of the idea of Peace in Islam is well known; this is what inspires resignation and generosity, the two key-virtues of Muslim piety. And again this same element manifests outwardly in liturgical phenomena such as the call to prayer from the height of the minarets, or in cultural phenomena such as the monotonous whiteness of Arab dress and towns;[8] this climate of soothing peace is prefigured in the desert which is inseparable from the Arab world—ancestrally the world of Hagar and Ishmael—and consequently from the Islamic world. In the Muslim Paradise, the chosen "say only Peace, Peace" (*illā qīlan salāman salāmā*); and "God calleth to the abode of Peace"

---

[7] In the climate of Christianity, we have encountered a similar opinion: God would have the "right" to impose what is nonsensical on the human mind, since, it would appear, He is "above logic"; but this too is impossible, for having created human intelligence "in His own image", God could not possibly wish to impose upon it contents incompatible with the ontological relationship between the mind and the truth, and therefore contents which are necessarily false. *Credo quia absurdum* quite clearly has in view apparent illogicalities only—ellipses touching on things that escape our earthly experiences or fragmentary reasonings.

[8] Leaving aside, of course, Turkish and Persian influences.

(*ilā dār as-salām*); the same fundamental idea is moreover contained in the word *islām*, which means "abandonment" to the Will of Him who, being the One (*ahad*), is the "absolutely Real" (*Wujūd mutlaq*).[9]

Certitude and serenity, we said; with these two attitudes are associated respectively combativeness and resignation. It is well known how important in the Path (*tarīqah*) are on the one hand spiritual "combat" (*jihād*)—prayer in all its forms (*dhikr*) being the weapon against the still untamed soul—and on the other hand "poverty" (*faqr*) "for the sake of God" (*ilā 'Llāh*), which render us independent both from the seductive world and the seducible soul. The Sufi is both *mujāhid*, "combatant", and *faqīr*, "poor"; he is always on a battlefield and, in another respect, in a desert.

The Testimony of Faith of Islam, according to which "there is no divinity except the one Divinity" is both sword and shroud: on the one hand it is a lightning-bolt in its fulgurating unicity, and on the other hand a sand dune or a blanket of snow in its peace-giving totality; and these two messages refer respectively, not only to the mysteries of Absoluteness and Infinitude, but also—in a certain fashion—to those of Transcendence and Immanence. In the final analysis, Immanence would be inconceivable without the Infinite: it is thanks to the Infinite that there is a cosmic projection enabling the Sovereign Good to be immanent; and it is starting from this projection that we can have the presentiment that all values and qualities have their roots in—and open out onto—necessary Being, which is the Good as such.[10]

---

[9] There is no point in objecting here that the personal God is not, strictly speaking, the Absolute since by definition He is already situated—He, the First—within universal Relativity; because He represents Absoluteness for all the subsequent contents of this Relativity. Similarly, when we speak of "necessary Being", we mean transcendent Reality as such, and not just the creating and personal Principle; the word "Being" has in fact two different meanings, namely "Reality" and "ontological Principle".

[10] If the first Testimony of Faith, which testifies to the Unity of God, is linked to Transcendence, the second Testimony, that of the Prophet or of the Logos, is in the final analysis the formula of Immanence.

Observations on Dialectical Antinomianism

There is a dialectical antinomianism just as there is a moral antinomianism; the latter is synonymous with "amorality"—not necessarily with "immorality"—whereas the former consists in presenting two opposing principles, not in order to choose between them, but to indicate an intermediary term which justifies them both; in which case, both affirmations become points of reference—each admissible in itself under certain conditions—serving to disclose an underlying truth which abolishes the contradiction. Thus one speaks of an "antinomian" theology[1] which consists in confronting two contradictory affirmations concerning God in view of a superior, possibly ineffable, truth, but without intending to negate either of the two affirmations, for the purpose is to confront, not a truth and an error—since that would not lead to a new conclusion—but two truths, each of which is valid in itself but insufficient as regards their antinomy.

The prototype of antinomian dialectics is furnished, all told, by the diversity of religions: apparently false in relation to one another, each is true in itself, and in addition each conceals—and provokes—a common and unifying truth which pertains to the plane of primordial and perennial wisdom.

But the absolute archetype of dialectical antinomianism is not situated on the plane of doctrines; it is found in the very nature of relative or contingent subjectivity, namely in the phenomenon of individuality, which is both evident and contradictory: evident because the "I" exists unquestionably—*cogito ergo sum*—and contradictory because while the "I" is unique by definition, it is nonetheless repeated; because there are "I's" which empirically are not "me", or rather, because no other "I" is "me".

Thus when a Muslim—and *a priori* an Arab—passes from one aspect of the real to another, he changes egos so to speak: either he sees only the divine Rigor, or he sees only the Gentleness; he is capable of loving one or more women while trembling at the idea of the Last Judgment—something which the Westerner is incapable of doing.

---

[1] We have come across this expression in a book on Palamite theology, if our memory is correct.

When a Westerner trembles at the idea of Judgment he enters a monastery or becomes a hermit; when he thinks he has the right to love a creature in the face of God, he does not tremble; trust then takes precedence over terror, once and for all.

Extreme fear and extreme trust: the underlying coherence of these opposite positions resides in the spiritual temperament of the Oriental, namely in a desire to go to the root of things, a desire for total commitment; in short, it is to perceive the aspects of the Revelation and the *Sunnah*, not according to their logical continuity and overall equilibrium, but according to a discontinuity that is mindful of penetrating each aspect taken by itself; the apparent incoherence may result from the fact that two different subjects are involved—in which case we would speak of a vocational disparity—but it may also be situated in one and the same subject. In the first case, the enigma lies in religion, which allows for such divergent and abrupt positions; in the second case, it lies in the mentality of the individual who changes egos, so to speak, according to his perception or state.

This question of the antinomy between fear and trust, or between Rigor and Clemency, leads us to the following consideration. According to the Koran, "God forgives whom He will and punishes whom He will", which for some people means that Justice depends upon the divine Will, whereas in reality it is the divine Will that is governed by Justice, for Being "precedes" Willing; otherwise the divine Name "The Just" (*Al-Hakīm*) would be meaningless. The Koranic verse we have just quoted could only mean: God forgives some people who, according to human measures, do not seem to be deserving of forgiveness, and He refrains from chastising some who, according to the same measures, seem to be deserving of punishment; and He acts in this manner not solely because "He wants to"—which precisely would not be a reason—but for reasons that we, not disposing of God's measures, cannot know; the apparent voluntarism of the Koran amounts therefore to a dismissal of the case. Notwithstanding, it is absurd to say that something is good simply because God does it, without implying that God, being the Sovereign Good, does it because it is good, just as He is Good; because it manifests the divine Goodness or some aspect of it.

God's Qualities precede His Willings, and not conversely; His Willings are inconceivable without His Qualities; "there is no divinity except God", and not: "except God's Will". If, Koranically speaking, "God doeth what He will", it is because metaphysically He does what He is.

In this connection, we would point out that, in speaking of God, the exegetists distinguish between "Desire" (*Irādah*)—or "Commandment" (*'Amr*)—and "Will" (*Māshīah*): God "wills" good and evil, but He "desires" or "orders" only good; now this point of distinction does not suffice to take us out of the vicious circle of a voluntarism which lends an almost human subjectivity to All-Possibility and which for that reason becomes morally unintelligible. It is true that Ghazzali alludes to "mysteries not to be disclosed", and doubtless he has in mind the complexity of the divine Nature, thus the degrees of principial Subjectivity, in short, all that could open the door both to polytheism and pantheism; still, the Sufis, who are supposed to know these mysteries, have too often lent their support to anthropomorphist voluntarism as well as to legalistic moralism, thereby assuming responsibility for all the pitfalls inherent in exoteric simplifications.

We must, for the sake of clarity, summarize here what may be termed—rightly or wrongly according to case—the doctrine of the "divine Will". The Supreme Principle is the Absolute, and in the final analysis it is from this quality that the existence of things derives; being the Absolute, the Principle is *ipso facto* the Infinite, hence All-Possibility, the supra-personal divine "Will", from which are derived the diversity of things, of creatures, of events, in short, of all that is possible. Being the Absolute and the Infinite, the Principle is also the Sovereign Good, and it is from this aspect that the positive qualities of things, on the one hand, and the regulating, legislating, and saving Will of God derive, on the other hand. But this is not to say that the same logical and moral subjectivity "wills" at one and the same time existence, the division into good and evil, and the realization of the good; the will that wants the good "superimposes" itself upon the ontological functions that "precede" it, which amounts to saying that this will is not the fundamental hypostasis of the divine Order, although it manifests its essence, otherwise it could not be the will of the Good.

If the hypostasis that most directly touches upon the human order is this will of the Good —thus the personal God who reveals and saves—it is precisely because the divine Essence, namely the Absolute with its aspect of Infinitude, is *a priori* the Sovereign Good; and this is so notwithstanding functional and transitory appearances to the contrary deriving from the limitlessness of Possibility.

— ∴ —

According to Muslims, God owes man nothing, but keeps His promises because He cannot lie. The key to this mystery is the combination—or parallelism—between two antinomic truths: firstly, God in Himself can owe nothing to man, for the Absolute can owe nothing to the contingent, and this is the relationship of incommensurability; secondly, God as Creator "wishes to owe" something to man, otherwise He would not have created him intelligent, free, and responsible, and this is the relationship of reciprocity. In ignoring the first relationship, man sins through casualness, through lack of fear; in ignoring the second, he attributes to God a tyranny and arbitrariness that are contrary to the divine perfection, and this borders on blasphemy; but depending on the social setting or circumstances, it may be opportune to stress one of these relationships more than the other. Monotheism, to the extent that it is "totalitarian", has the tendency to reduce divergent realities to a single relationship, that of the "will" of God.

Analogously: on the one hand, man possesses intelligence, thus he has the right to think and cannot help doing so; on the other hand, God alone is omniscient, thus man cannot know more than God, nor understand better than God; he can know and understand only through God. Wisdom consists in being aware of both relationships.

Let us return now to the abrupt juxtaposition between fear and trust: the first is motivated by the idea of Judgment, and the second, all things considered, finds its immediate expression in the integration of sexual pleasure in the Way. The Islamic insistence on the religious value of sexuality is readily understandable: according to the Prophet, marriage is a schooling in generosity and patience, leaving aside the concern of procreation; it comprises a mystical function because, again according to Tradition, sexual union prefigures celestial beatitude and, we may add, contributes to the sense of the Infinite to the extent that man is contemplative, which he is supposed to be. Besides, when a Junayd says that he needs to unite with woman as he needs to eat—an illogical comparison, objectively speaking, since man can live without woman but not without food—he has in mind the experience of sexual *barakah* and not a biological necessity; this experience, thanks to its affinity with the mysteries of Infinitude and Extinction, had become for him as necessary as daily bread. What takes precedence here is the compelling association of ideas for the contemplative, and not a concern for logic; the ill-sounding character of the expression proves the implausibility of its literal meaning—in accordance with the principle *credo quia absurdum*—given that one is dealing here with a saint.

A marginal note may be useful in this vein of thought, so as to forestall difficulties that could arise when reading certain texts: according to Ghazzali and others, one of the advantages of marriage is that it allows one to "vanquish" the goad of the flesh; now by "victory" is meant simply appeasement inasmuch as it enables one— through the absence of carnal distraction, precisely—to draw closer to God by direct and positive spiritual means that compensate for what might seem to be a defeat, and which it would be without said compensation; another element of "victory" lies moreover in the sexual experience itself: the extinctive and unifying consciousness of the metaphysical or mystical transparency of the sensible phenomenon.

But the great enigma of the average Sufic mentality is not the accentuation of sexuality and thereby of the perspective of trust or hope, it is the excessive accentuation—even though only incidentally—of the perspective of fear and thus of legal scrupulousness.[2] It must be said that the ideas of sin, Judgment, hell, and Predestination were unknown to the pagan Arabs, or were known to them only as "tales of the men of old" (*asātīr al-awwalīn*); the new, insistent, and striking presentation gripped their imagination all the more powerfully. Even so, the over-accentuations of the perspective of fear—of which Ghazzali provides examples—which logically induce despair, are compatible neither with the "good tidings" (*bushrā*) which is the purpose of Revelation, nor with the spiritual quality and right to hope of those who make themselves the spokesmen of these excesses; for, after all, when a man who is supposed to be a great saint declares that he would rather be a wisp of straw when he thinks of the Judg-

---

[2] See *Le Soufisme, voile et quintessence*, the chapter "Paradoxes d'un ésotérisme". As a matter of fact, we repeat ourselves from book to book, and sometimes even from one chapter to the next, but do not deem it necessary to excuse ourselves for doing so given that the need for clarity has its rights.

ment than be a human being, one is tempted to think that under such conditions religion virtually loses all meaning—despite Pascal's wager—even though one will guess that, in such a case, we are dealing with a subjective experience eluding the laws of logic or language. As for what the limits—by right or in fact—of symbolism, metaphors, and hyperboles should be, they are somewhat hazy, especially in the Oriental atmosphere.[3]

No doubt, there is a blind fideism that abolishes intelligence, as there is a pedantic legalism that ruins the moral sense, but it would be imprudent, to say the least, to attribute such aberrations to all those whose language and comportment err on the side of excess. Be that as it may, we find ourselves here in the setting of *bhakti* and *karma-yoga*—to speak in Hindu terms—and certainly not in that of *jnāna*;[4] we are thus in a setting favoring mystical individualism, not liberating knowledge. The expressly anti-intellectual tendency of a certain bhaktism, infatuated more with efficacy than with truth, can moreover explain many paradoxical and disappointing phenomena, on the practical as well as theoretical planes.

We must return once again to the case of the saint who wishes, from excess of fear, to be a wisp of straw rather than a man: from the symbolist point of view, we could assume that subjective expressions have in this instance an objective meaning, as if one were saying, "If ye knew what the Day of Judgment is, ye would want to be wisps of straw"—but the books do not specify this intention; in any case, there seems to be a preference for a nonsensical utterance, which has a catalyzing effect, or supposedly so. The matter of symbolism notwithstanding, we could also surmise that the expressions in question

---

[3] In *Mahāyāna* Buddhism, the desire to deliver the last blade of grass is absurd in many respects when taken literally, but it expresses an intention of generous impersonality and in the final analysis refers to the Apocatastasis.

[4] It would be a naive illusion to believe that at the beginning of a religion all the apostolic personages had to be *jnānīs*; *jnāna*—gnosis—possesses the deepening and transforming virtue resulting from its very nature, which is both intellective and unitive; but this does not mean that it has the expansive impetus required by a newborn religion.

were uttered when under the sway of a mystical state or during a particular period; but such an argument is not used except in the case of theopathic exclamations—like "I am the Truth" or "Glory be to me"—that run the risk of disturbing the faith of the believers, whereas edifying extravagances are supposed to stimulate it, even though they defy common sense.[5]

Keeping to the image of the wisp of straw and analogous images and sayings, there is also this hypothesis to be considered: according to Ghazzali, men have to be whipped into Paradise, and that is why the Koran contains threats; now this reasoning, plausible in itself, opens the door to every exaggeration, including the most implausible and scandalous. But this is not all: in order to endow the threat with a maximum of authority, it is placed in the mouth of a great saint; it is believed that a maximum of persuasive force is achieved thereby, whereas in fact one simply falls into absurdity. In other words, attributing the saying of the straw to a saint to whom it could not possibly apply might be a pious fraud; in fact, it seems impossible for us to rule out this hypothesis completely, even though it would discredit many traditional sayings;[6] by compensation it has the merit of sparing men from being perplexed who know that sound logic is a gift of the Holy Spirit.[7] Now, having said this, we do not underestimate the argument that symbolism has its rights—even when the symbolism is outrageous to the point of absurdity—for this argument is no doubt sufficient in many cases; yet pious frauds exist nonetheless.

---

[5] One has to know that the Koran contains nothing that authorizes eschatological terror on the part of pious men, and still less on the part of the Companions of the Prophet: "Is it not true (regarding) the saints of God (*awliyā Allāh*)—no fear shall be on them, neither shall they sorrow? Those who believe and who fear Him—for them are good tidings in this life and in the next. There is no changing in the Words of God: that is the supreme happiness" (*Sūrah* "Jonah" [10]:63-65). "Who believe and who fear Him": these are those who on the one hand accept the Truth and on the other respect the Law, which has no connection with a "totalitarian" mysticism of fear, or rather of dread.

[6] A "sincere fraud", sincere since it is based—as Massignon rightly or wrongly supposes for certain *ahādīth*—on a mystical "mediumship" which, even if it is not illusory, has in any case nothing to do with historical truth.

[7] "Sound logic": that which operates starting from intellection and with certain and sufficient data—something rationalism does not do.

To return to Ghazzali's "whippings": when the Koran specifies that in hell sufferings "shall not be lightened", one is tempted to think that this is metaphysically impossible since all duration comprises cycles, hence alternations, and that an absolutely "compact" punishment is inconceivable;[8] but it is not this cosmic law that the Koranic passage has in view, the explanation being much more simple: it is solely a question of forestalling the unfortunate tendency men have of devising means of escape that could neutralize the threats of the Scriptures. The same principle applies when the Koran rejects the opinion of unbelievers that in the fire "their days will be numbered"; which is metaphysically true but morally false, if one may express it thus, all the more so in that the unbelievers who put forth this argument are certainly not metaphysicians.

An example of symbolism which is at first glance arbitrary and excessive, but plausible in the final analysis, is the *hadīth* that dooms painters and sculptors to the depths of hell. It will of course be objected that the plastic arts are natural to man, that they exist everywhere, and that they can have a sacral function—that this is even their most fundamental reason for being—which is true, but misses the essential intention of the *hadīth*. For the literal meaning of the saying represents, by its very violence, a "preventive war" against the ultimate abuse of human intelligence, namely naturalism in all its forms: artistic naturalism on the one hand and philosophical and scientistic naturalism on the other; hence the exact imitation of appearances, both exteriorizing and "accidentalizing", and recourse to logic alone, to reason alone, cut off from its roots. Man is *homo sapiens* and *homo faber*: he is a thinker and therefore also a producer, a craftsman, an artist; now there is a final phase of these developments that is forbidden to him—it is prefigured by the forbidden fruit of Paradise—a phase therefore that he must never reach, just as man may make himself king or emperor but not God; in anathematizing the creators of images, the Prophet intended to prevent the final subversion. According to the Muslim conception, there is only one sin

---

[8] The same is true—but conversely—for paradisiacal bliss, with the difference that there is no symmetry between Paradise and hell, and that the shadows in Heaven have nothing to do with punishment. Let us note that Buddhism insists on the omnipresence of Mercy; this idea also follows from the Koran, for the divine *Rahmah* "encompasseth everything".

that leads to the depths of hell—that is to say, which will never be forgiven—and that is the fact of associating other divinities with the one Divinity; if Islam places such creators in Gehenna, it is because it seems, quite paradoxically, to liken the plastic arts with the same mortal sin, and this disproportion is precisely proof that it has in view not the arts in their normal state—even though it forbids them, assuredly—but the reason for forbidding them; in other words, it has in view the naturalistic subversion of which the plastic arts are, for the Semitic sensibility, the symbols and prefigurations.[9]

This example, which we have dwelt on to some extent, shows how excessive formulations can serve as a vehicle of correspondingly profound intentions, which leads us once again to the principle *credo quia absurdum*.

In order to properly situate the problem of man's sentiments before God, it is important to specify that fear refers to the relationship "Lord-servant", and to the Law; Christ, who insisted upon love and inwardness, advocated the relationship "Father-child" which, being in the nature of things, must also find a place in Islam, *a posteriori* at least; not on the plane of legalism, but on the plane of gnosis and of love.

Still on the subject of fear and referring to the Gnostic terminology, one could also put forth the argument that for the "hylic" or "somatic" type, it is primarily threats that determine the will; for the "psychic" it is primarily all of the promises or the imagery of religion in general; whereas for the "pneumatic", it is the metaphysical idea. But given that man is not an absolute unity, we may also speak of man "inasmuch as" he is this or that, so as to avoid the idea that threats concern the "hylic" exclusively, or that the "psychic"—always in connection with volitive assimilation—is necessarily closed to the language of universal principles.

---

[9] In condemning images, Islam—which is blessedly "sterile"—refuses at the same time "culturism"—the plague of the West—with its torrents of artistic and literary creations, which puff up souls and distract them from the "one thing needful".

—— .:. ——

Dialectical antinomianism is characteristic of Sufism because it springs from the very character of the Arabs, which—as we have suggested above—tends to enclose the mind in a particular aspect of things to the detriment of the homogeneity of the overall vision of the real; negatively, this is to be incoherent; but positively, it is to do nothing by halves.[10] Thus the ancient Arab was wholehearted in everything, which explains his propulsive force—a force not by itself capable of miracles, but that is enhanced by supernatural factors.

Yet there is something else. A language that is both abstract and logical is something that can only be acquired through long experience; originally, language is concrete and allusive or associative: concrete because it expresses principles through images, and allusive or associative because instead of relying on a logical sequence it makes use of associations of ideas or of analogies; it readily replaces complex demonstrations with impact images, of which a classical symbol might be Alexander cutting the Gordian knot. An example of this manner of proceeding—common in Islam on account of its quasi-Bedouin origin—is this saying of Ibn Abbas: "The best of Muslims is he who has the most wives"; now, in order not to be scandalized,[11] one has to know the Arabo-Islamic implications, which are at once practical, psychological, moral, and contemplative. We are here in the presence of a dialectical procedure that consists in suggesting what is most substantial by what is most accidental; a two-edged sword if ever there was one, yet it is an efficacious language for a mentality accustomed to elliptical, implicit, and multi-dimensional symbolism; the scandal of a crude and, if need be, quantitative image serves here as a catalyst, something that in fact is encountered in all mythologies.

[10] Someone has told us the story that one day Saint Teresa of Ávila had prepared a turkey for dinner, and that one of the nuns was astonished at it; the saint is said to have replied: "When I fast, I fast, and when I eat, I eat." This is what is called doing things wholeheartedly, whatever one does; but without exaggeration.

[11] David and Solomon would not have been able to disavow this opinion. It is a question of the spiritual significance of polygamy, which we do not have to analyze here, all the more since we have done so elsewhere. We have no choice but to admit that human possibility is diverse.

Doubtless, there would be no need to speak of antinomic dialectics if it were merely a question of exaggeration in one subject only; but what allows us to speak of antinomianism is precisely the fact that such exclusive overemphasis is duplicated in the case of different and contradictory subjects, and takes place all within the same human consciousness. It is this fact, and not some fragmentary exaggeration, that places us before a phenomenon *a priori* unintelligible and exasperating; yet, although it is logically unacceptable, it is psychologically decipherable in the final analysis, and instructive in the sense that it teaches us about one more modality in the range of indefinitely diverse possibilities of the soul and the mind.

Unquestionably, there is a passional element intervening in antinomic dialectics—in this curious capacity to switch egos according to the trajectory of a thought—and this element also explains another tendency, that of gratuitous argumentation: a given truth can be conceived perfectly, and one assumes that one owes it some kind of proof, but this proof can be literally anything at all, and this "anything at all"—in the mind of the thinker—is justified by the truth; the proof is good since the thing to be proved is true.[12] Many defective and disappointing reasonings of theologians, metaphysicians, and mystics are explained by this pious intention to fly to the rescue of a truth that often has no need of this solicitude and that in any case would deserve to be buttressed by serious arguments. It is as if what matters is less to furnish an objective proof than to create some kind of mental satisfaction; from such a point of view, a proof and a semblance of proof are equivalent, for in any case, the truth is what it is.

A particularly disconcerting aspect of a mentality that is too unilaterally symbolist is the omission of necessary information: something is affirmed that is not understandable or plausible unless one knows in what connection it is being considered, but this connection is left out; such dialectical deficiencies presuppose, quite clearly, a reader who has an intuition of the non-formulated intentions, whose hidden meaning is not supposed to present any kind of a problem within the framework of the ethnic mentality wherein this phenomenon takes

---

[12] An example of this procedure is, in Sufism, the subjectification of evil with the intention of showing that God wills only the good. Similar reasonings are encountered—as regards their gratuitousness—in the Christian climate, for example in order to prove that God cannot but comprise three Persons.

place; this is a mentality that combines allusive language with a need for absoluteness, and the elliptical with the explosive.[13]

In addition, as we have already mentioned, the mental and moral antinomianism of the Arabs and other peoples—especially those who are Arabized—is not unrelated to the symbolist mentality for which the symbol takes precedence over the fact, either relatively or absolutely: rightly so in the first case, and mistakenly in the second; this does not mean that the second case cannot be legitimate in its turn, for instance when the fact denied has no importance from the point of view of the symbolism affirmed, as is often the case in religious dogmatisms.

Be that as it may, there are *grosso modo* two kinds of symbolist thought: one respectful of facts and at the same time mindful of preserving the homogeneity of the overall view of the real, and the other infatuated with the essence of the symbol—infatuated with the absolute within the limits of a given symbolism—to the point of neglecting the exactitude of facts and, furthermore, isolating the symbolism by cutting it off from all other aspects of reality. It is in fact a certain need for absoluteness that explains, in the Arab, the tendency on the one hand to isolate an idea or an image from every compensatory context, and on the other to exaggerate the specific coloration of the image, making of it an absolute, precisely; which is yet another way of "doing nothing by halves" and of "doing everything with the heart". If on the one hand this predisposition gives rise to a curiously dynamic way of thinking—at least on the plane of religion and outside the Greek influence—on the other it opens the way to a unitive mysticism that goes straight to the mark, with the simplicity of the forces of nature.

[13] Aside from tautology and platitude, born from the need to depict things, to implant them in the imagination, or to be able to picture them, as it were.

Diversity of Paths

One of the chief distinctions in Sufic methodology is that between the path of "stations" (*maqāmāt*) and the path of "attraction" (*jadhb*); the first is systematic and proceeds from stage to stage under the vigilant eye of a master (*murshid*)—there may be several of them—whereas the second is subject to no rule other than the spiritual intuition (*dhawq*) of the mystic and the divine aid (*tawfīq*) or Grace (*Rahmah*) that answers it and at the same time provokes it. The difference of principle between the two paths does not exclude combinations made possible by the nature of things, since man is one, and, above all, because God is one; hence there could be no absolute boundaries between these two paths, despite the rigor of certain conditions.

The first path, which is initiatic in the proper sense, and hence methodical, is based essentially on the idea that in the human soul there are defects which have become natural owing to the loss of the earthly Paradise, and that the "Path" (*Tarīqah*) or the "Journey" (*Sulūk*) consists in eliminating them successively; and this explains the need for a master who must define these obstacles, indicate the remedies, and, if necessary, validate the cure, and then take necessary or useful measures to prevent the victory—when too individualized—from turning into a defeat, and even the most serious defeat of all.

The main obstacle, it is said, is the unconscious attachment to "secondary causes" (*sabab*, pl. *asbāb*); by this term two things are meant: firstly, natural, verifiable causes, and secondly, human causations, particularly the means of sustenance; work, for example, is a "cause" (*sabab*) of our gain just as the sun is the "cause" of heat. All "secondary causes" are "veils" (*hijāb*, pl. *hujub*) hiding the "First Cause" (Tustari: *as-Sabab al-Awwal*),[1] the only one which is; the path

---

[1] Regarding matters of terminology, we will refer readers interested in Arabic to Louis Massignon's *Essai sur les origines du lexique technique de la mystique musulmane* and to Jean-Louis Michon's *Le soufi marocain Ahmad Ibn ʿAjība et son Miʿrāj*. Let us note here—since we are on the topic of Sufism—that it is absurd to have the esoterism of Islam coincide with Shiite "imamology" and "gnoseology", as Corbin would have it; then to reduce metaphysics to an inspirationist exegesis, as if intellection—which is also supra-rational—did not exist or had no role to play. Authentic esoterism derives from the nature of things and not from a dynastic institution; its seeds are everywhere

consists in overcoming the optical illusion of relative and multiple causes, in order to allow for the final perception of the only Cause in all things, including our own acts, which "veil" the true Agent; not "such and such an agent" but the "Agent as such".

The "Remembrance of God" (*dhikru 'Llāh*), of which the Koran says that it is "greater" than the prescribed prayer, or that it is the "greatest thing of all", is basically a spontaneous awareness of the divine causality, within ourselves as well as around us. Every moral defect, and even every innocently individualistic attitude, is a for-getting of God, whether naively habitual or perverse; this is the "forgetfulness" (*ghaflah*) mentioned by the Koran and referred to by the Sufis; conversely, each moral quality coincides with a way of remembering the divine Cause, which is the Good and the Norm. And that is why, to conquer the superstition—or idolatry—of secondary causes amounts to acquiring the virtues; it is also to render the natural virtues supernatural. Superstition or idolatry; but we could also say: "association" (*shirk*) of something else with God—of a second reality with the one and only Reality—for it is there, in the Koranic perspec-tive wherein everything converges on Unity, that lies the sin of sins, together with "unbelief" (*kufr*), which implies the idea of ingratitude and blasphemy.

Thus, in order to obtain the spiritual cure, the disciple (*murīd*) or the traveler (*sālik*) will have to detach himself from "secondary causes" as far as possible in practical life, for this awareness needs

---

present, sparks can flash from every flint; to make of esoterism a religious program and a theological argument is a contradiction in terms. Of course, fundamental truths were expressed initially by those whom the Shiites consider to be imams; however, Sunnite Sufism refers to these sages, not insofar as they are supposed to be imams in the theo-logical sense of Shiism, but insofar as they are "poles" (*qutb*, pl. *aqtāb*) of Islam as such, outside all confessional interpretation or annexation; *Spiritus autem ubi vult spirat.* Be that as it may, it could be admitted that the Persians, being Aryans, are *a priori* more apt for metaphysical speculation or formulation than the Arabs, who are Semites; but the Arabs having assimilated the Greek influence—like the Hellenized Jews as well—did not need the Persians to have *a posteriori* the aptitude in question. What the Iranian spirit was able to confer upon the Shiites, the Greek spirit was able to confer upon both the Sunnites and the Shiites; this may be said without forgetting that several of the greatest Sunnites were Iranians, and that the indirect, or direct, founders of Shiism were Arabs. It should also be specified that the general tone of Muslim philosophy allows us to include it in the religious thought—in the widest sense—of Islam; with some reservations, depending on the case.

to be concrete and thorough: for example—although this is only a symbol of attitudes exhibiting the greatest variety and, at times, the greatest subtlety—the disciple will refuse alms because "God alone provides", or he will refuse a remedy because "God alone cures". This is the virtue of "trust" (*tawakkul*), which is crucial, but which in fact has led to many abuses; doubtless it is better to be absurd than to be impious, and it is better to overdo than to stop halfway; nonetheless, exaggeration is a double-edged sword. However, if the realists of spirituality are right in thinking that a philosophical awareness of divine causality is insufficient, and strictly speaking that it amounts to "hypocrisy" (*nifāq*)—for the usual behavior of the mere "thinker" hardly corroborates his sublime convictions—they all too often make the mistake of forgetting the "supernaturally natural", and in principle efficacious, role of intelligence; a forgetfulness that can be explained primarily by the fact that they address themselves to the average—albeit normally endowed—man and not to the "pneumatic", and do so according to the voluntaristic and *a priori* anthropomorphic perspective of common religion. In Sufism, extreme popularization and initiatic elitism go hand in hand; each has its place but there are also paradoxical and problematic blends. The excuse could be made that not only profane or passional men are being addressed, but the profane or passional aspect of man as such; in which case everything comes down to a question of proportion and opportuneness.

An objection that could be raised against this therapy consisting in eliminating "secondary causes" is the following: if it is not the sun that gives light, fire that burns, food that nourishes, medicine that cures—on the "pretext" that God alone does it all—the object of the operation should also be placed in the divine Order, because the sufficient reason for physical causes is that God contacts the physical domain only through them—except in the case of miracles—and He does this precisely because the causes are physical.[2] Consequently, the problem to overcome is not the fact that man attributes earthly effects to earthly causes, but that he does not perceive at the bottom of these causes the immanent divine Cause, as he ought to perceive, in the final analysis, the divine Self in the depth of his own spirit.

---

[2] In the Aristotelian sense of the word, embracing the entire order of "nature", at least logically and *de jure*.

The idea of divine intervention in natural causality brings up the following considerations: if on the one hand God does not "enter" the physical order except in the case of a miracle, on the other hand He does not "leave" the divine Order except in the case of creation; He "enters" without stepping outside of Himself, and He "leaves" without entering into what is other than Himself; the first miracle being Revelation, and the first creation being the Logos. Or again: if we say that divine "causes" do not enter directly into the created order, except in cases of a miraculous intervention, we could also say correlatively that the "effects" of these causes are situated, like the causes themselves, in the divine Order, except in the case of creative projection.[3] From still another standpoint, we may say that if the Uncreated does not "enter" into the created except through theophany, conversely the created does not "enter" into the Uncreated except through the Apocatastasis; both "entries" being only apparent, quite evidently, for the Principle and manifestation cannot mingle; we are here at the outward limit of what is expressible.

The distinction between the path of methodical "progression" (*sulūk*) and that of mystical "attraction" (*jadhb* or *jadhbah*) means, not that there are only these two paths in Sunnite Islam, but that each of them is a category encompassing an almost indeterminate number of possible paths; according to a Sufi adage, "There are as many paths towards God as there are human souls". An example of this diversity is the difference, on the plane of the "stations", between a positive method, that of a Qushayri, and a negative method, that of an Ibn al-Arif; in the first case, one is expected to overcome the illusion of "secondary causes" by means of the corresponding and corrective virtues, whereas in the second case virtue itself is considered as an attachment to such a "cause", and it must be overcome by an "extinction" that puts God in place of the virtue, or more exactly, by an "extinction"

---

[3] Which is to say that *in divinis* the relationship of cause to effect and the nature of the two poles appear altogether differently than they do in the physical order, the meta-cosmic archetype of all causality being the relationship—in Sanskrit terms—between *Brahma* and *Īshvara*, and then between *Purusha* and *Prakriti*.

having the effect of rendering God present there where "common man" (*'awwām*) places his virtue or, what amounts to the same, his "station". Our intention here is not to comment on this point of view which is characteristic of the Sufic tendency towards subtle eliminations and "unveilings", but simply to take account of the complexity of the paths, or of the Path.

Again, concerning the fact of replacing the superstition about secondary causes with the awareness of divine causes, or with God-as-Cause, the main pitfall of this alchemy is the definition of the divine Will, on the one hand, and, on the other, of the object of this Will; that is to say, the idea—quite elliptical, to say the least—that God is the only cause of cosmic or natural effects leads us straight to the question of evil as object of the Will of God.

We have often said, and doubtless will repeat, that God could not will evil as evil, that He wills it only in a connection where, precisely, evil ceases to be an evil. A phenomenon that is an evil, at its own level and in our experience, does not form part of the divine Will except as a fragment or phase of a good, but not when taken separately; the possibility of what is an evil at its own level does not stem from the Will of God as a Person who creates, legislates, and metes out justice, but from divine All-Possibility, which is evidently impersonal since it pertains to the divine Essence. Or again, if it is affirmed that God is the only Agent of every act, it ought to be specified then that He is, in every act, the Agent of the act as such, but not of a particular act.

Be that as it may, in pure theosophy there is no question of wishing to remove from God His mysteries by means of unveilings and specifications; for however acute our discernments, the divine mystery remains complete by reason of the Infinitude of the Real.

Whatever the ideological or moral excesses that the disciple may find useful to adopt in the course of his way, the method consists, as we have seen, in divesting oneself progressively of profane prejudices that amount to so many forgettings of God—namely, the well known "breaking of habits"—and in realizing "sincerity" (*sidq*) of faith in the One; each divestment being a "disappearance" (*fanā'*) before the real Cause, or, in other words, an "extinction". Yet it is here, according to Ibn Arabi, that the major temptation of the Path occurs: having obtained the awareness of a given aspect of divine causality, man, due to his individualism or inveterate egoism, risks appropriating this victory for himself, and forgetting that the subject as well as the object of the victory is God; now "pride" (*kibar, istikbār*) kills all the other virtues. Thus it is a question not only of eliminating the superstition about a given secondary cause—of a given causality experienced outside God—but also of uprooting all temptation to luciferianism on the part of the subject who risks wishing, with a satisfaction that is spiritually paralyzing, to settle into a given "station" (*maqām*), the awareness of which he individualizes; therein lies the whole danger of spiritual narcissism. Symbolically, it will be said that each station tempts the "traveler" with a particular treasure which he must refuse if he does not want to lose everything; numerous initiatic stories—from myths to fairy tales—relate this spiritual drama, and this is also one of the meanings of the "extinction of extinction" (*fanā' al-fanā'*), although this term applies primarily to an extrinsic aspect of the supreme goal.

Some precisions are necessary here, for one should not fall into disproportionate fears or into a blind humilitarianism refractory to all objectivity with respect to oneself. The danger of the "pride" in question results on the one hand from the natural ambition of the man who is voluntaristic by temperament, and on the other hand from the idea that one must "personally" attain a transcendent goal and a perfect realization, whence a perfectionistic obsession, or an ambitious subjectivism that ends up practically speaking putting the "I"—in the form of a particular "realization"—in place of God. The whole remedy for this can be summarized with the so to speak Vedantic meaning of the *Shahādah*, and consequently by the *neti neti* of the *Vedānta*: "not this, not this"—the implication being: "*Ātmā* alone". This is also expressed, in the Koran, by the story of the child Abraham: seeing a star, he believes it is God; but when he sees it set, he is aware of his error; likewise with the moon and the sun (*Sūrah* "Cattle" [6]:76-78). Unquestionably, this story—like analogous symbolisms—comprises both a specifically initiatic as well as a generally human meaning.

The point to be made here is that one ought to distinguish carefully between an "abode" (*manzil*) which one believes is supreme and which one takes pride in, and an "abode" in which one finds contentment in all piety and in all humility. When certain texts blame those who stay at a given "abode" we can guess that this staying stems from pride since we are told that it causes one to lose everything, according to Ibn Arabi; for it goes without saying that contentment with little— a little that in reality is immense—does not result in such a loss, otherwise there would be neither a hierarchy of saints nor degrees in Paradise.

It is possible that we have simplified somewhat the problem of "renouncing something in order to obtain more"—renouncing a particular treasure or dignity—and that this question is in reality much more subtle and complex than we seem to acknowledge, all the more as it pertains to the initiatic order; but what in any case justifies our simplification, if it be one, is the theme of "loss" or "fall", which always indicates a luciferian attitude, so that the most convoluted analyses can add nothing substantial to our interpretation.

Be that as it may, there is another version of this myth found in a German folktale, with a different meaning since it comprises no luciferianism or fall: the hero goes off to seek adventure on his white horse—which in reality is the spiritual guide or the protective genius, like Al-Khidr in Islam—and he sees on the ground a peacock feather of marvelous beauty; he dismounts in order to pick it up, but the horse tells him: "Leave it on the ground." After some time, the incident repeats itself; the hero renounces a still more beautiful feather; but the third time, he cannot resist and picks up the feather, despite the repeated warnings of the horse. The horse then lists, in ascending order, the glories that the hero has renounced, to his advantage in fact; but the greatest glory has escaped him because he has not been able to renounce the preceding glory, which was lesser. The implication here is thus an initiatic possibility altogether different from the one that entails the risk of a fall, even though the symbolism is almost identical.

After having experienced—as far as possible and up to the edge of the absurd—the rejection of secondary causes, which entails the practice of all the forms of asceticism, the disciple has the right to return to these causes without hesitation or suspicion. Henceforth he sees in them—existentially, not philosophically—the divine causation, and as a result will have access to the mystery of Immanence; this new awareness renders asceticism—but not healthy sobriety—superfluous, and opens the door to a spiritualization of the most noble and there-fore most fundamental pleasures, by supernaturalizing and disindividualizing them, precisely.[4] Neither Islam in general nor Sufism in particular can be understood without taking into account this perspective of Immanence which completes, whether paradoxically or harmoniously, the exclusive and austere perspective of Transcendence.[5]

It follows from all the preceding that the two major infirmities of the human soul are the forgetting of God—of the immanent divine Cause—and the appropriation, by the individual, of qualities, merits, and glories; in other words, profanity on the one hand and pride on the other; or "association" (*shirk*) both objective and subjective. A phenomenon that seems to contradict this verdict is the fact that many Sufis have not feared to speak of the sublimity of their station, which *a priori* can give the impression of a strange boastfulness; in reality, it is the reverse that is true: they speak, well or ill, of themselves as if they were speaking of others; and they do so in order to express a victory made miraculously possible, hence in order to glorify God or to exalt the Path, and not in order to attribute a merit to a personality which, to the extent that this is possible, is no longer their own.

But let us return to the question of secondary causes and their spiritual reduction to the one Cause: each religion possesses an energetic aura—a *barakah*—producing phenomena that are consonant with the perspective of that religion; in a Sufi climate, miraculous phenomena occur—or have occurred—which corroborate supernaturally the perspective we have described, namely trust in the single divine Cause, and which may encourage recourse to attitudes that are generally senseless but heroically pious. Many facts of this kind seem implausible from the Christian point of view, but that is because the style of Christianity is different and consequently produces different marvels; thus it is appropriate to be prudent when judging phenomena situated in a religious world foreign to our own, and whose apparent

---

[4] Which Ibn Arabi has dealt with in his *Fusūs al-Hikam*, in the chapter on the "Muhammadan Wisdom".

[5] Meister Eckhart has expressed the in principle sacramental character of the gifts of nature by which we live; a character that is unveiled or actualized according to the sanctity or wisdom of the subject.

implausibility merely illustrates in a particularly concrete fashion the profound difference between traditional universes.[6]

The path of mystical "attraction" (*jadhb*), to which we alluded at the beginning of this chapter, is more direct than that of the methodical "journey" (*sulūk*), but it deprives the faithful soul who follows it of the experiences he needs if he wishes to guide others. The path of those who are "attracted" (*majdhūb*, pl. *majādhib*) requires in fact only two conditions, aside from the necessary qualification and vocation: on the one hand the religious framework, without which one risks being deprived of divine aid (*tawfīq*), and on the other hand the practice of the fundamental virtues, and this brings us back to the "stations" and to "secondary causes", but independently of all methodical succession. Of course, this path also implies, like the other, accomplishment of what—in principle or in fact—draws one closer to God, and abstention, by the same token, from what—in principle or in fact—takes one away from Him; "in principle", namely by its nature, and "in fact", namely by our disposition or our capacity. For there are good things that are not good for everybody, just as conversely, there are things reputed to be dangerous or harmful—but not intrinsically bad—that are not harmful to everybody; this is evoked, notably, by the symbolism of wine.

As in the "regular" path of *sulūk*, everything in this exceptional path of *jadhb* is based on the sacramental and almost Eucharistic ternary *Madhkūr-Dhikr-Dhākir* ("Invoked-Invocation-Invoker"), and then, correlatively, on the ternary *Makhāfah-Mahabbah-Ma'rifah* ("Fear-Love-Knowledge"); these diverse elements can be subdivided and combined indefinitely. But everything in this second path is more independent and spontaneous than in the first; the sense of the nature of things takes precedence over the concern for rules or conventions. The emphasis is upon "taste" (*dhawq*) and upon "state" (*hāl*), although, of course, they are not taken for criteria, since the criteria

---

[6] The phenomena in question are doubtless the origin of poetic legends on the one hand and hagiographic absurdities on the other, and yet they do not excuse the latter despite extenuating circumstances.

derive in the final analysis from the fundamental Idea (the *Shahādah*) understood in depth, and from the "Remembrance of God" accomplished with sincerity and perseverance; spiritual intuition and the sense of the sacred being more important here than ascetic practices,[7] unless one includes in this latter category the retreat (*khalwah*), accomplished in solitude and combined with fasts and vigils. The music and dance of the dervishes—supposed to favor, if not ecstasy as such, at least its anticipation—pertain to this same perspective of "tastes" and "states", although not exclusively; this is a question of affinities, not of prerogatives.

At the outermost limit, the *majdhūb* appears as a "fool" (*majnūn*), of whom one accepts a behavior situated more or less outside the Law; but at the opposite extreme one finds on the contrary the man who conforms to the primordial nature (*fitrah*), the "knower through God" (*'ārif bi-Llāh*), with similar intrinsic—and possibly practical—consequences as regards the literal Law.[8] This is to say that "attraction" is not necessarily a phenomenon of emotional mysticism, it can equally pertain to pure gnosis, given that in Sufism there is *Ma'rifah* as well as *Mahabbah;*[9] one will recall here the two ternaries mentioned above. In other words, the path of liberating attraction can be the fact not only of a Grace coming as it were from without and from above, and which occasionally can cloud the mind, it can also act *ab intra* and through the pure Intellect—"uncreated" center of the immortal soul—and bring about an awakening made of clarity or evidence.

---

[7] Hasan ash-Shadhili, father of the Shadhilite line, did not require his disciples—in spite of the problem of secondary causes—to renounce their livelihood, even a princely one, or to ostentatiously scandalize a society that was, after all, honorable since it was composed of believers.

[8] It is appropriate not to forget that in any case legalism comprises the danger of pharisaism: the replacement of virtues by prescriptions and the forgetting of what the nature of things requires or allows.

[9] It seems almost superfluous to add, firstly, that it is not enough to have no master in order to be one of the "attracted", and secondly that the fact of being "attracted" does not prevent one from having one or more masters; all the more so in that all combinations are possible. Let us add that the superior type of the "attracted"—extremely rare in fact—is none other than the "solitary" (*fard*), who more or less corresponds to the *Pratyeka-Buddha* of the *Mahāyāna*.

Transcendence and Immanence
in the Spiritual Economy of Islam

Dogmatic and exoteric Islam insists fiercely on Transcendence, which by definition is separative; esoterism, on the contrary, is based on Immanence, which is unitive. Basically, exoterism admits only its own point of view—due allowance being made for some nuances—whereas esoterism by definition admits two complementary perspectives, its own and that of exoterism, which is that of the Law. But esoterism has erected, of necessity, a barrier between them that is at once protective and disconcerting; this barrier is the ascetic zeal, which on the one hand clothes esoterism with a mantle of religious intelligibility—since this zeal presents itself as the "sincere" consequence of the Law—but on the other hand risks taking the means for the end, that is, it risks favoring a confusion between asceticism and gnosis. The Arabic word *barzakh* means "isthmus": it is a dividing line between two domains, and this line appears from the standpoint of each side to belong to the other side;[1] and that is why excess of legalistic scruple can seem like esoterism from the standpoint of legalism—the excess of scruples being a way of sublimating legalism through sincerity, hence by the absence of hypocrisy—whereas from the vantage point of gnosis excessive scruple appears on the contrary as an element of exoterism, given that no formalistic zeal can lead to knowledge. This ambiguity, which has its basis in the complexity of a society dominated by an inevitably anthropomorphic, voluntaristic, and sentimental religion, is the permanent source of misunderstandings and confusions; it is even what may be termed the classical misunderstanding of average Sufism.

We have just noted that the "exoterization of esoterism" is the reduction of esoterism to religious zeal, notably to legal scrupulousness, and to asceticism. This simplification or this confusion perforce

---

[1] The archetype of the *barzakh* is the half-divine and half-cosmic frontier separating Manifestation and the Principle and yet, in another respect, uniting them; it is the "divine Spirit" (*Rūh*) which is Manifestation, when seen "from above", and Principle, when seen "from below". Consequently, it is *Māyā* in both its aspects; the same thing appears, in a certain manner, in the Christian expression "true man and true God".

goes hand in hand with an "esoterization of exoterism", namely the mystical sublimation of ritual acts—by associating them with "degrees of contemplation"; from this standpoint, it is as if believers who perform the prescribed acts while being unaware of these mystical interpretations were insincere, or it is as if their acts were invalid, or again, as if mystical graces were the criteria of ritual validity, *et cetera.* However, religion cannot require believers to walk on initiatic stilts, for by definition it is addressed to all; and conversely, initiates, who by definition are situated at the center and in the inward, should have no need for projecting their spiritual tension into an outward zeal, all the more so in that such a projection, inasmuch as it cannot be avoided, will be manifested by the spiritual quality of the prescribed acts. All the errors under consideration here result from the strange idea that "the common Law (*shari'ah*) is esoterism (*tarīqah*)", an idea in which mystical sublimism meets legalistic scruple and confessional zeal.

Obviously, Sufi asceticism is in itself free from these misinterpretations and abuses. Its normal function is to be at once a discipline, an argument, and a veil; a discipline rightly intended to make the soul more supple in view of knowledge; then an argument intended to make Sufism plausible in the eyes of the doctors of the Law; and finally, a veil intended to hide gnosis and its "extra-territoriality", hence all that is dangerously and blessedly above the narrownesses of the "letter that killeth". The latter two intentions are extrinsic and result from the immanent wisdom which regulates the economy of sacred things but which does not forestall the classical misconception that consists in connecting to the domain of Transcendence factors which in reality pertain to that of Immanence. In a word, the moral incoherence—whether real or apparent—that is encountered in Islam is due in the final analysis to the presence of two domains that are at once complementary and relatively antinomic, that of the Transcendent and that of the Immanent; of obediential and separative piety on the one hand, and of participatory and unitive spirituality on the other.

These three elements, Transcendence, Immanence, and intermediary asceticism, are prefigured in the personality of the Prophet, and even explain it; they are to be found in him in an intrinsically homogeneous and substantial manner, quite obviously, and this homogeneity has allowed Islam to realize an unshakable equilibrium, from its beginnings down to our times; and necessarily so since we are dealing with a religion. However, this equilibrium cannot preclude partial, and in a certain sense providential, disequilibria, as we have just shown.

As for asceticism, it is necessary to distinguish between an ascesis that is physical, and indirect in relation to its end, and another that is moral, and direct in relation to its end: the physical is purificatory and aims to master the passional element, but not to destroy it inasmuch as it is pure energy, whereas the moral ascesis, on the contrary, aims at enabling the conformity of the soul to the demands of contemplation and thus seeks to develop receptive and participatory perfection; it affects not only the character but also the intelligence, in the sense that lack of virtue—or of a particular virtue—limits or paralyzes the very organ of knowledge. It is in fact a matter of common experience that the capacity for knowledge or for comprehension depends upon character: this comprehension can suddenly and "mysteriously" cease to function in an intelligent man who lacks a particular moral quality, and who for that reason falls into aberrant opinions that are logically inexplicable because they are incompatible with his intellectual scope. The essential—and not merely vocational—virtues are both moral qualities and contemplative attitudes, hence they are beauties of soul and of mind, and for that reason keys for gnosis; whence precisely the traditional notion of the *maqāmāt*, namely of the "stations", which are at once simultaneous and successive.

It has been said that "Sufism (*tasawwuf*) is sincerity (*sidq*)"; now sincerity is the passage from the cerebral to the cardiac, from the intellectual to the existential, from the partial to the total. The content of this transfer is the idea of Unity, and it is realized with the concurrence of the virtues, which for their part are so many modes or proofs of sincerity, even appearing in average Sufism—along with the practices of prayer and asceticism—as the pre-eminent means; however this is often achieved to the detriment of the purely intellective and contemplative keys, whose sacramental and transformative efficacy is then underestimated.

This last remark obliges us to pause for a moment, and once again,[2] on the problem of excess. One Sufi master requires his disciple, an eminent man about town, to wear a partially torn robe and a ridiculous cap and to beg at the door of the great mosque, on Friday, the day when the entire city attends. Our objections: firstly, a man who needs such treatment, or for whom such treatment is useful, is not qualified for esoteric knowledge; secondly, because such a spectacle—that of an eminent man of the highest esteem having to beg dressed in extravagant garb—is totally lacking in charity towards the community and has no other effect, aside from the scandal caused, than to render Sufism and its representatives odious and deserving of scorn, all the more so that such excesses are perfectly contrary to the principles of Islam, all question of "sincerity" notwithstanding. Another example: a Sufi is entreated by his friends to leave a city with his family because there is a danger of epidemic, and if the epidemic is declared he will no longer have the right to leave the city, according to the law; now, this Sufi refuses to leave on the pretext that "everything is written"; the epidemic arrives, and the ten children of the Sufi die from it. And yet, the Prophet had said to someone: "Tie your camel and trust in God", in other words: Heaven helps those who help themselves.

One of the greatest Sufi masters, Hasan ash-Shadhili, was in no way partial to such extravagances; deeming Sufism to be an inward treasure, he allowed his disciples to live like everyone else, to wear elegant dress and to fill high and lucrative positions. And similarly Rumi who, like David, preferred music and dance inspired by God and offered to Him, to sensationalistic exhibitions of poverty and virtue; all the more so in that the Prophet, though poor, was so beautifully and without ostentation.

Non-Muslims have great difficulty in grasping the spiritual or typological originality of the Arab Prophet, whereas they have no difficulty in grasping that of Christ or the Buddha; this is because the latter two each represent a synthetic radiance easy to perceive in its dazzling simplicity and directness, whereas the Prophet manifests a range of very diverse virtues that are close to human experience; and it is precisely this unfolding of humanly graspable qualities, both

---

[2] We have done so above all in our book *Le Soufisme: voile et quintessence*; the excesses in question are precisely the veil.

noble and imitable, which constitutes the Muhammadan originality. Thus the cult of the virtues and their ramifications is a salient feature of the Arabo-Muslim mentality, and this explains—but does not always excuse—the inordinately moralizing symbolism of Islamic hagiography; whereas the Christian is inspired by the ternary humility-charity-sacrifice and does not analyze the more relative or more situational virtues except *a posteriori.*

In Immanence as well as in Transcendence, it is necessary to distinguish two aspects, one objective and one subjective: objective Transcendence is that which is indicated by the word itself; but it may be termed "subjective" when it is located at the core of our personality where it indicates the Transcendence of the Self which, though subjective by definition, is nonetheless transcendent in relation to the "I". As for Immanence, it is termed "subjective" when it indicates the Self which is situated within us, and that there is continuity in principle between the "I" and the Self, or more precisely, between the latter and the former; but Immanence may be termed "objective" when, in the beings and things surrounding us, we discern Immanence as the existentiating and qualifying Substance.

Now esoterism, by contrast with the exoteric perspective, is based on this double Immanence, without thereby failing to recognize the validity of the complementary perspective. Thus the *Shahādah*—"there is no divinity (reality, quality) but the sole Divinity (Reality, Quality)"—which signifies first of all the exclusive and thereby extinguishing primacy of the Sovereign Good, assumes in esoterism an inclusive and participatory meaning; when applied to a positive phenomenon, it will mean: this particular existence or this particular quality appearing before us—this miracle of being or of consciousness or of beauty—cannot be other than the miracle of the Existence or the Consciousness or the Quality of God, since precisely, according to the very terms of the *Shahādah*, there is no other Existence, Consciousness, or Quality. And it is this truth that lies at the basis of such theopathic expressions—at the highest level—as "I am the Truth" (*anā 'l-Haqq*) of the illustrious Hallaj, or "Glory be to me" (*subhanī*) of the no less illustrious Abu Yazid.

It goes without saying that in ordinary language, the first *Shahādah*—of which we have just spoken—is connected with Transcendence, without in any way excluding a certain causal, existentiating, and efficient Immanence which is essential for Islamic unitarianism; but it is in the second *Shahādah*—"Muhammad (the perfect Manifestation) is His Messenger (His unitive prolongation)"— that we meet with the direct expression, or the formulation-symbol, of Immanence and thus of the mystery of Union or Identity.

The same difference in divine dimensions, so to speak, is expressed by these two formulas of the Koran: "God is greater (*Allāhu akbar*)"; "And verily the remembrance of God is greater (*wa la-dhikru 'Llāhi akbar*)."[3] These formulas establish symbolically the identification of *Allāh*, God, with *Dhikru 'Llāh*, the remembrance of God; this remembrance being quintessential orison or unitive concentration. In fact, *Dhikru 'Llāh* is one of the names of the Prophet, who in the Koran is presented as "a fair example for him who invoketh God much", and of whom this saying is related: "Who hath seen me, hath seen God (Truth or Reality: *man rā'anī faqad rā'a 'l-Ḥāqq*)"; and this brings us back to the mystery of the theopathic expressions of a Hallaj, an Abu Yazid and others; above all, it testifies to the presence of the mystery of Immanence in the soul of the Prophet of Transcendence.

There is a realm of "sobriety" (*sahw*) and a realm of "intoxication" (*sukr*)[4] and although Sufism claims both climates, and although Islam as such recognizes itself in the former, it may be said that sobriety pertains to Transcendence, and intoxication to Immanence.[5] Whence the reason for the prohibition of wine, music, and dance in exoterism, and whence, in esoterism, the reason for the symbolism of wine, the

[3] "Greater" (*akbar*) than the canonical prayer, according to the text. It should be noted that the word *akbar* expresses, not merely a comparative, but also a superlative; God is "supremely great", and so is the remembrance of Him.

[4] The word *sahw* means literally "lucidity", as opposed to the obnubilation of "intoxication". As for the word *sukr*, it contains on the one hand the idea of sweetness and on the other hand it indicates, in another form of the same root, a connection with death (*sakrat al-mawt*), which evokes a very important spiritual symbolism, that of "disappearance" (*fanā'*) or "extinction", or of ecstatic "death".

[5] It should be noted that Shiism, by its personal dramatism and its claim to esoterism, tends to introduce the element intoxication into exoterism itself, whereas Sunnism, on the contrary, tends to ignore it—even to excess when it confronts esoterism—in accordance with the general intention of Islam.

practice of music and of dance, not to mention poetry. Here lies the whole difference between the domain of the "outward" (*zāhir*) and that of the "inward" (*bātin*), or between the "Law" (*sharī'ah*) and the "Path" (*Tarīqah*) or the "Truth" (*Haqīqah*).

All this certainly does not mean that "sobriety", or "lucidity", pertains exclusively to the Law, and "intoxication" to the Path, for metaphysical discernment, and consequently esoteric science, pertains essentially to "lucidity", whereas exoteric piety with its aspects of sentimentality, excessiveness, and fanaticism is unquestionably to be found on the side of "intoxication", on a purely psychological level, of course. This is yet another illustration of the principle of compensatory inversion, of which the most well-known symbol is the *Yin-Yang* of the Chinese tradition.

The reason for linking "sobriety" to Transcendence, and "intoxication" to Immanence—aside from the compensatory inversion just pointed out—is that Transcendence is objective and static in the sense that the element object dominates everything, whereas Immanence is subjective and dynamic since it engages the subject; now the divine "Object", the content of Transcendence, is immutable, and as a consequence the adequacy, the "objectivity", precisely, of our intellective perception is also immutable; whereas the divine "Subject", which comes into play in Immanence, along with the human subject, which is its plane of refraction, are dynamic owing to their very unitive reciprocity—mystical union being our participation in the "divine Life". If, on the one hand, the Transcendent fixes, immobilizes, and crystallizes us, in keeping with "fear", on the other hand, the Immanent attracts, vivifies, and, in the final analysis, reintegrates us in keeping with "love"; this is the "dilating" and "intoxicating" return of the accident to the Substance, or of the drop to the Sea.

The Question of Perspectives in Muslim Spirituality

The fact that Islam intends to represent a terminal synthesis, implies that it must contain and emphasize in its fashion all spiritual possibilities; now there are fundamentally three paths: that of works and asceticism, then that of love and trust, and finally that of gnosis and unitive contemplation. The first, when taken separately, pertains to exoterism; the second extends from exoterism to esoterism; the third cannot but be esoteric in its substance, but must include elements that in one way or another pertain to the two preceding paths, namely the elements of operative and ascetic activity, and those of affectivity or love.

The first perspective is, basically, that of "fear" (*makhāfah* = *karma-mārga*); in the context of an anthropomorphist, voluntaristic, individualistic, and sentimental piety, it will give rise to the emphasis upon fear of chastisement and consequently to an excess of formalistic and legalistic scruple; it is here that is situated the surprising mysticism of sadness encountered in some Sufis.[1] It is very tempting, in a climate of religious solidarity and exoteric-esoteric symbiosis, to insert the path of fear, obedience, and works as such into esoterism, namely without any modifications; as if knowledge could be the fruit of action—which the Vedantists expressly deny —and as if an extravagant piety could serve as metaphysical adequation.

The second of the three fundamental perspectives, that of "love" (*mahabbah* = *bhakti-mārga*), gives rise, again at the level of a *de facto* individualistic piety, to a practically unrestrained sentimentalism, hence contrary to pure and discerning intelligence, something which no euphemism can understate; intelligence is likened then to the sin of pride, for only belief and zeal count. It goes without saying that this perspective can readily be combined with the preceding one, in a manner suiting its own viewpoint.

By contrast, the third path, that of "knowledge" (*ma'rifah* = *jñāna-mārga*), excludes by its very nature the excesses of the other

---

[1] This kind of sensibility can attach itself formally to a given fragmentary teaching of the Tradition, but not to its integral teaching—setting aside the question of the necessarily relative rights of mystical subjectivism, which is vocational and not normative.

two; rather, its excess will be an overemphasis upon theory to the detriment of practice; upon speculation to the detriment of contemplation. Nonetheless, this way could never exclude either realizational activity or purgative ascesis, nor *a fortiori* the element "love": namely, the sense of the sacred as well as intellective and contemplative serenity, not to mention the ecstatic modes of union.

It is easy to understand why an exclusive perspective of love has no choice but to reject gnosis out of an instinct for self-preservation, when one takes into account the fact that the path of love as such is dualistic and based upon Revelation, whereas gnosis is monistic and based upon Intellection; the latter implies the immanence of the whole Truth in the pure Intellect.[2] Thus *mahabbah* allies itself to *makhāfah*—penitential asceticism—insofar as it closes itself to *maʿrifah*, and this is something that can be observed in Islam as well as elsewhere, even though oppositions of this kind are not at all systematic in Muslim spirituality.[3]

Gnosis contains everything, but it does not follow that everything can enter gnosis, disappointing as this may be to those who confuse it with confessional fanaticism and who seem to wish to say, in the name of the *sophia perennis*, that "all that is sublime is ours". It is not enough to exaggerate a religious practice to be a Sufi, any more than one is profane for not exaggerating it.

When Semitic monotheism is envisaged as a great cycle comprising three successive religions—which does not preclude their being simul-

---

[2] Some Catholic zealots have even said that gnosis is worse than all other sins taken together, a position that goes even farther than Thomist sensualism, and that in any case implies a singular limitation of the power of the Holy Spirit, to say the least.

[3] Vishnuite *japa-yoga* as well as devotional Buddhism are examples of a *bhakti* (= *mahabbah*) that in a certain respect—and paradoxically at first glance—is closer to *jnāna* (= *maʿrifah*) than to *karma-mārga* (= *makhāfah*), owing to the fact that the emphasis upon Mercy and trust is based in the final analysis on the idea, not of a transcendent Judge, but of the immanent Self. It should be noted that the Sanskrit terms quoted are not in every respect the equivalents of the corresponding Arabic terms, but what is in question here are fundamental principles and not modalities.

taneous in another respect[4]—a certain analogy between them and the triad "fear-love-knowledge" can be noted, and this is corroborated by the Islamic feeling that, in the face of the preceding religions, it is the Truth pure and simple, or that it is the Truth more than anything else. The most direct expression possible of this awareness is the testimony of faith, the *Shahādah*, which is like the very symbol of the element Truth.

Now, just as the perspective of knowledge contains the two perspectives that prepare and introduce it, as a final synthesis and by essentializing them, so Islam intends to be a synthesis of what has preceded it; in consequence, it intends to include quintessentially and in an appropriate manner, both the perspective of love and that of fear. Moreover, beyond Judaism and Christianity, Islam aims at rejoining primordial Monotheism, that of Abraham and the patriarchs; but whereas Abrahamism was undifferentiated, Islam is differentiated, precisely because it recapitulates, more or less separately, the perspectives actualized by Moses and Jesus.

And this explains to a certain extent the tendency, on the part of average Sufism, to bring the entire religion into esoterism; this is because Islam, while analogically corresponding to the element "knowledge" in the triad of the Semitic messages, is nonetheless a religion and not a gnosis. It is a religion: that is to say, a system destined to save the largest possible number of souls, and to realize, according to this very intention, a social equilibrium capable of withstanding the trial of centuries; such an intention, however, has no direct connection with knowledge. In wishing *a priori* to esoterize exoterism, Islam will necessarily tend to exoterize esoterism; not gnosis in itself, which is inviolable, but Sufism as a general phenomenon; already the mere fact of its enormous diffusion is completely disproportionate from the point of view of gnosis. In such a context, esoterism becomes synonymous with moral sublimation, while at the same time ending in a mystico-political sectarianism.

Be that as it may, the fact that the perspective of fear was the first to be manifested in Sufism, or in Islam as such, is a reflection of the initial position of the "purgative path" in the initiatic order: "The beginning of wisdom is the fear of God", which is to say that one cannot approach the unitive path without having acquired the sense of

---

[4] Given that every religion, by definition, is a closed, self-sufficient system.

the divine Majesty and without having satisfied its requirements; it is above all a matter of removing "the rust from the mirror of the heart". Just as in the cycle of monotheism, legalistic and formalistic Mosaism has to precede mystical and interiorizing Christianity, so likewise the perspectives of fear and love have to succeed each other within Islam, notwithstanding the fact that there has to be simultaneity as well, there being nothing absolute about the order of succession. Islam, as we have noted, intends to represent "knowledge" in the monotheistic cycle; and similarly, within the Islamic tradition, the perspective of gnosis will be the last to blossom.

But there is also a more contingent reason for the impossibility of gnosis to assert itself widely at the outset of the religion: if on the one hand religion must save souls, on the other it must educate the collectivity; it must forge a mentality and therefore an ambience allowing for the flowering and radiation of superior spiritual possibilities. The mysticism of love, on Islamic soil, had to await the coming of a Rabiah Adawiyah and a Hallaj to be able to expand fully; and similarly, gnosis could not explicitly assert itself prior to the coming of an Ibn Masarra, a Niffari, an Ibn Arabi; not to mention the philosophers who—quite paradoxically in some respects—pertain more or less to the same family. It is true that all the spiritual possibilities were able to manifest themselves from the beginning of Islam, but they could only do so elliptically, almost inarticulately, and so to speak sporadically.

—— ·⋮· ——

What is curious in Islam is not that it comprises the three perspectives, but that they are manifested in a manner which is *de facto* incoherent; that is, they appear to be incompatible and on many points seem to ignore the overall teaching of the Koran and the *Sunnah*, while fervently basing themselves upon particular isolated elements of this teaching. As regards incoherence—whether doctrinal or simply dialectical—one has no doubt to take into account the fact that the ancient Arabs possessed no intellectual culture and that their thought was much more impulsive and empiricist than logical.[5] The Prophet

---

[5] Although the ancient Arabs were rationalists in their fashion, but on a very elementary and outward level.

sensed this when he said: "Seek knowledge, be it in China" (= to the ends of the earth); in fact, "China" was ancient Greece, the legacy of Plato, of Aristotle, and of the Neoplatonists. Be that as it may, the disappointing features of a certain type of pious literature—undisciplined impulsiveness, gratuitous exaggeration, platitude, infantilism combined with mercantilism—plainly had their roots in the mentality of the human group to which the religious message was addressed;[6] yet the simple fact that the religion had to educate a rather barbarous collectivity and over time bestow upon it a certain congeniality—we speak of the collectivity as such, not of every individual in it— explains the fact that at the beginning of Islam, dialectics could not have been satisfactory from the standpoint of an impeccable logic; this is an extenuating circumstance for many an instance of clumsiness and extravagance.

Incoherence, it has to be stressed, does not in any way stem from diversity pure and simple; it stems from a thinking which on the one hand tends to isolate and to be discontinuous, and on the other tends to intensify and overemphasize. It is as if in average Sufism different religions exist side by side; according to some adherents—let it be said without euphemism—God appears to be a capricious and vindictive tyrant, *quod absit*; according to others, the very substance of God is the desire to forgive, even mountains of sins; moreover, the sincere believer cannot be damned—even though he may pass through a purgative fire—whereas fire could never even touch those affiliated with a given *Tarīqah*, and so on and so forth. The distant and positive cause of the disparity in standpoints is, as we have said, Islam's character as a terminal synthesis; the near and negative cause is an undisciplined sense of the Absolute, combined with an impulsive temperament; in short, a kind of "henotheism" plunging into one mystery while forgetting all others.

But there is yet something else: to say that each of the fundamental perspectives had—or has—to be manifested within the Islamic tradition, means practically that each had—or has—to find a saint

---

[6] A curious phenomenon that must be taken into account is the recurrence, even in the greatest writings, of imperfections of this kind; a recurrence which in a sense is inevitable since the cult of the ancients obliges one to close one's eyes to their shortcomings, or even to take these shortcomings as an example. As in the case of Christian art or in the case of scientific and other kinds of progress, the absence of a critical sense becomes a virtue.

personifying it; the first Sufis had to incarnate "provisionally necessary" attitudes in a quasi-sacrificial manner and in order to "clear the way"; certain excesses had to be manifested by way of examples, in order to be exhausted through being manifested. The most problematical aspect of pious incoherence is that "a given perspective equals a given God"; it is true that all the divine qualities are mentioned in the Koran, but they are in equilibrium or are mutually compensated, whereas the exclusive and excessive emphasis upon one of them by a particular perspective amounts to presenting a particular God, and one who is exclusively severe in most cases; whereas gentleness, which is obviously more plausible in the context of sanctity, does not give rise to some of the more flagrant absurdities.

If the perspective of *makhāfah* incites some to weep almost methodically at the idea of the Last Judgment—which is unrelated to the "gift of tears" of Christian mystics—the perspective of *mahabbah* on the contrary does not make much of the notions of heaven and hell: it allows one, in other words, to disdain both heaven and hell in virtue of the love of God alone, so that one would rather go to hell loving God than to be in Paradise without loving Him, or without loving Him enough, since there are the houris and other delights. Such extravagances—and such irreverence—are explained in part by a turn of mind that replaces logic and the sense of proportions with associations of ideas or images, and that is more attached to symbols than to exact facts; a turn of mind moreover that is fundamentally moralistic; never mind common sense so long as the moralizing intention and efficacy are preserved. It is as if one devoted one's ingenuity to think of all that is thinkable, provided it be to the glory of the one God or in the interest of a moralizing piety, or that it serve some religious sublimation or other.

Be that as it may, there is a point one must not lose sight of: if stereotypical opinions—showing a pious automatism in thinking—are encountered even among eminent spokesmen of the perspective of *maʿrifah*, this may be in large part due to a religious solidarity which sacrifices the critical sense to the sentiment of spiritual fraternity, given that the boundary between truth and charity is often not well-defined in a religious climate. It is difficult for us to believe that a Ghazzali, for example, could be the dupe of all the naiveties he repeats, unless in his mind the symbolism and the basic intention compensated for shortcomings of form; however, this does not exclude a concern for charitable concession. Nonetheless, this hypothesis has a limited bearing, for it applies to stories or images of religious or Sufi "folklore" and not to all theologico-mystical speculations.[7]

As for the question of Paradise—since we broached it above—we shall add that it gives rise to two points of view that are logically opposed but that sometimes can be combined in fact: according to the first point of view, Paradise is a place of pleasure which the true lover of God ought to disdain; according to the second, the idea of Paradise lends itself to extensions or transpositions in meaning, which is to say that the "Garden" (or "Gardens", *Jannāt*) comprises degrees and that it opens onto the most demanding Union; we shall say without hesitation that it is the second point of view that is objectively correct and traditionally legitimate, since it safeguards the symbolism, and therefore the dignity, of Scripture.

Some Sufis, and not the least, have believed it possible to affirm that Islam is the "religion of love", which is surprising to say the least, but which indicates two things: firstly, that Islam inasmuch as it is a "synthesis" (*jam'*) intends to emphasize every fundamental spiritual possibility and, secondly, that it has the tendency—in Sufism—either to reduce or to bring the entire religion to esoterism; this tendency is

---

[7] According to Jili, evil-doers are happier in hell than they were on earth, for on earth they forgot God, whereas in hell they remember Him, since they encountered Him at their particular judgment; now nothing is sweeter, argues Jili, than the remembrance of God. In the same style of thought, some have asserted that Satan will be forgiven since, in refusing to prostrate himself before Adam, he attested to the divine Oneness, God alone being worthy of adoration; it seems to be forgotten that the refusal to do homage was prompted, not by the idea that God alone merits a prostration, but by Satan's conviction of being better than Adam. This does not prevent the opinion from referring to the Apocatastasis and joining thereby other symbols expressing a truth; an analogous excuse could be made for the Sufic opinion according to which Pharaoh was pardoned, in the sense that this thesis can refer to the orthodoxy of the Egyptian tradition, of which Pharaoh was after all the incarnation.

particularly marked in the Shiites, who go so far as to make of gnosis a confessional article of faith. What seems to be lost sight of is that the Law could not of itself be esoteric, but that it nonetheless participates in esoterism to the extent that one's attitude is esoteric, and not otherwise.[8]

It is perhaps not superfluous to insist, once again, on the following point: at the beginning of Islam and during the periods immediately following, there was the need to counter pagan tendencies—to thwart their heedlessness, self-sufficiency, and horizontality; that is why in certain Sufis there is a propensity, rather astonishing when taken in itself, towards sadness and pessimism that is alien to the overall teaching of the Koran and the *Sunnah*. There was a need to awaken in very profane men the awareness of the divine Majesty; for the idols did not commit anyone to anything, they were asked only to fulfill earthly desires. The sense of the sacred is everything: after having provoked in souls the fear of the divine Majesty (*Jalāl*), the way was clear for allowing one to speak of the divine Beauty (*Jamāl*), and finally of the mystery, at once forbidding and peace-giving, of liberating Immanence.

The element "knowledge" which, according to the theory of the three religious phases of the monotheistic cycle, determines in a certain fashion the Islamic religion, is manifested not only by the saving importance of the idea of Unity or of the Absolute, which is the prototype of metaphysical discernment; it is also manifested by way of consequence in contemplative serenity which confers upon the believer "resignation" (*islām, taslīm*) to the Will of the One; a resignation which precisely gives Islam its name. Now serenity of soul, like the sense of the Absolute, pertains quintessentially to Intellection; it is a conformation to the nature of things, hence to the nature of That which is, and That which alone is.

---

[8] The canonical prayer of Islam, like the Lord's Prayer, is a discourse addressed to God; now Sufism managed to distinguish three degrees in this discourse: "service" (*'ibādah*), "proximity" (*qurb*), and "union" (*ittihād*). That prayer enables a "proximity" follows from the reason for its existence; but we do not see how it could be merely a "service", and still less how it could accede to the dignity of "union" when by definition it is a dialogue; unitive alchemy disposes of other supports. However, it is plausible that the prayer of the "sage" (*'ārif*) has a quality different from that of the "common man" (*'awwām*), which does not mean that the latter's prayer cannot be fully agreeable to God.

The Mystery of the Prophetic Substance

There are several relationships between a substance and its accidents: first of all, it must be borne in mind that the accidents necessarily manifest the substance; and then, that they can manifest it in varying degrees or in different ways. For gold projects its royalty into an object, not only by its matter but also to the extent that the object is royal by its form and its function, which is precisely why it is made of gold; however, not every object made of gold is necessarily a throne, a crown, a scepter or a chalice, it may also be an implement that by its nature neither requires nor justifies the use of this noble metal; nonetheless, gold transmits its radiance even to modest objects.

"By their fruits ye shall know them": this saying expresses in the most concise manner possible the relationship of cause and effect that exists between substantiality and accidentality. It is by the properties of the drop, the wave, or the fountain that we recognize the nature of water; it is by the properties or effects of the flame, whether warming or devouring or illuminating, that we recognize the nature of fire. The same holds true for every spiritual manifestation: the substance it conveys will be transmitted through the accidentality, no matter what the latter's mode may be—direct or indirect, evident or paradoxical, open or veiled. And this diversity of modes is ontologically necessary—and thus should not surprise us—given the play of *Māyā*, that is to say, given the inexhaustible diversity within divine and cosmic Possibility.

The concrete content—and thus the origin—of Islamic spirituality is the spiritual substance of the Prophet, the substance whose modalities Qushayri, Ibn al-Arif, and others have tried to classify by means of the notion of "stations" (*maqāmāt*). What is Sufism if not the realization of Union, starting not only from the idea of a Unity that is both transcendent and immanent but also, and correlatively, by being reintegrated into the hidden and yet ever-present Muhammadan substance, either directly or indirectly or in both ways at the same time. In other words, the mystical "traveler" (*sālik*) "can follow the example of the

Prophet" in a way that is either formal or non-formal, hence indirect or direct; for the *Sunnah* is not just the multitude of precepts, it is also the "Muhammadan substance"[1] of which these precepts are the reflections at various levels, and which coincide with the mystery of the "immanent Prophet". The intrinsic qualities are, in principle or in themselves, independent of the different modes of outward comportment, whereas the latter's entire reason for being lies in the qualities; this is akin to the Shaykh al-Alawi's indication that the sufficient reason of the rites is the remembrance of God, which contains all rites in an undifferentiated synthesis.

Man has two kinds of relationships with the divine Order, one direct and the other indirect: the first encompasses prayer and, more esoterically, intellectual discernment and unitive concentration; the second goes to God through the door of the human Logos, and it comprises the virtues of which the Logos is the personification and model. At issue here are not only the elementary virtues which may be natural to man or which he can draw from himself, but also and above all the supernatural virtues, which on the one hand are graces and on the other require that man transcend himself and even cease to "be" in order to "become". No path exists without reference to a human manifestation of the Logos, just as, with all the more reason, no path exists without a direct relationship with God.

Outwardly, the Prophet can readily be seen and understood in his role as Legislator; inwardly, in his substance, he represents esoterism at every level, whence a duality that is at the source of certain antinomies and which in the last analysis determined the schism between Sunnites and Shiites. The Legislator points out the way and sets the example on the formalistic plane of legality and morality, whereas the Muhammadan substance—the soul of the Prophet insofar as it is accessible in principle—is a concrete and quasi-sacramental presence that prefigures the state of Salvation or of Deliverance and that calls us, not to legality or to the social virtues, but to self-transcendence and transformation, hence to extinction and to a second birth.

—— ⁖ ——

[1] "And verily thou art of a supereminent nature" (*la ʿalā khuluqin ʿazīm*): that is, of a most lofty character (*Sūrah* "The Pen" [68]:4).

The governing idea of Islam is the concept of Unity; it determines not only the doctrine and the organization of society but also the entire life of the individual and in particular his piety which, moreover, cannot be dissociated from his legal conduct. It is not merely a question of accepting the idea of Unity but also of drawing from this idea all the consequences that it implies for man; this is to say that one has to accept it "with faith" and "sincerity" in order to benefit from the saving virtue it contains. Thus, in the last analysis, the idea of Unity fundamentally implies the mystery of Union; and likewise, in a related order of ideas, Unicity implies Totality by complementarity. To be able to grasp the geometric point is to be able to grasp all of space; the Unicity of the divine Object demands the totality of the human subject.

And yet, despite the clarity of this relationship of cause and effect, Islamic spirituality presents an enigma in that its theoretical and practical expressions often seem to move away from Islam as such,[2] notwithstanding the efforts of Sufi authors to emphasize the legality of their opinions and methods, even those most foreign to the overall perspective of Islam. The entire enigma lies in the fact that there is here a dimension that the Law has not articulated, or which it only suggests covertly; this enigma stems from the very person of the Prophet, who privately—if one may say—practiced an asceticism which he doubtless recommended to some but did not make mandatory, and which moreover in his own case could not signify a "purgative way" as it did with those who have emulated him. This asceticism, which is readily confused with Sufism—whereas it can only be a preparatory trial at the threshold of the mysteries—is far from constituting the substance itself of the Messenger; given that the Prophetic substance is a spiritual beatitude and thus a state of consciousness, it remains independent from all formal conditions, even though the formal practices can be rightly considered as paths towards participation in it.

---

[2] Not that we must therefore accept the inadmissible hypothesis of borrowings from Christianity and Hinduism.

The spiritual nature of the Prophet is determined, illuminated, and vivified by two poles that could be designated, quite synthetically, by the terms "Truth" and "Heart": the Truth of God, of the Sovereign Good, and the Heart-Intellect which mysteriously harbors it; Transcendence and Immanence.

The Muhammadan substance comprises all the qualities or excellences which the Sufis term "stations" (*maqāmāt*) and which are in principle innumerable given that it is always possible to subdivide them and thereby to extract new modes from them. But simplicity also has its rights: starting from a given plurality, one can always proceed from synthesis to synthesis towards pure substantiality, which here is none other than the love of God in the widest as well as the deepest meaning of the word; we are then at the source, but without the differentiated points of reference that could impart to us the internal riches of this love. It is appropriate therefore to find a golden mean between synthesis and analysis, and this mean, far from being arbitrary, is offered by traditional symbolism as well as by certain cosmic structures: Paradise contains four rivers flowing from the Throne of *Allāh*, and there are four Archangels at the summit of the angelic hierarchy; the Kaaba has four sides, and space has four cardinal points.[3] But before considering the Muhammadan substance in its aspect of quaternary, we must explain the meaning of the numbers that precede it: from the perspective of unity, this substance is the love of God; with respect to duality, it is the tension between the two poles Truth and Heart, Transcendence and Immanence; and with respect to trinity, this same substance reveals the mystery of the Prophetic quality: this quality comprises first of all perfect conformity and receptivity towards the Lord, then the prophetic Message as "content" of the Prophet and as the quasi-hypostatic link between him and God, and finally the perfect knowledge of Him who gives the Message.

The odd numbers are "retrospective" in the sense that they express an infolding towards Unity, or the divine Origin, whereas the even numbers are "prospective" in the sense that they express on the contrary a movement in the direction of Manifestation, the world, the Universe. In the First *Shahādah* ("There is no divinity but

---

[3] When a believer is outside the Kaaba, whether near or far, he prays towards it, hence towards one of its four walls; but when he is inside it, he must pray towards each of the cardinal points.

God alone"), which in Arabic comprises four words, the Truth of the Principle penetrates so to speak "prospectively" into the world; in the Second *Shahādah* ("Muhammad is the Messenger of God"), which in Arabic comprises three words, the Prophet is defined "retrospectively" in relation to his divine Source. The number four in particular (the words of the First *Shahādah: lā ilāha illā 'Llāh*) expresses the radiation of the Principle with respect to the world and is therefore the number-symbol of Radiation. When, correlatively, we consider the Source—or the Center—of the Radiation, we arrive at the symbolism of the number five; and when we take into account the two poles determining the quaternary, namely the Transcendent and the Immanent, we come to the symbolism of the number six.

As for the quaternary, which is the mean of our synthesis or analysis—because every number is to be found between these two poles—its inner significance becomes clear in the light of the symbolism of the cardinal points: the North is negative perfection, which is exclusive, surpassing, or transcending; the South is positive perfection, which is inclusive, vivifying, and deepening; the East is active perfection, which is dynamic, affirming, and realizing and, if need be, combative; and the West is passive perfection, which is static and peace-giving. We say "perfection" rather than "principle" since we have in view the Prophetic nature, which is human.[4]

Leaving aside for now these more or less abstract preliminaries, let us consider concretely the principal aspects of the spiritual substance of the Prophet, which sum up all the "stations", and by the same token all the *Sunnah*, at least as regards its subjective and spiritual motivations. In the soul-intelligence of the Prophet there is, first of all, the quality of serenity; this perfection rises above the turmoil of the contingencies of the world and is linked to the divine mystery of Transcendence; to be serene is to situate oneself above all pettiness, just as in the divine Order—in Vedantic terms—*Ātmā* is above *Māyā*. Serenity is, accordingly, not only an elevation, but also an expansion (*inshirāh*, "dilation of the breast");[5] hence it evokes the limitlessness

---

[4] But "like coral amongst pebbles", according to an ancient formula.

[5] "And whomsoever God willeth to guide, He dilateth his breast unto Islam" ("resignation" to the will of God) (*Sūrah* "Cattle" [6]:125); "He (Moses) said: Lord, dilate my breast. . ." (*Sūrah* "Ta Ha" [20]:25); "Have We (God) not (O Prophet) dilated thy breast?" (*Sūrah* "The Dilation" [94]:1).

of heights as well as the luminosity that suffuses them and gives them their natural and glorious content. This station—or category of stations—is often represented, in various traditional symbolisms, by the eagle soaring above the accidents of a landscape, in majestic solitude before the singleness of the sun. Snow is another image of this station; pure and celestial, it covers the accidents of a landscape with a white, crystalline blanket, thus reducing all diversity to the indifferentiation of *materia prima*. This same mystery of elevation, limitlessness, and transcendence finds a religious expression in the call to prayer from the height of the minarets, which reduces all earthly agitation and turmoil to a celestial indifferentiation—an indifferentiation that is the opposite of leveling, for the former is qualitative while the latter is quantitative. These considerations pertain to the mystery of Purity,[6] symbolized by the North and thus also by the pole Star;[7] and to this order of ideas belong the sacrificial attitudes of abstention, renunciation, poverty, and sobriety; or the virtues of detachment, patience, resignation, and impassibility; or again, the conditions of solitude, silence, and emptiness—qualities or stations that are found, not in sadness but precisely in the calm and already celestial joy which serenity represents.

Although the "vertical" complement of the North is the South, we prefer to consider first the message of the West which, being static and pertaining to "passive perfection", prolongs in a certain manner the likewise static message of the North, while differentiating itself from the North owing to the quality of mildness that it shares with the South; by contrast, both the North and the East pertain to the quality of rigor.

The message of the West, then, is that of recollectedness, contemplation, peace. Like serenity, recollectedness implies holy resignation, but in a manner that is gentle, not rigorous, so that immobility here is conditioned, not by a void, or by the absence of the world with its noise and turmoil, but on the contrary by a plenitude, namely the inward and peace-giving Presence of the Sovereign Good. Recollectedness is closely linked to the sense of the sacred; within the realm

---

[6] By "mystery" we mean a spiritual reality inasmuch as it is rooted in the divine Order.

[7] One can see the relationship with the Holy Virgin, who is *Stella Maris*: immutable and primordial in her inviolable purity, and at the same time inspiring hope and certitude.

of material things, it evokes not the luminous and cold heights of the boundless sky, but rather the sacred and enclosing intimacy of the forest or the sanctuary; it thus evokes that reverential awe—both fascinating and immobilizing—which holy places, works of sacred art, and also various manifestations of virgin nature can awaken in the soul. The idea of recollectedness evokes all the symbols of contemplative immobility, all the liturgical signs of adoration: lamps or votive candles, bouquets or garlands of flowers, in short, all that stands before God and offers itself to His Presence which is Silence, Inwardness, Beauty, and Peace. It is this atmosphere that is suggested and created in mosques by the prayer niche (*mihrāb*)—often adorned with a lamp recalling the tabernacle of the Blessed Sacrament in Catholic churches—the same prayer niche which is the abode of the Virgin Mary, according to the Koran; now Mary personifies mystical retreat and prayer, hence the mystery of recollectedness. All this refers to that holy repose (*itmiʾnān*, "appeasement of hearts") of which the Koran conveys the echoes.[8]

Recollectedness, like serenity, is indicated by the word "Peace" in the formula of eulogy about the Prophet: "Upon him be Blessing and Peace" (*ʿalayhi as-Salātu wa as-Salām*); from the element "Blessing" stem the two qualities of which we shall now speak, namely fervor and certitude. Fervor—in spatial symbolism—is the "horizontal" complement of recollectedness, certitude being the "vertical" complement of serenity; on the one hand, the East is the complementary opposite of the West, as, on the other hand, the South is that of the North. These considerations, while not indispensable, can nevertheless be useful for those sensitive to the language of symbolism and analogies.

The quality of fervor seems to be opposed to that of recollectedness, as action seems opposed to contemplation; nonetheless, without sacramental and actualizing activity, contemplation would lack support, not necessarily in the present moment, but as soon as the impact of duration is felt. The quality of fervor is in fact the disposition of soul inducing us to perform what can be termed "spiritual duty"; if this duty is made compelling by an outward law, that is because it

---

[8] "Those who believe and whose hearts are set at peace by the remembrance of God; is it not by the remembrance of God that hearts are set at peace?" (*Sūrah* "The Thunder" [13]:28); "O thou soul at peace, return unto thy Lord, satisfied and accepted" (*Sūrah* "The Dawn" [89]:27-28).

is inwardly compelling and *a priori* so given our own "supernatural nature"; a Hindu would say that it is our *dharma* to liberate our soul, just as it is the *dharma* of water to flow or of fire to burn. In Islam this immanent law is manifested as the "Remembrance of God" (*dhikru 'Llāh*); now the Koran specifies that it is necessary to remember God "much" (*dhikran kathīran*)— "without ceasing", in the words of the New Testament—and it is this frequency or this assiduousness, together with the sincerity of the act of orison, that constitutes the quality of fervor.[9] For not only must the sacred act dominate the moment in which it arises, it must dominate duration as well; the perfection of the act requires perseverance as its logical consequence and complement; it is not enough to be a saint "now", one must be one "always", and that is why the Sufi is the "son of the moment" (*ibn al-waqt*). The comparison between spiritual activity and holy war (*jihād*) will be readily understood: for establishing the sacred in the soul that is by nature exteriorized—namely, dispersed and at the same time lazy—necessarily entails combat, and one could even say a fight against the dragon, to use an expression belonging to initiatic symbolism. All spirituality requires therefore the virile virtues of vigilance, initiative, and tenacity; thus fervor is a fundamental quality of the Man-Logos, and it can be said that the immensity of the victory of Islam proves the immensity of the strength of soul of the Prophet.

As for the quality of certitude, which takes precedence over that of fervor since it provides fervor with its reason for being, it is the liberating "yes" to realities that transcend us and to the consequences they require of us; whether this "yes" be a gift of heaven or a merit of our own—and the one, of course, does not preclude the other—makes no difference psychologically. Certitude of God implies certitude of our own immortality, for to be able to know the Absolute is to be immortal; only the immortal soul is proportioned to this knowledge. Moreover, he who appeals to the divine Mercy must

---

[9] "O Maryam, remain in prayer before thy Lord; prostrate thyself and bow with those who bow" (*Sūrah* "The Family of Imran" [3]:43). It is in these terms that the Koran presents fervor as belonging to the very substance of Mary, the divine Command being here, not an order given *a posteriori*, but an existential determination. It is noteworthy that the Virgin is *Stella Matutina*, an allusion to the East, which in our symbolism denotes fervor. Aside from this particular meaning, the East expresses the coming of light, and it is thus that the Christian tradition interprets the Marian title "Morning Star"; now fervor derives from light just as in principle light and heat go together.

himself be generous, in accordance with the *hadīth*: "Whosoever hath no mercy, unto him shall be given no mercy" (*man lam yarham lam yurham*). And this defines the connection between faith in God and charity towards the neighbor, or between hope and generosity, all the more as the acceptance of the Sovereign Good implies or requires the gift of self, hence a kind of generosity towards Heaven.

It is true that on the plane of metaphysical intellection the transcendent Invisible presents itself so compellingly to our mind that we cannot but accept it; but this impossibility of resisting the Truth lies then in our nature, hence the gift of self to the divine Real lies in our very substance; the *a contrario* proof of this is that there are men who, while capable in principle of admitting the highest Truth, refuse to admit it owing to the tendencies of their passional nature. The sincere "yes" to that which transcends us always presupposes beauty of soul, just as the capacity of a mirror to reflect light presupposes its purity; it is the *fiat* of the Virgin Mary—she is essentially beautiful and pure—at the Annunciation; the "yes" to the supernatural and to the incommensurable, to that which slays us and at the same time delivers us.

Thus, whether it is a matter of elementary belief, ardent faith, or metaphysical knowledge, certitude always goes hand in hand with beauty and goodness of soul. Closely related to faith is trust and therefore hope: to trust in the divine Mercy, without a moment's despair and yet without temerity—while abstaining from what is contrary to it and accomplishing what is in conformity to it—is a way of saying "yes" to the Merciful, and no less so to the deiform nature of our immortal soul; it is to say "yes" at once to God and to immortality. And it is in this sense that the Koran tells the believers: "Verily ye have in the Messenger of God a fair example for him who hath hope in God and in the Last Day, and who remembereth God much" (*Sūrah* "The Clans" [33]:21); a saying that combines the mystery of certitude with that of fervor. "I am black, but beautiful", says Wisdom in the Song of Songs: she is black because she transcends and thereby negates our all too human plane, but she is beautiful because, in revealing herself to us, she reveals the Sovereign Good and thereby its saving Mercy. If the Koran testifies to the "supereminent nature" (*khuluq ʿazīm*) of Muhammad, it is because as a Prophet he realizes the greatest possible receptivity with regard to the highest Reality.

—— ⋮ ——

Even in pure intellection there is place for the "obscure merit of faith": there remains in all speculative knowledge a gap between the knower and the known, otherwise the knower would be identified with the known, which indeed has to be the case in a certain dimension, that of intellection precisely; but intellection does not encompass the entire being of the subject, or at least it does not encompass it at every moment. Besides, passive union is one thing, while active union is another; therein lies all the difference between a "state" (*hāl*) and a "station" (*maqām*). At all events, to have certitude is not yet, in every respect, to be that of which one is certain.

Clearly, the value of faith is more than simply moral; not only is faith good because of the merit entailed by its aspect of obscurity, it is good also—and above all—because of the certitudes it sparks in souls of good will; otherwise expressed, not only does faith imply that its object is hidden from us because our nature comprises a veil, but also that we see this object despite the veil, and through it; the element of obscurity remains since the veil is always there, but at the same time this veil transmits certitude because it is transparent. Thus, if the *Shahādah* signifies *a priori* that a given quality is unreal since God alone is the Good, it signifies *a posteriori* that a given quality, since it is not non-existent, is of God; either the created quality "is not", or else it is of God to the extent that it "is"; for to "exist" is a manner of "being"; seen from this perspective, the divine Beauty manifested through earthly beauties never ceases to be itself, in spite of the limitations of relativity. It is within this context that one must situate that feature of the Muhammadan substance which could be called "Solomonian" or "Krishnaite", namely its spiritual capacity to find concretely in woman all the aspects of the divine Femininity, from immanent Mercy to the infinitude of universal Possibility; the sensorial experience, producing in the ordinary man an inflation of the ego, actualizes in the "deified" man an extinction in the divine Self.

But the "obscure merit of faith" includes still another and altogether different meaning resulting from the relationship between the subject and the object: on the one hand, the subject—being contingent—has limits that prevent it from knowing in an absolute, hence exhaustive, manner; on the other hand, there appears to be, on the part of the object, a "wish" as it were to elude examination after a certain point, a desire not to be known totally, of not being despoiled of all mystery of aseity, or violated and emptied so to speak by the knowing subject.[10] The relative subject as such cannot know everything, which amounts to saying that it does not need to know everything, even from the standpoint of the adequacy of knowledge; this also amounts to saying that the object is by definition inexhaustible, and that the more one dissects and seeks to systematize it improperly, the more it will avenge itself by depriving us of its "life", namely of that something which, precisely, is the "gift" of the object to the subject. Total knowledge exists, certainly—for otherwise the very notion of knowledge would lose all its meaning—but it is situated beyond the subject-object complementarity, in an inexpressible "beyond" whose foundation is the ontological identity of the two terms; for neither term could be other than "That which is", and there is but one Being. Total knowledge means that the absolute Knower knows Himself, and that there is within us a door which opens onto this knowledge; "within ourselves", yet "beyond ourselves".

In metaphysics there is the principle of the "sufficient point of reference", namely the awareness of the limit separating a thinking that is sufficient and useful from a thinking that is excessive and useless; it is the former that furnishes us with points of reference enabling us in fact to transcend the indefinite plane of thought as such. For the man who is not aware of the provisional character of concepts it is natural to ask of thinking to provide what it cannot, and to reach the conviction that thinking is vain and that man can know nothing; but it is not normal for man to take thinking as an end in itself.

These reflections may all help to clarify the idea of certitude; but a clearer idea of certitude may also be obtained by recalling what its contrary is, namely doubt: "For the man subject to doubt", the *Bhagavad Gītā* says in substance, "there is no salvation either in this world or in the next". To have doubts about what is ontologically certain is not to want to be; it is thus a kind of suicide, that of the mind; and to doubt in the divine Mercy is a disgrace as great as to doubt in God. Spiritual certitude implies the liberating "yes" to that which transcends us, and which in the last analysis is our own essence; whence the relationship

---

[10] There is a certain connection here with the principle of tithing, or of sacrifice in general; to guarantee fertility, the divine gift must not be exhausted.

between self-knowledge and the knowledge of God, and also between the knowledge of God and the workings of Mercy.

Serenity, recollectedness, fervor, certitude; this quaternary summarizes the Muhammadan substance—although other systems of synthesis-analysis are equally possible—and unfolds, as described earlier, between two poles, the Truth of the Transcendent and the Heart as seat of the Immanent. Thus, in space, the four cardinal points are situated between the Zenith and the Nadir; strictly speaking, it is not the substance of the human Logos which retraces the features of the cosmic order, rather is it the cosmic order that in reality testifies to the "supereminent" and universal nature of the Man-Logos.

In order to correctly situate the diverse relationships between the contemplative qualities and the virtues properly so called—the moral and social ones—it is necessary to start with the following universal Qualities: Purity, which governs serenity and resignation; Strength, which governs fervor and vigilance; Beauty, which governs recollectedness and gratitude; Goodness or Love, which governs certitude and generosity. Resignation to trials—namely to the "Will of God"—and serenity both derive from Purity since they transcend all pettiness and weaknesses, but resignation concerns personal experiences whereas serenity transcends the world as such, and this constitutes a critical difference despite the appearance of a common identity. And likewise for vigilance and fervor: both stem from Strength, but the first in a moral and social mode, and the second in a spiritual, operative, sacramental, and alchemical mode: vigilance is the strength of soul focused upon duty, the capacity to be implacable in connection with duty, and this is a crucial virtue, for goodness is a virtue only so long as it is not weakness;[11] fervor, by contrast, concerns spiritual activity alone, it is Strength directed solely towards God.

---

[11] Some have reproached the Prophet for his harsh treatment of traitors, and they have not always resisted the temptation to make *ad hominem* accusations against him or to falsify history, while losing sight of the fact that generosity does not apply in every case—otherwise justice could never be exercised—and also that generosity can be relevant even within the framework of justice, of which the life of the Prophet, precisely, offers us a number of examples.

As for gratitude and recollectedness, both of which pertain to Beauty, their difference lies in the fact that gratitude responds to men and objects, whereas recollectedness is turned exclusively towards God; nonetheless, this latter quality or attitude is unthinkable without the virtue of gratitude, thanks to which man appreciates, like a child, the value of small things; the man who is noble, who has a sense of the sacred, is the diametrical opposite of the jaded and trivial man who respects nothing. Whoever does not appreciate the gifts of God in the world is incapable of appreciating them in the heart; there is no contemplativeness without gratefulness, hence without humility. "Suffer the little children to come unto Me."

As for the relationship between generosity and certitude, the Bible furnishes us the key: the first Law is to love God with all our faculties, and the second—which is "like unto it"—is to love our neighbor as ourself. This is to say that the acceptance of the Truth, hence the certitude of God—be it moral or intellective—coincides with the love of God to the extent that it is sincere or real; to know God is to love Him, and not to love Him is not to know Him; and the love of God includes or requires *ipso facto* the love of the neighbor, hence generosity.[12]

We have said above that the four qualities of the substance of the human Logos are to be found between two poles, the Truth and the Heart; one could also say: between intelligence and holiness. To the first of these poles pertains the virtue of veracity, while sincerity pertains to the second: veracity is the inclination to accept the primacy of the true or the real, thereby acknowledging that no right is superior to the right of the Truth, whereas sincerity is the tendency to accept and realize totally that which by its very uniqueness requires totality; sincerity is likewise to do what is just, and not simply what flatters, and to do it to please God, not men.

These four spiritual qualities or attitudes are at the same time beatitudes, and this calls to mind the four rivers of Paradise, consisting

---

[12] However, as has often been repeated, love of the neighbor cannot be absolute or unconditional in the way the love of God is, that is to say love of the neighbor is subordinate to the love of God which, precisely, determines it; one loves "in God", and one loves that which by its nature is lovable to God; and yet, in another respect, there can be an element of charity in what our love has the right or the duty to exclude.

of water, milk, wine, and honey.[13] It is easy to conceive the relationship between serenity and water, and between fervor and vivifying wine; then, between recollectedness and milk—here suggesting maternity and the Marian mystery of *lactatio,* which Saint Bernard experienced. What remains is the relationship between certitude and honey: nothing is sweeter than certitude of the Sovereign Good and of the Salvation which it implies, not forgetting that honey is a medicinal nourishment, just as certitude is what heals us and makes us live.[14]

The qualities, attitudes, or virtues of which we have spoken are rooted in the Logos and consequently pertain also to the "Muhammadan substance", which can be defined as a crystallization of the love of God, in a mode that unfolds, like a fan, the fundamental qualities of the soul. According to Aisha, the "favorite wife", the soul of the Prophet is similar to the Koran; in order to understand this comparison, one has to know that this Book possesses, alongside the literal wording and in an underlying fashion, a supra-formal "magic", namely a "soul" extending from the moral qualities to the spiritual mysteries; whence the sacramental function of the Text, its *mantra* nature, if one will, but a function that is independent from its form and contents.

While this magic, for a person sensitive to it, can be used as a way of approaching the Muhammadan substance, there is nevertheless another way of this kind, more readily accessible because far less demanding, and this is the concrete example of holy men in Islamic

[13] The Koran speaks of rivers in the plural for each of the four substances, whereas other versions mention four rivers springing, in the form of a cross, from beneath the Throne of *Allāh.* In Jewish and Christian texts describing the same four rivers, oil takes the place of water, which is not surprising considering, on the one hand, that water is precious for the Arabs of the desert but not—empirically speaking—for Palestinians or for Europeans, and on the other hand, that oil, a sacramental substance, symbolizes purification and enlightenment.

[14] These contemplative beatitudes are symbolized not only by the four rivers but also by the "pool" and the "fountain" of Paradise, *Kawthar* and *Tasnīm,* which no doubt represent a principial complementarity; according to the commentaries, the pool evokes the idea of "proximity", and the fountain that of "inexhaustibility"; the Absolute and the Infinite, in beatific vision.

countries; certainly not hagiography with its stereotypical moralism and its extravagances, but rather the living men who can communicate the perfume of the *barakah muhammadiyyah* of which they are the vessels, witnesses, and proofs. For without the qualities of the Prophet, these men would not exist—neither in his time nor, with all the more reason, a millennium and a half after him.

Another testimony of this order—and it will come as a surprise to those who fail to see the profound connections between the most diverse traditional phenomena—is of necessity provided by the arts and crafts of the Muslims, especially in architecture and dress, which relate respectively to ambience and to man. As with Christian or any other traditional art, the important thing to know is not from what source the Muslim peoples took the *materia prima* of their art; what is decisive as regards worth and originality is what they have made of this *materia*, the spirit and the soul they have manifested by means of it, or starting from it. Now Muslim art in its most authentic and thus most characteristic realizations—such as calligraphy, architecture, mosque ornamentation, and dress—is the very expression of the soul and the spirit of the Prophet, of his serenity and his recollectedness before God ever-present.

In summary, and leaving aside all considerations of the mystical character of Muhammad, we can say with historical accuracy that the Prophet was generous, patient, noble, and profoundly human in the best sense of the word; no doubt, there are those who will point out that this is all fine and well but hardly significant and the least that could be expected of the founder of a religion. Our reply is that on the contrary, it is something immense if this founder was able to inculcate these qualities into his disciples, both near and distant, if he was able to make of his virtues the roots of a spiritual and social life and to confer upon them a vitality that could bridge centuries. Herein lies everything.

According to a *hadīth* as enigmatic as it is famous, "women, perfumes, and prayer" were "made lovable" (*hubbiba ilayya*) to the Prophet; since that is so, we have to admit that these three loves, at first sight unrelated, necessarily enter into the Muhammadan substance and consequently into the spiritual ideal of the Sufis. Every religion has to integrate the feminine element—the "eternal feminine" (*das Ewig Weibliche*) if one will—into its system, either directly or indirectly; Christianity virtually deifies the Mother of Christ, despite exoteric reservations, namely the point of distinction between *latria* and *hyperdulia*. Islam for its part, and beginning with the Prophet, has sacralized femininity, on the basis of a metaphysics of deiformity; the secrecy surrounding woman, symbolized by the veil, basically signifies an intention of sacralization. In Muslim eyes, woman, beyond her purely biological and social role, incarnates two poles, unitive "extinction" and "generosity", and these constitute from the spiritual point of view two means of overcoming the profane mentality, made as it is of outwardness, dispersion, egoism, hardness, and boredom. The nobleness of soul that is, or that can be, gained by this interpretation or by this appreciation of the feminine element, far from being an abstract ideal, is clearly detectable in representative Muslims, namely in those still rooted in authentic Islam.[15]

As for the love of "perfumes" mentioned by the *hadīth* quoted, it symbolizes the sense of the sacred and in a general way the sense for ambiences, emanations, and auras; hence it is connected with the "discernment of spirits", not to mention the sense of beauty. According to Islam, "God loves beauty" and He hates uncleanness and noise, as is shown by the atmosphere of freshness, harmony, and equilibrium— namely of *barakah*—to be found in Muslim dwellings which have remained traditional, and above all in the mosques; an atmosphere which also is clearly a part of the Muhammadan substance.

The *hadīth* then mentions prayer, which is none other than "remembrance of God", and this constitutes the fundamental reason for all possible loves, since it is love of the source and of the archetypes; it coincides with the love of God, which is the very essence of the Prophetic nature. If prayer is mentioned in third place, it is by way of conclusion: in speaking of women, Muhammad is essentially speaking of his inward nature; in speaking of perfumes, he has in mind the world around us, the ambience; and in speaking of prayer, he is giving expression to his love of God.

---

[15] It is always this Islam we have in mind, and not so-called "revivals" which monstrously combine a Muslim formalism with modernist ideologies and tendencies.

Regarding the first of the three enunciations in the *hadīth*, an additional explanation is called for, and it is fundamental. The apparent moral inconsistency in Islam has its source not only in the antagonism between the public Law on the one hand, with its concern for equilibrium and harmony, and private ascesis on the other, enthralled with detachment and self-transcendence, it has its source also in the personality of the Prophet himself, in what appears at first sight as the divergence between his ascesis and his sexual life; tradition mentions in fact the virile power of the Prophet as well as his voluntary poverty, his virtually constant hunger, and his habitual vigils. This apparent contradiction, which in reality is a positive bipolarity, could not be particular to Muhammad alone—although it characterizes him among the Semitic founders of religions—since it manifests a universal phenomenon and thereby an archetype: Hindu mythology in fact presents Shiva, god of destruction as well as of generation, as the model of ascetics as well as of lovers. This is because Shiva expresses both Transcendence and Immanence, and, in like manner, the Prophet of Islam pertains typologically to the same mysteries, if one may say; his Message testifies to the Transcendent, whereas his personality—his *barakah*—manifests as it were a "Krishnaitic" participation in the Immanent.

Islam, like Hinduism, considers two aspects of femininity: glorified woman and woman as martyr;[16] it situates two examples outside Islam, in the past, and two other examples at the beginning of its own history. The martyrs are Asiyah, the believer-wife of Pharaoh the unbeliever, and Fatimah, harshly treated by her father and her husband, and unjustly—from a certain point of view—by the first caliph;[17] whereas the glorious women are Maryam—whom "God hath purified and chosen above all women"—and Khadijah, first wife of the Prophet and his guardian angel so to speak, as well as "protectress" of the Revelation at the outset of his career.

---

[16] In Hindu mythology, the story of Sita is characteristic of this second aspect; other myths illustrate the glorious aspect.

[17] It is partly from this drama of frustration and misunderstanding, which also involved the sons of Fatimah and above all her husband, that Shiism has arisen. The antagonism between these historical figures stems from a providential and inevitable antagonism between perspectives; the exclusivism and the ostracizing tendency of the exoteric spirit completes the process.

But let us return to the third enunciation of the *hadīth*, the love of prayer: a frequently used canonical formula proclaims that "prayer is better than sleep";[18] now the Koran enjoins the Prophet to keep vigil part of the night in order to devote himself to prayer, and this reference to the night signifies far more than mere practical advice: more profoundly it means that knowledge is born in the night of the soul, that is, in the perfect receptivity that is "poverty", "humility", "extinction" or *vacare Deo*; a gift can be given only to a hand that is "below" and opened to what is above, according to Eckhart. From another perspective, wisdom is a night compared with the profane mentality, just as it is "folly" in the eyes of the world; the same holds true, within the framework of religion, for esoterism, which transcends religious, formal, and psychological limitations; thus there is a certain relationship, at once principial and historical, between the Prophet's nights of prayer and esoterism in Islam. This also brings us back to the two caves of the Prophet, that of Mount Hira where he used to meditate prior to his mission, and the cave of Thawr where during the Hegira he taught his companion Abu Bakr the science of the divine Name; within the same order of ideas, and preeminently, one should mention the *Laylat al-Qadr* and the *Laylat al-Mi'rāj*, the night of the "Descent" of the Koran and the night of the "Ascension" of Muhammad during the "Night Journey".[19]

This vigil that God imposed upon His Messenger has two contents, the recitation of the Revelation and the remembrance of God: "Keep vigil a part of the night, a half thereof or a little less or more thereof, and recite the Koran with care. . . . Invoke the Name of thy Lord and devote thyself with a total devotion" (*Sūrah* "The Enshrouded One" [73]:1-4, 8). The difference between the two practices—the recitation of the Koran and the Invocation of the divine Name—is that between the qualities and the essence, the formal and the non-formal, the outward and the inward, thought and heart; and it is this passage concerning the two nocturnal practices which basically inaugurates the Sufic tradition. It is to be noted that the recitation must be done "with

---

[18] The *tathwīb*, which is uttered during the call to the dawn prayer (*fajr*). Sleep is profane heedlessness, and prayer, spiritual wakefulness.

[19] A saying analogous to the *tathwīb* is the following Koranic verse, which also refers to a "best" and to an "awakening": "And in truth, the Hereafter is better for thee than the here-below" (*Sūrah* "The Morning Hours" [93]:4).

care" (*tartīlā*), whereas the invocation demands that the worshiper "devote himself totally" (*tabtīlā*) to God, the first expression referring to the zeal that satisfies the requirements of the formal plane, and the second, to the totality of dedication needed for the realization of the supra-formal element, this being the Essence, or the immanent Unity.

——— .:. ———

The Prophet of Islam possesses two hundred and one names and titles; the most fundamental, those summarizing all the others, are the two names *Muhammad* and *Ahmad*, and next, the designations or titles *'Abd*, *Nabī*, *Rasūl*, and *Habīb*.

The name *Muhammad* designates more particularly the mystery of Revelation, of the "Descent" (*tanzīl*), hence of the "Night of Destiny" (*Laylat al-Qadr*) during which this Descent took place. The name *Ahmad* designates correlatively the mystery of the Ascension (*mi'rāj*), hence of the "Night Journey" (*Laylat al-Mi'rāj*) which transported the Prophet before the Throne of *Allāh*.

The title *'Abd*, "Servant", refers to the quality of Rigor (*Jalāl*) and expresses the ontological and moral submission of the creature to the Creator, hence "fear"; whereas the title *Habīb*, "Friend", refers to the quality of Gentleness or "Beauty" (*Jamāl*) and expresses on the contrary the participation of the deiform being in its divine Prototype, hence "intimacy".

The title *Rasūl*, "Messenger", refers to the quality of Activity and expresses the affirmation of the True and the Good; whereas the title *Nabī* (*ummī*), ("unlettered") "Prophet", refers to the quality of Passivity and expresses receptivity with regard to the heavenly Gift.[20] The first function relates to "duty", and the second to "qualification".

The initiatic means of assimilating the Muhammadan substance[21] is the recitation of the "Blessing on the Prophet" (*Salāt 'alā'n-Nabī*),

[20] These two titles correspond respectively, in the universal order, to the supreme "Pen" (*Al-Qalam al-a'lā*), which writes out the cosmic possibilities, and to the "Guarded Tablet" (*Al-Lawh al-Mahfūz*), upon which they are inscribed.

[21] *Barakatu Muhammad*, the "spiritual aura"—beneficent and protective—of Muhammad. The terms *Nūr Muhammadī* and *Haqīqah Muhammadiyyah* refer, with different shades of meaning, to the Logos itself.

whose constituent terms indicate the different modes or qualities of this substance;[22] these terms are the following: *'Abd, Rasūl, Salāt,* and *Salām;* "Servant", "Messenger", "Blessing", and "Peace". Now the disciple, "he who is poor before his Lord" (*al-faqīr ilā Rabbihi*), must realize the perfection of the *'Abd,* following in the footsteps of the Prophet, by a thorough consciousness of the relation between contingent being and "necessary Being" (*Wujūd wājib* or *mutlaq*), which is *ipso facto* "Lord" (*Rabb*); correlatively, the perfect and normative man is "messenger", that is to say "transmitter" of the divine Message, owing to his radiation, for a perfectly pure mirror will reflect the light. This precisely is expressed by the terms *Salāt* and *Salām*—the latter being the purity of the mirror, and the former, the ray of light. Now purity is also a gift of God; it includes all the receptive, stabilizing, preserving, and peace-giving graces; without it, as the Shaykh al-Alawi pointed out, the soul could not bear either to receive or to carry the "vertical", illuminating, and transformative graces offered by the divine "Blessing" (*Salāt*).

Other points of reference for the knowledge of the Prophetic nature are to be found in the words of the Second Testimony of Faith: *Muhammadun Rasūlu 'Llāh;* "Muhammad is the Messenger of God". The first word—the name of the Prophet—indicates Immanence, and by way of consequence Union; the second word connotes the perfection of Conformity or of Complementarity, one could say Piety; and the third—the Name *Allāh*—indicates Transcendence, and more especially the Muhammadan knowledge of this mystery.

— ·:· —

The Muhammadan substance is the love of God combined, by the nature of things, with contemplativeness and nobleness of character; as also with a sense of outward or practical values, such as the beauty

---

[22] One could say as much for the *Ave,* whose expressions *gratia plena* and *Dominus tecum* refer respectively to the perfections of container and content, hence to *Salām* and *Salāt,* and also in a certain fashion to *'Abd* and *Rasūl.* The first term denotes the primordial state—the "immaculate conception"—and the second, the divine gift and the mission.

of forms and cleanliness,[23] or the rules of propriety infused with generosity and dignity. The sense of outward things—although in no wise "vain" for being so—stems in the final analysis from the emphasis on "discernment", hence from the element "Truth"; for one who discerns initially between the Absolute and the contingent, between necessary Being and possible being—and this is the very content of the *Shahādah*—will readily apply analogous discernments in the sphere of contingency. As for the sense of beauty, it is related to the mystery of Immanence.

It is from this substance and its deepest dimensions, as we have said, that Sufism draws its life, with a sense for following through with things that sometimes contradicts—or seems to contradict—the general formalism of Islam. Thus the *'ulamā*, for whom Sufism is alien, are all too prone to insist that it is contrary to tradition, in which they are mistaken, though with extenuating circumstances; Sufis for their part affirm the contrary, and sometimes with too much zeal since esoterism, while formally rooted in the traditional system, constitutes by definition an independent domain, its essence being situated outside all temporal or "horizontal" continuity.[24]

We can liken the particular mode of inspiration and orthodoxy that is esoterism to the rain falling vertically from the sky, whereas the river—the common tradition—flows horizontally in a continuous current; in other words, the tradition springs from a source, it goes back to a given founder of a religion, whereas esoterism refers in addition—and above all *a priori*—to an invisible filiation, one which in the Bible is represented by Melchizedek, Solomon,[25] and Elijah, and which Sufism associates with Al-Khidr, the mysterious immortal.

---

[23] These last betoken an element of primordiality; they are to be found, moreover—with the same meaning and long before Islam—in Hinduism, for example, and notably also in Shinto.

[24] Zen Buddhism offers a particularly striking example of this spiritual and structural "extra-territoriality".

[25] Who was also "king of Salem", as his name indicates; but in biblical History he is presented in terms of the exo-esoteric antinomy.

APPENDIX

Selections from Letters and
Other Previously Unpublished Writings

1

The peculiarity of Muhammad is to be the synthesis of all spiritual possibilities; this makes his image, as seen from without, somewhat unintelligible, compared with the formal unequivocalness of other prophets; Muhammad's unequivocalness lies precisely in his many-sidedness. Christ represented quite unequivocally—in relation to the Jewish cult of the Law—spiritual inwardness; and therefore he has this meaning for the Sufis also; he is the Prophet of the Heart, not of outward works; and Mary has the same meaning, with this difference that she founded no religion and is "Mother of All the Prophets", hence well-spring of all the religions. The image of the Prophet is clear and unequivocal—provided one has the key to it—insofar as he is an open fan of all the virtues.

2

The Message (*Risālah*) of Christ is the Gospel and the Eucharist, then His Name. The Message of the Holy Virgin is her Son; not the Message of her Son, but her Son in Himself; now this Son, viewed outside of His Message is the Logos as such, which is represented by the Child Jesus; the Logos-Child being the Logos in itself. To say that the Virgin is the Mother of the Logos in itself, of the Logos viewed before or outside every articulated Message, is to say that she is the Mother of all the Prophets. For her Son, not yet being "such and such a Prophet" since he had not yet articulated a Message, was "all of the Prophets", or "the Prophet as such".

Every law-giving *Risālah* is a Message of Truth. The non-formal and non-law-giving *Risālah* of the Virgin is a Message of Sanctity: or rather, it is the Message of Sanctity; of the Sanctity which coincides with non-formal, essential, primordial Truth.

3

I could be asked this question: how could a Catholic, even an esoteric one, accept the "intrinsic orthodoxy"—not "extrinsic"—of Protestantism? And someone could ask, with all the more apparent reason, this other question: how could a Catholic accept the intrinsic orthodoxy of Islam? Because Islam rejects Christianity, just as Protestantism rejects Catholicism, but even more fundamentally so; and if esoterism allows one to understand why and how Islam can do this, then esoterism allows one also to understand why and how Protestantism can do so likewise, *mutatis mutandis.*

4

Obviously the artistic (not merely pictographic) representation of living beings cannot be primordial—the Native Americans have no images of the gods—however, it is esoteric by nature, and precisely because of this, a two-edged sword; what is equally obvious, late Semitic iconoclasm is *a priori* exoteric, but it nevertheless recreates a primordial state, and in this way expresses the *Religio Perennis;* and thus, however contradictory it may sound, there is no profound opposition between Islam and a pictorial art that is esoteric; thus the two are compatible on the plane of esoterism if circumstances permit or demand it. The painting of the Iranian and Indian Muslims proves this in its way.

5

God is the Sovereign Good, and this Good—the Good in itself—is absolute and infinite. This supreme truth is to be found inscribed in our immortal spirit; but exteriorized man has lost the immediate access to his spirit. That is why he has need of revelation and teaching, hence of lights coming from without.

The Reality of God produces in us Certitude and Serenity; the latter being the irradiation of the former. Serenity is to Certitude what Infinitude is to Absoluteness.

The Certitude of God produces as its effect the Certitude of Salvation; for knowledge of the Sovereign Good in a certain manner encompasses the soul in this Good, as light encompasses the mirror which it illuminates. Moreover, the unicity of the object demands the totality of the subject; our Certitude must reside in our heart, and consequently it must encompass our entire being; the result of this is virtue. The Certitude of God produces Serenity in God, and at the same time demands—or entails—virtue, namely, conformity of the entire soul to the Truth of which it is aware.

In a certain sense, Certitude corresponds to the Absolute, and Serenity to the Infinite; in an analogous manner, virtue corresponds to the Sovereign Good.

Since the Certitude of God must be situated in the heart, and in consequence must encompass our entire being, for that very reason it gives rise to virtue and also, and even above all, to love of virtue; all the more so, that without virtue there could be no Certitude of Salvation. Without virtue, the heart is absent, and in the absence of the heart, there could be no question of Certitude of Salvation.

It is indeed marvelous that Certitude of God—springing either from Gnosis or from Faith—implies Certitude of Salvation, which it does to the extent that Certitude of God is sincere—and consequently rooted in the heart—and that it gives rise thereby to virtue.

6

Knowledge is at once inexpressible and expressible; to deny the second term would amount to saying that no metaphysical doctrine is possible, that the only doctrines possible would be theological specu-lations, namely those marked by a "passional" element and which therefore are "not disinterested", as Guénon would say. That the most rigorously metaphysical doctrine is not supreme knowledge as such, no one will argue, but this could not mean that short of this doctrine there are nothing but speculations of a confessional type, or let us say metaphysical speculations that are more or less subject to the direc-tives of theology, and to the psychology resulting from it. The theo-logical limitations for which I reproach some Sufis are not reducible to the natural and therefore general limitations of human language, otherwise any language possible would be theological; in a word, to reproach a Shankara for the limitations inherent to language, which he has to make use of on pain of not being able to express anything at all, would amount to reproaching a man for being a man.

Someone who is purely and simply an exoterist has no choice but to accept, at the risk of heresy, some errors or half-truths that are providential; he will accept them in the context of a fundamental and compensatory truth. These canonical errors are never gratuitous, they are functional or, in other words, their reason for being is to ward off dangers that are likely or certain to happen, given the collective nature of the human recipient; in that sense, they are indirectly and symbolically "truths", at least *de facto*. Be that as it may, "there is no right superior to that of the truth"; this amounts to saying that an esoterist is never obliged before God to accept points of view he knows are false, were it even a canonical point of view; I mean: to accept them with respect to their falseness, for he can obviously accept them with respect to their symbolism and their role, but this reduces everything to a question of terminology. A religion is an *upāya*, a "salvific mirage" or a "divine means"; however no religion can do without some defect, and the esoterist cannot be unaware of this; the proof of this defect or of this error, if one may say, being precisely the quasi-canonical obligation to revile the religion of one's neighbor.

7

Ghazzali points out that God creates bad things for reasons unknown to us and does so with wise intentions; Ashari and Ibn Arabi would say that these things are intrinsically good since God created them, which is plausible from a certain point of view, but which nonetheless robs words of all their meaning. I have dealt with this matter in more than one book; what this comes down to is to know where one draws the line between the form and the essence of a thing or a being; what always remains good in phenomena is obviously their existential substance, then their positive qualities, their faculties of understanding, sensation, and action if we are talking about creatures, but not necessarily their characteristic particularities. Evil is not transcended simply because one denies it; God could not ask this of us.

To qualify an animal as bad because it bites us makes no sense; an animal species can be bad even if it does not harm us, and another can be good even if it harms us; one does not like the hyena, but one admires the lion. It is really too simple to reduce our assessment of the qualities of creatures to a matter of subjective opportunity; one can, metaphysically, save the intrinsic goodness of creation at less cost, that is to say without abdicating the rights of intellectual discernment. Because the notion of evil must have a meaning; God Himself proposes it in His Scriptures; and before there is the notion, there is obviously the concrete phenomenon, which we know from experience, on the aesthetic plane as well as on the moral plane and on other planes; what matters is to know how to distinguish between an intrinsic and an extrinsic evil. To say that the devil is "good in himself" makes no sense, unless by that one means that he is good in his transpersonal essence; but in that essence, precisely, he ceases to be the devil. Clearly, one must account for the essential goodness of the whole creation, but one must do so in keeping with the nature of things and according to the principle of All-Possibility, and not by means of the simplifications theologians envisage. If the reason for being of ugliness is the possibility—rendered necessary by the limitlessness of divine Possibility—of a privation of beauty within the confines of universal relativity, then, to safeguard the absoluteness and universality of divine Beauty, it is not enough to declare that the ugly is the beautiful "in itself". This Beauty—I am repeating the formulation—can be safeguarded "at less cost"; or, if one wishes, "at a greater cost". If theologians are afraid of Mazdean dualism, that is their business, not that of the metaphysicians.

There are two pitfalls that must be avoided: to maintain that there are two gods, one good and one evil; and to maintain that evil does not exist, either objectively or intrinsically. Now, to avoid the first pitfall one need not choose the second; Koranic language does not shy away from the boldest elliptical expressions, for example when one finds in the text that "God leads into error whom He will"; but God reestablishes equilibrium *a priori* in defining Himself as *Rahmān* and *Rahīm*; and the other Names.

God created man "in His own image", and He "taught him the names" of things and of creatures; this means that He gave us discernment—which is adequate by definition—and that as a result we are the measure of all things. We notice that some creatures embody *sattva*, others *rajas*, and yet others *tamas*; this is an adequation, hence the perception is objectively valid, outside any question of knowing whether or not these creatures are useful to us, or whether or not they are harmful to us. I keep on returning to this same point, so strangely misunderstood by certain pious simplifiers. The argument of the snake that bites—abusively applied to the whole question of evil—applies only to extrinsic harm, thus to what is conditional or subjective; this should be as clear as day.

What we term evil—not due to a bias but because it is really an evil on its plane of manifestation—has its ontological root in All-Possibility inasmuch as All-Possibility requires the manifestation, one the one hand, of a portion of the good presented in a contrasting fashion and, on the other, the absence of the good which, according to Ibn Arabi, is "non-existence". Now All-Possibility, quite obviously, is an aspect of the Sovereign Good, and so is the universal Radiation. "Possibility of the impossible", or "existence of the non-existent" resulting from the Infinite, and by definition within relativity: this is the answer to the problem, insofar as it can be expressed. "He is God, there is none other except him; He knoweth the hidden and the manifest; He is the Ever-Compassionate and the Ever-Merciful."

8

The invocation, like any action and *a fortiori* so, requires an intention; a spiritual motivation or, if one wishes, a metaphysical or mystical point of view. The basis for this doctrine is provided by the ternary *makhāfah-mahabbah-maʿrifah*; each of these elements can be polarized into various modes, and a plurality of spiritual attitudes is thus obtained to which, moreover, the virtues (*fadhāʾil*) correspond, as well as the contemplative states (*ahwāl*), and the spiritual stations (*maqāmāt*), which have been discussed by Qushayri, Ibn al-Arif, and others.

9

The Christian Message refers to the primordial Religion in teaching that what counts is the inward, not the outward; the essence, not forms. The Islamic Message refers to the primordial Religion in the sense that Islam harmoniously takes into account all points of view or all the natural and spiritual possibilities of man, and does so in view of Unity, thus of the Absolute.

There is an esoterism which is indirect, relative, mitigated, and another which is direct, absolute, pure: the first intensifies, deepens, and refines exoterism, whereas the second, which is esoterism as such and not such and such an esoterism, refers to the supraformal and thereby universal Truth, to the nature of things, to the *Religio Perennis*, while relying extrinsically upon the central elements and the fundamental symbols of the historical Revelation. Pure esoterism is the direct manifestation of the one and universal primordial Religion, within some particular religious framework.

10

In Catholicism there is a strange disproportion between the initiatic, and consequently very demanding, character of the "means of grace", and the completely profane level of the masses for whom they are destined; a proof of this level is the almost "traditional" worldliness of the laity, something which can be seen even in their dress.

The remote and fundamental cause of this disproportion is the fact that Christianity, esoteric in its origin, crystallized into an exoterism—of necessity, otherwise it could not have become a world religion; whence the growing concern to specify dogmatic details and elaborate the liturgy, thus distancing itself more and more from the Eastern Church. In Islam, Christianity is reproached for offering only an esoterism, and consequently for lacking an exoterism; in other words, for having improvised an exoterism which in fact is not one, or which is one *de facto*, but not *de jure*.

The celestial archetype of an exoteric sacramentality—namely one that offers only the indispensable minimum necessary for elementary salvation—can in certain circumstances project into the human world supports that are adapted to this need; and this is exactly what happened in and through Protestantism. Strictly speaking, Luther did not attack the sacraments—least of all the Mass—in themselves, he attacked the Catholic way of looking at them and handling them. He called the Catholic Mass an "abomination"—though he believed in the real Presence and the necessity of the rite—just as some orthodox Buddhists call the *nembutsu* of Amida Buddhism an "abomination", such as, in practice, would merit hell; something Luther never said of the Catholic practice.

The relationship between Protestantism and Catholicism is completely analogous to the relationship between Amidism and the other Buddhist schools; but whereas Amidists, conscious of possessing a way capable of saving the average man and even the "worst of sinners", are content to say that the other schools—Zen, Tendai, Shingon, etc.— are for superior souls and can only trouble the simple, Protestants reject Catholicism in itself, in keeping with the Western and Semitic "either-or" attitude and exclusivism. For their part, Catholics reject Protestantism, that is to say, they deny its saving efficacy, whereas if they were Hindus, they would be content to admit that this way was suitable for the simple, but not for the aristocrats of spirituality.

If the archetype of the Protestant perspective had been able to manifest itself within Catholicism, it would have been much less abrupt, and much more gentle than it was outside the Catholic tradition. One ought to have listened to Savonarola, who was the Catholic prophet of this perspective; the condemnation of Savonarola was one of the papacy's great crimes. Since it had to manifest itself outside the Catholic tradition, the Protestant perspective had of necessity to be radicalized. As an independent *upāya*, it could not avoid taking liberties which it would not have taken within the framework of the Roman church. An *upāya* is absolute to the extent that it is independent.

Let us return to the question of the Mass. In the *Abrégé de Théologie dogmatique et morale* by Father J. Berthier, we read: "The sacrifice of the Mass is the same as that of the Cross. It is one and the same host, the same sacrifice as offered itself on the Cross, which is now offered by the ministry of priests." Now for Luther, there is only one sacrifice, that of Calvary, and the rites carried out by pastors "participate" in it but do not "create" it, something which is indicated precisely by the word "commemoration"; but for Catholics, the sacrament is "repeated", which does not impair the underlying idea that this repetition is related to the historical sacrifice of Christ. One might also say that this sacrifice "enters" into each Mass; but what upsets Protestants is that, in spite of this notion, the material cause of the rite is the officiating priest, since he operates fully *in persona Christi*, whereas the cause of the historical sacrifice is Christ himself. One could argue indefinitely about these nuances, but the essential here is to understand that the Protestants have extenuating circumstances, the Catholic formulations being much too absolute; something which—from the point of view of *upāya*—is their right, but which nevertheless contains the seeds for a shattering, given the complexity of the total truth.

Luther was very sensitive to the disproportion between the Mass—considered by Catholics to be practically speaking the equivalent of the historical sacrifice—and the casualness with which it was handled; the Orthodox have the same sentiment and this explains the central and immutable place accorded to their majestic liturgy, for their refusal to apply the Mass for this or for that intention, for their refusal to permit private masses, and so on. When Luther, at Rome, was celebrating Mass, an Italian priest called out to him: "Hurry up!" For Luther this was a shock from which he never recovered, he who believed he was reciting the Mass *in persona Christi*!

We can stop here, for most of the important arguments are given in the chapter "Divergences chrétiennes". The essential is not to lose sight of the notion of the "relatively absolute": in other words, that the necessarily absolute character of theological formulations does not prevent them from having a relative status from a higher point of view—that of the *religio perennis*—otherwise there would be no denominational divergences, or religious divergences, *a priori*.

EDITOR'S NOTES

Numbers in bold indicate pages in the text for which the following citations and explanations are provided.

Foreword

xi: *Religionswissenschaft*, or "the science of religions", is the comparative and academic study of religions; the term was popularized by the German philologist and Indologist, Max Müller (1823-1900).

xii: In the author's writings, the Latin term *religio perennis*, or "perennial religion", refers to "the essence of every religion . . . the essence of every form of worship, every form of prayer, and every system of morality" (Frithjof Schuon, "The Perennial Philosophy", in Harry Oldmeadow, *Frithjof Schuon and the Perennial Philosophy* [Bloomington, Indiana: World Wisdom, 2010], p. 312); see also the author's chapter, *"Religio Perennis"*, in *Light on the Ancient Worlds: A New Translation with Selected Letters*, ed. Deborah Casey (Bloomington, Indiana: World Wisdom, 2006), pp. 119-126.

The Decisive Intuition

4: *Mythological traditions*, in contradistinction to later so-called historical traditions, have variously been referred to as "primal", "primordial", and "archaic"; they include indigenous traditions such as the Native American Indians and Japanese Shintoists, about whom the author has written extensively in *The Feathered Sun* (Bloomington, Indiana: World Wisdom, 1990) and Part 2 of *Treasures of Buddhism* (Bloomington, Indiana: World Wisdom, 1993). For more on the distinction between myth and history in religious traditions, see the author's *Gnosis: Divine Wisdom: A New Translation with Selected Letters*, ed. James S. Cutsinger (Bloomington, Indiana: World Wisdom, 2006), pp. 9-14.

5: A *categorical imperative* refers to an absolute or unconditional requirement; the phrase is most commonly associated with the work of the German philosopher, Immanuel Kant (1724-1804) and his *Groundwork for the Metaphysics of Morals* (1785).

Note 1: *Asharite thesis*: the Asharites comprised an early school of speculative

Islamic theology, based on the teaching of Abu al-Hasan al-Ashari (873-935), which taught that anthropomorphic descriptions of God in the Koran should not be interpreted as metaphors, but accepted at face value, that is, "without asking any questions" or "without asking how" they apply to God. For further commentary on Asharism, see the author's "The Exo-Esoteric Symbiosis", in *Sufism: Veil and Quintessence: A New Translation with Selected Letters*, ed. James S. Cutsinger (Bloomington, Indiana: World Wisdom, 2006), pp. 31-33.

6: Note 3: *Pascal's wager.* Blaise Pascal (1623-62) was a French philosopher, mathematician, and scientist. His "Wager" is to be found in the posthumously published *Pensées* (1669), and posits that there is more to be gained from a belief in God than from atheism, even though the truth cannot be decisively established.

Note 4: *Mazdean dualism* refers to the metaphysical and cosmological tenets of Mazdaism, also called Zurvanism, a now-defunct branch of Zoroastrianism.

7: Note 5: Jean-Jacques *Rousseau* (1712-78) was a French philosopher and writer associated with Enlightenment ideas about "natural goodness" and the "noble savage".

Augustine (354-420), the Bishop of Hippo, was perhaps the greatest of the Church Fathers; he was the author of numerous works, including *On Christian Doctrine, Confessions, The City of God,* and *On the Trinity.*

8: *Platonic anamnesis* refers to the doctrine, notably presented in Plato's dialogues *Phaedo* and *Meno*, according to which real knowledge is inscribed in human intelligence from eternity and needs merely to be "recollected" (*anamnesis*) though intellectual intuition.

Note 6: The Roman poet *Virgil* (70-19 B.C.) was the author of the *Aeneid*, the *Eclogues*, and the *Georgics*, from which last comes the adage cited (2:490).

9: Note 7: For a fuller treatment of *Buddhist* non-theism—notably explaining why they are not "*atheists*"—see the author's "The Originality of Buddhism", in *Treasures of Buddhism*, especially pp. 21-22, and *To Have a Center* (Bloomington, Indiana: World Wisdom, 1990), pp. 135-136.

The Ambiguity of Exoterism

11: "And Jesus said unto him, *Why callest thou me good?* there is none good but one, that is, God" (Matt. 19:17, Mark 10:18).

"*God alone is good*": "Good, O Asclepius, is in none else save in God alone; nay, rather, Good is God Himself eternally" (*Corpus Hermeticum,* VI:1; cf. Matt. 19:17, Mark 10:18).

12: *The "letter" and the "spirit"*: "The letter killeth, but the spirit giveth life" (2 Cor. 3:6).

13: Jacob *Boehme* (1575-1624), a German Lutheran mystic and theologian, was author of *Aurora, oder die Morgenröte im Aufgang* (1612) and *De Signatura Rerum* (1622). The *Ungrund* is the "ground" or root of all mysteries, the "abyss" from whence come forth all divine manifestations. In metaphysical terms it corresponds to the First Cause, the divine Essence, or Beyond-Being.

14: *A collective soul determined by particular racial and ethnic factors*: for some explication of this subject, see the author's "The Meaning of Race", in *Language of the Self* (Bloomington, Indiana: World Wisdom, 1999), pp. 147-175.

"*True man and true God*": the doctrine of the "two natures" of Christ was ratified at the Council of Chalcedon in 451 and is a foundation-stone of Christian theology.

15: Note 2: Muhyi al-Din *Ibn Arabi* (1165-1240) was a prolific and profoundly influential Sufi mystic, known in tradition as the Shaykh al-Akbar ("great master"). He is the author of numerous works, including *Meccan Revelations* and *Bezels of Wisdom.*

Note 3: The author's *Sur les traces de la Religion pérenne* ("In the Tracks of the Perennial Religion") (Paris: Le Courrier du Livre, 1982) was incorporated into his English work, *Survey of Metaphysics and Esoterism* (Bloomington, Indiana: World Wisdom, 1985, 2000), where the second chapter is entitled, "Dimensions, Modes, and Degrees of the Divine Order" ("*Dimensions, modes et degrés de l'Ordre divin*").

Note 4: *Meister Eckhart* (c. 1260-1327) was a German Dominican theologian and mystic, regarded by the author as the greatest of Christian metaphysicians and esoterists.

16: Note 5: *Pope Honorius I*, pontiff from 625-38, was anathematized by the Third Council of Constantinople (680-81) for his failure to refute the *Monothelite thesis* that Christ had two natures, but only *one divine will.*

Note 6: *The Koranic doctrine of the divine "signs"* (āyāt) *in the world*: "We [God] shall show them Our signs on the horizons and within themselves until it will be manifest unto them that it is the Truth" (*Sūrah "Ha Mim"* [41]:53); "In the earth are signs for those whose faith is sure, and (also) in yourselves. Can ye then not see?" (*Sūrah "Winnowing Winds"* [51]:20-21 *passim*).

17: The most significant of the *sun-worship cults* were the Mithraic mystery cults in Babylonia and Persia.

The Koran speaks of the sun, moon, and stars as slaves upon whom God has imposed forced labor (sakhara) *in the service of men, and then it enjoins men not to bow down to the heavenly bodies:* "And He hath constrained (*sakhara*) the . . . sun and the moon to be of service unto you, and the stars are made subservient by His command" (*Sūrah "The Bee"* [16]:12; cf. 7:54); "Worship not the sun nor the moon; but worship God who created them" (*Sūrah "Ha Mim"* [41]:37).

Agni is the Vedic deity of fire, while *Surya* is the Vedic solar deity.

Francis of Assisi (1181-1226), founder of the Order of Friars Minor, or Franciscans, took the admonition of Christ to abandon all for his sake (Matt. 10:7-19) as a personal call to poverty and holiness, and was noted for bearing the stigmata of Christ. He is also well known for his love of the beauty of nature as expressed in the *Canticle to the Sun*, a hymn in praise of the radiation of the Divine in creation.

Note 7: The spiritual practice of the *Hesychast* monks of the Christian East is aimed at attaining a state of *hesychia*, or inner stillness, through the practice of the Jesus Prayer or other "prayers of the heart".

"He that raiseth up himself shall be brought low" (Luke 18:14).

Note 8: *Heraclitus* (c. 535-c. 475 B.C.) of Ephesus was a pre-Socratic philosopher and author of *On Nature*.

18: *"God is the Light of the heavens and the earth"* (*Sūrah "Light"* [24]:35).

In the Koran, the sun is described three times as a "lamp" (sirāj): "Blessed be He who hath placed in the heaven mansions of the stars, and hath placed therein a great lamp [the sun] and a moon giving light!" (*Sūrah "The Discernment"* [25]:61); "See ye not how God hath created seven heavens in harmony, And hath made the moon a light therein, and made the sun a lamp?" (*Sūrah "Noah"* [71]:15-16); "And We have built above you seven strong (heavens), And have appointed a dazzling lamp [the sun]" (*Sūrah "The Announcement"* [78]:12-13).

This word [lamp] *is also applied to the Prophet, whence his name* Sirāj: "O Prophet! Lo! We have sent thee as a witness and a bringer of good tidings and a warner. And as a summoner unto God by His permission, and as a lamp (*sirāj*) that giveth light" (*Sūrah* "The Joint Forces" [33]:45-46).

19: *In Muslim imagery, rain holds a privileged rank, as is easily understood in a desert country; the Koran misses no opportunity to mention it with praise:* "And, O my people! Ask forgiveness of your Lord, then turn unto Him repentant; He will cause the sky to rain abundance on you and will add unto you strength to your strength" (*Sūrah* "*Hud*" [11]:52); "Seek pardon of your Lord. Lo! He was ever-Forgiving. He will let loose the sky for you in plenteous rain, And will help you with wealth and sons, and will assign unto you Gardens and will assign unto you rivers" (*Sūrah* "Noah" [71]:10-12 *passim*).

Esoterism is "*open to all forms*", *as Ibn Arabi expressed himself in speaking of his heart*: "My heart is open to every form: it is a pasture for gazelles and a cloister for Christian monks, a temple for idols, the Kaaba of the pilgrim, the tables of the Torah, and the book of the Koran. I practice the religion of Love; in whatsoever direction His caravans advance, the religion of Love shall be my religion and my faith" (Ibn Arabi, *Tarjumān al-ashwāq*). For a commentary on these verses, see the author's *Understanding Islam: A New Translation with Selected Letters*, ed. Patrick Laude (Bloomington, Indiana: World Wisdom, 2011), pp. 30-31.

For *the theological excesses of Ashari*, see editor's note for "The Decisive Intuition", p. 5, Note 1.

Note 10: *Hanbalite* fideism refers to the perspective of Ahmad Ibn Hanbal (d. 855), whose school of Islamic law accentuates a literal interpretation of the Koran.

20: *It is better to reach Paradise with a limb missing than to be thrown into hell with all of one's limbs*: "If thy right hand offend thee, cut it off, and cast it from thee: for it is profitable for thee that one of thy members should perish, and not that thy whole body should be cast into hell" (Matt. 5:30).

Note 13: The *Hanafite theologian* Muhammad Abu Mansur al-*Maturidi* (853-944) was a Turkish theologian, exegete, and scholar of Islamic jurisprudence who elaborated the teachings of Abu Hanifa (699-767), the founder of the Hanafite school of law.

Mutazilites were members of an early Islamic theological school that insisted on the importance of reason in establishing a middle way between the extremes of unbelief and fideism.

Zeno of Elea (c. 490-c. 430 B.C.) was one of the pre-Socratic philosophers of ancient Greece, best known for his paradoxes, which were designed to show that multiplicity and change are illusory.

21: The *Kaaba* is a cube-shaped construction located in the Great Mosque of Mecca, the most sacred site of Islam and destination of the *hajj* or pilgrimage; the *Black Stone* is one of the Kaaba's cornerstones and is revered by Muslims as a primordial relic.

Note 14: Abu Hamid Muhammad al-*Ghazzali* (1058-1111) was an Islamic jurist and theologian who entered upon the Sufi path in search of a direct confirmation of God, which he described in his *Munqidh min al-Dalāl* ("Deliverance from Error") and *Mishkāt al-Anwār* ("The Niche for Lights"), among other works.

Sunnites comprise one of the two main streams within Islam, the other being Shiism. While Shiites look to Ali and his descendents—the Imams—as the legitimate and authoritative representatives of the Prophet Muhammad, Sunni Muslims accept the validity of the entire historical line of caliphs.

23: For his most extended critique of the *modern philosophers*, see the author's *Logic and Transcendence: A New Translation with Selected Letters*, ed. James S. Cutsinger (Bloomington, Indiana: World Wisdom, 2009).

The Two Problems

28: Christian theologians such as Clement of Alexandria (c. 115-c. 210), Origen (185-254), and Gregory of Nyssa (c. 335-c. 395) taught a doctrine of universal salvation called the *Apocatastasis*, or "restitution".

In Hindu cosmology the universe is periodically reabsorbed into the undifferentiated Absolute during a "*Night of Brahmā*". In the Hindu *Trimūrti* ("triple form"), Brahmā is the Creator-God, along with Vishnu (the Preserver), and Shiva (the Destroyer).

"*God alone is good*": "Good, O Asclepius, is in none else save in God alone; nay, rather, Good is God Himself eternally" (*Corpus Hermeticum*, VI:1); "Why callest thou me good? There is none good but one, that is, God" (Matt. 19:17; Mark 10:18).

30: "*God doeth what He will*" (*Sūrah* "The Family of Imran" [3]:40 *passim*).

The Notion of Eternity

33: *The Koran calls hell "perpetual"* (khālid), *but adds "unless God should will otherwise"*: "And whoso disobeyeth God and His messenger, lo! his is fire of hell, wherein such dwell forever (*khālid*)" (*Sūrah "Jinn"* [72]:23); "As for those who will be wretched (on that day) they will be in the Fire; sighing and wailing will be their portion therein. Abiding there so long as the heavens and the earth endure unless thy Lord willeth otherwise" (*Sūrah "Hud"* [11]:106-107).

The Prophet even declares explicitly that hell will have an end: "The flames of hell will grow cold" (*hadīth*); "By the God in whose hands is my soul, a time shall come when the gates of hell shall be closed and watercress [symbol of coolness] will grow on its soil" (*hadīth*).

For *Ashari*, see editor's note for "The Decisive Intuition", p. 5, Note 1.

Note 2: The *Dhyāni-Bodhisattva Jizo* (*Kshitigarbha* in Sanskrit) is widely revered in Buddhist East Asia, where he is usually depicted as a monk and regarded as the protector of hell-beings, especially deceased children.

Note 3: "God *doeth what He will*" (*Sūrah* "The Family of Imran" [3]:40 *passim*).

34: For *Ibn Arabi*, see editor's note for "The Ambiguity of Exoterism", p. 15, Note 2.

Thomas Aquinas (c. 1225-74) was an immensely influential Italian Dominican priest and scholastic theologian, known in Catholic tradition as the "Angelic Doctor". His best-known works are the *Summa theologiae* and the *Summa Contra Gentiles*.

35: In this context *Brahmanists* refer to Hindus.

36: *"It is not God that wrongeth them, but they wrong themselves"* (*Sūrah* "Jonah" [10]:44).

37: *Man courts perdition unless he grasps a particular "lifeline", as a verse of the Koran says*: "And hold fast, all of you together, to the lifeline of God, and do not separate" (*Sūrah* "The Family of Imran" [3]:103).

Paradise . . . will be transcended—or "absorbed"—in the end by the mystery of Ridwān, *the divine "Good Pleasure"*: "God promiseth to the believers, men and women, Gardens underneath which rivers flow, wherein they will abide—blessed dwellings in Gardens of Eden. And—greater (far)!—[is] God's good pleasure (*ridwān*). That is the supreme triumph" (*Sūrah* "Repentance" [9]:72).

"*Unless God should will otherwise*": see note above, p. 33.

Origen (c. 185-c. 254) was a Church Father of the Catechetical School in Alexandria which exhibited strong Platonic tendencies and a preference for mystical and allegorical interpretations of Scripture.

38: Note 7: In Orthodox Christianity an *iconostasis* is a wall of icons and religious paintings separating the nave from the sanctuary of a church.

39: "*Faith that moves mountains*": "If ye have faith as a grain of mustard seed, ye shall say unto this mountain, Remove hence to yonder place; and it shall remove; and nothing shall be impossible unto you" (Matt. 17:20).

Paul says that the pots must not argue with the potter. "Nay but, O man, who art thou that repliest against God? Shall the thing formed say to him that formed it, Why hast thou made me thus? Hath not the potter power over the clay, of the same lump to make one vessel unto honor, and another unto dishonor?" (Rom. 9:20-21; cf. Is. 45:9).

For *Shiva and Vishnu*, see editor's note for "The Two Problems", p. 28.

40: "*Water takes on the color of its container*" is a saying attributed to Abu al-Qasim al-Junayd (830-910), a *Sufi* mystic of Persian extraction who taught in Baghdad.

For "*true man and true God*", see editor's note for "The Ambiguity of Exoterism", p. 14.

The Complexity of Dogmatism

43: Note 2: *Wisdom of Christ:* "We preach Christ crucified . . . unto them which are called, both Jews and Greeks, Christ the power of God, and the wisdom of God" (1 Cor. 1:24).

"We speak wisdom among them that are perfect: yet not the *wisdom of this world*, nor of the princes of this world, that come to nought" (1 Cor. 2:6).

Plato (c. 427-c. 347 B.C.) was a student of Socrates, teacher of Aristotle, and the greatest of the ancient Greek philosophers.

"I beseech you, that I may not be bold when I am present with that confidence, wherewith I think to be bold against some, which think of us as if we walked *according to the flesh*" (2 Cor. 10:2); "Though we have known Christ *according to the flesh*, yet now henceforth know we him no more" (2 Cor. 5:16).

44: In the author's original French, the word here rendered *Protestantism* is *Évangélisme* or "Evangelicalism", a term used in a European context to refer either to Lutheranism or to the union of the Lutheran and Reformed churches, or again to Protestant bodies in general.

46: *The denial in the Koran of the crucifixion of Christ*: "And . . . [the Jews] saying: We slew the Messiah Jesus son of Mary, God's Messenger—They slew him not nor crucified [him], but it appeared so unto them" (*Sūrah* "Women" [4]:157). For a fuller explanation of this "denial", see the author's *Gnosis: Divine Wisdom: A New Translation with Selected Letters*, p. 7n.

The story of *Abraham* being *thrown into the blaze* by Nimrod is recounted in *Sūrah* "The Prophets" [21]:51-70.

The story of *Daniel in the lions' den* is recounted in Dan. 6:10-28.

Note 4: The *Law of Manu* (*Mānava Dharma Shāstra* or *Manu-smriti*) is an ancient collection of moral, social, and legal prescriptions understood to be binding on all orthodox Hindus.

Amitabha (Sanskrit), or *Amida* (Japanese), is the Buddha of "infinite light" who, as a *Bodhisattva* named Dharmakara, vowed not to enter *Nirvāna* until he had brought all who invoked his Name into the *Paradise* of his Pure Land.

Amidism is the Buddhist *Jōdo* or Pure Land sect, whose central spiritual practice is the invocation of Amida, the Buddha of "infinite light".

Christian Divergences

49: For the word *Protestantism* throughout this chapter, see editor's note for "The Complexity of Dogmatism", p. 44.

Dante Alighieri (1265-1321), the author of *The Divine Comedy*, composed his *De Monarchia* (*Treatise on Monarchy*, 1313) in honor of Emperor Henry VII.

Note 2: The author's longest and most detailed study of Protestantism (*Évangélisme*) was first published in English as "The Question of Evangelicalism" in his book *Christianity/Islam: Essays on Esoteric Ecumenicism*

(Bloomington, Indiana: World Wisdom, 1985), pp. 15-53; a second edition, subtitled *Perspectives on Esoteric Ecumenism: A New Translation with Selected Letters*, ed. James S. Cutsinger, was published by World Wisdom in 2008, and translates the essay "*La question de l'Evangélisme*" as "The Question of Protestantism", pp. 23-54.

50: For the *Lutheran denial*, see note below, p. 51.

For *Amidists*, see editor's note for "The Complexity of Dogmatism", p. 46, Note 4.

50-51: *Augustinianism*, or the teaching of *Augustine* of Hippo (see editor's note for "The Decisive Intuition", p. 7, Note 5), taught that before the fall man was "able not to sin" (*posse non peccare*), but that fallen man "is not able not to sin" (*non posse non peccare*).

51: Martin *Luther* (1483-1546), a leading figure in the Reformation, was a German monk, priest, and theologian. He believed that man is wholly under the power of evil and can do nothing but sin, justification itself being a kind of legal fiction whereby the righteousness of Christ is imputed to the Christian.

52: *It is necessary to love God with all our faculties*: "Thou shalt love the Lord thy God with all thy heart, and with all thy soul, and with all thy mind" (Matt. 22:37; cf. Deut. 6:5).

"It is profitable for thee that one of thy *members* should perish, and not that thy whole body should be cast into hell" (Matt. 5:29).

Note 3: For *categorical imperative*, see editor's note for "The Decisive Intuition", p. 5.

For *Thomistic intellectuality*, see editor's note for "The Notion of Eternity", p. 34.

"*Those who have ears to hear*": "Who hath ears to hear, let him hear" (Matt. 13:9 *passim*).

53: Ulrich *Zwingli* (1484-1531) was a leader of the Reformation in Switzerland who believed that the Eucharist was merely a memorial service and that Christ was not really present in the bread and wine.

According to the Catholic doctrine of *transubstantiation*, the essence of the elements is changed, though they still appear in their "accidents" to be bread and wine; Luther preferred a doctrine of *consubstantiation*, according to which the body and blood of Christ co-exist with the essence or substance of the bread and wine.

John *Calvin* (1509-64) was a leading figure in the Reformation who believed the faithful communicant receives the virtue or power of the Body and Blood, a doctrine proclaimed in the fourth book of his *Institutes of Christian Religion* (1536).

54: *Bernard* of Clairvaux (1090-1153) was a Cistercian monk and author of numerous homilies on the *Song of Songs*.

"*In my Father's house are many mansions*" (John 14:2).

"*Gloria in altissimis Deo* et in terra pax hominibus bonae voluntatis" is the Vulgate text of Luke 2:14, "Glory to God in the highest, and on earth peace, good will toward men".

The very transcendence of the Eucharist entails terrible dangers, as Saint Paul attests: "He that eateth and drinketh unworthily eateth and drinketh damnation to himself, not discerning the Lord's body" (1 Cor. 11:29).

Note 7: For *Asharite ways of reasoning*, see editor's note for "The Decisive Intuition", p. 5, Note 1.

56: The term *impanation*, literally a "turning into bread", is sometimes applied to Eucharistic doctrines which seek to safeguard a belief in the Real Presence with the idea that the Son of God "becomes bread" in the sacrament even as he "became flesh" (cf. John 1:14) in Jesus.

The consecrating words of Christ: "Take, eat; this is my body" and "Drink ye all of it; for this is my blood of the new testament" (Matt. 26:26-28; cf. Mark 14:22, 24, Luke 22:19-20, 1 Cor. 11:24-25).

John Damascene (c. 675-c. 749), also known as John of Damascus, wrote on the Eucharist in his influential treatise *An Exact Exposition of the Orthodox Faith*, which is the third part of his *Fountain of Knowledge*.

58: "In vain they do worship me, teaching for doctrines the *commandments of men*" (Matt. 15:9, Mark 7:7).

For *High Church Anglicanism*, the author's French reads "*l'Anglicanisme du type* High Church".

The *Talmud* is a collection of the principal texts of Rabbinic Judaism, comprising commentaries on the *Torah* and other traditional works.

Note 12: The *Tridentine Mass*, promulgated by Pope Pius V in 1570, was the liturgical form of the Roman Catholic Church until the Second Vatican Council (1962-65).

59: The *Seventh* Ecumenical *Council* was held at Nicea in 787.

For the proper relationship between the Pope and the other *patriarchs, who are his brothers*, the author elsewhere says this: "Regarding the question of ecclesiology, the most ancient Christian texts sometimes uphold the Latin thesis and sometimes the Greek; the ideal, or rather the normal situation, would therefore be an Orthodox Church recognizing a pope who was not totally autocratic, but in spiritual communion with all of the bishops or patriarchs; this would be a pope without *filioque*, but having nonetheless the right, in theology, liturgy, and other domains, to certain particularities that are opportune or even necessary in a Latin and Germanic setting" (*Form and Substance in the Religions* [Bloomington, Indiana: World Wisdom, 2002], p. 203).

Note 13: As a test of authentic tradition, Vincent of Lérins (d. before 450) proposed the three-fold Latin formula *quod ubique, quod semper, quod ab omnibus creditum est*, that is, "what has been believed *everywhere, always, by all*".

Note 14: One reason for the schism between Orthodoxy and Roman Catholicism was the unilateral decision of the West to interpolate the word *filioque* into the Latin text of the Nicene Creed, thus expressing a double procession of the Holy Spirit from the Father "and the Son".

Note 15: *Pius V* was pontiff from 1566-72 and was later canonized by Pope Clement XI in 1712.

60: "God is a Spirit: and they that worship Him must worship Him *in spirit and in truth*" (John 4:24).

Note 16: In the French text of the Gospel cited by the author in this note, the passage from Matthew 23:10 reads, "*Ne vous faites pas non plus appeler Docteurs: car vous n'avez qu'un Docteur, le Christ*", thus making the phrase "Doctors of the Church" (*Docteurs de l'Eglise*) rather more problematic than it may seem in English translation.

61: *Bramante* (1444-1514) was a Renaissance painter and architect. He developed the original plan for Saint Peter's Basilica in Rome and designed the Vatican's Belvedere Courtyard.

Michelangelo (1475-1564) painted the celebrated frescoes on the ceiling of the Sistine Chapel in the Vatican Palace.

Peter the Great (1672-1725), Czar of Russia, was enamored of European culture and science, and brought his efforts to "modernize" the country into the very heart of the Church—for example, by replacing traditional Byzantine and Kievan plainchant with Western polyphonic music imported from Italy.

62: Note 20: *The Encyclopedists* were a group of French philosophers who produced the twenty-eight volume *Encyclopedie*, or *Systematic Dictionary of the Sciences, Arts, and Crafts* (1751-1772). Led by Diderot, and including contributions by the likes of Montesquieu, Rousseau, Voltaire, and D'Alembert, it presented the worldview of the eighteenth century French Enlightenment.

63: *Gamaliel* was a teacher of the Apostle Paul (Acts 22:3) who advised his fellow members of the Sanhedrin not to put Peter and the other Apostles to death, on the grounds that "if this counsel or this work be of men, it will come to nought: but if it be of God, ye cannot overthrow it" (Acts 5:38-39).

The *Council of Trent* (1545-63) was convened in response to the Reformation and embodied the ideals of the *Catholic Counter-Reformation*, aiming to eliminate abuses in the Roman Church and to put forward a comprehensive system of Catholic doctrine and practice.

Note 22: The *Inquisition* was a powerful group of institutions within the medieval Roman Church which fought intransigently against perceived heresy.

64: *"But thou, when thou prayest, enter into thy closet, and when thou hast shut thy door, pray to thy Father which is in secret"* (Matt. 6:6).

"One is your Master, even Christ; and *all ye are brethren"* (Matt. 23:8).

64: In speaking to Christ about the *Samaritan* practice of worshipping God "in this mountain", that is, on *Mount Gerizim* (cf. Joshua 8:33)—a practice that conflicted with the Jews' worship of God "in Jerusalem"—a "woman of Samaria" prompted *the injunction of Christ* concerning true worship: "God is a Spirit: and they that worship Him must worship Him *in spirit and in truth"* (John 4:24).

For *Shiism*, see editor's note for "The Ambiguity of Exoterism", p. 21, Note 14.

Bernard insisted that churches of his Cistercian Order should be plain in character and that vestments and ornaments should not be made of precious materials.

Teaching, like Luther, that man cannot attain salvation by his own efforts, but must place absolute faith in the help of Heaven—manifest, in this case, by the Buddha Amida—the Japanese Buddhist priest *Shinran* (1173-1262) was noted for advocating the marriage of monks, since he wished to minimize the distance between the clergy and laity.

Note 24: For *Hesychasts*, see editor's note for "The Ambiguity of Exoterism", p. 17, Note 7.

Note 25: *The Fedeli d'Amore* (Italian for "the faithful of love") were a group of medieval poets, including Dante, who transposed the courtly ideal of love for the earthly beloved—in Dante's case, Beatrice—into a means of deepening one's love for God.

65: *The kingdom of God which is within you*: "The kingdom of God is within you" (Luke 17:21).

For *Platonic anamnesis*, see editor's note for "The Decisive Intuition", p. 8.

Note 26: The *Essenes* were a Jewish *ascetical* and quasi-mystical *sect* of the first and second centuries.

Note 27: For full bibliographical information concerning the author's *Christianisme/Islam: visions d'Œcuménisme ésotérique* (Milan: Archè, 1981), see editor's note above, p. 49, Note 2.

66: *"For where two or three are gathered together in my Name, there I am in the midst of them"* (Matt. 18:20).

The Seat of Wisdom

67: The Latin *Rosa Mystica*, or "Mystical Rose", is one of the traditional epithets of the Blessed Virgin.

The *Litany of Loreto* is a traditional Roman Catholic litany in honor of the Virgin, often recited at the Benediction of the Holy Sacrament and consisting of a series of invocations of Mary, each followed by the petition "Pray for us".

Peter Damien (1007-72) was a Benedictine prior and Cardinal Bishop of Ostia.

That wondrous throne: According to 1 Kings 10:18, Solomon "made a great throne".

Although never defined as dogma, popular recognition of the Blessed Virgin as *Co-Redemptress* dates from ancient times and can be found in both the Eastern and the Western Churches; echoing the belief of many Christians, Louis Marie de Montfort writes, "Let us boldly say with Saint Bernard that we need a mediator with the Mediator himself and that the divine Mary is the one most able to fulfill this office of love" (*True Devotion to the Blessed Virgin*).

Note 1: The *Bible* appears to have *condemned* Solomon, for example, in 1 Kings 11:9.

"I have remembered thy Name, O Lord, in the night, and have kept thy Law" (Ps. 119:55): Quoting a French translation of this passage, the author has used the divine "Name" Yahweh: "Je me rappelle dans la nuit ton Nom, *Yahvé*, afin que j'observe ta Loi."

68: *Cabalists* are Jewish esoterists and mystics.

Note 3: Again *Yahvé* appears in the French for *Lord.*

69: *Magnificat* is Latin for "magnify" and is used in reference to the Virgin's words in the Gospel: "And Mary said, My soul doth magnify the Lord" (Luke 1:46).

Vincit omnia Veritas—Latin for "truth conquers all"—is a traditional maxim, often quoted by the author, based upon the words of 1 Esdras 3:12: *super omnia autem vincit veritas*, "But truth conquereth over all" (cf. 1 Esdras 4:35, 41).

Note 7: The *Vulgate*, the Latin translation of the Bible most often used in the West, is based on the work of *Jerome* (c. 342-420).

In the Authorized Version, 2 Chronicles 9:18 speaks of a "footstool of gold", rather than a *golden lamb.*

Flavius *Josephus* (c. 37-c. 100), also called Joseph ben Matityahu, was the author of *Antiquities of the Jews* (c. 94) and won the favor of *Vespasian* (reigned from 69-79) by prophesying that he would become emperor.

Islam and Consciousness of the Absolute

75: "And God said unto Moses, *I am that I am*" (Ex. 3:14).

"*God alone is good*": "Good, O Asclepius, is in none else save in God alone; nay, rather, Good is God Himself eternally" (*Corpus Hermeticum*, VI:1); "Why callest thou me good? There is none good but one, that is, God" (Matt. 19:17, Mark 10:18).

The Augustinian notion that it is in the nature of the good to impart itself, hence to radiate: Augustine (see editor's note for "The Decisive Intuition", p. 7, Note 5), expressed the principle of the "diffusion of the Good" (*bonum diffusivum sui*) in his renowned formula, "Because God is good we exist" (*De doctrina christiana*, 1:31).

Note 1: *The chapter "Les deux problèmes"* appears in this volume as "The Two Problems".

77: For "*true man and true God*" see editor's note for "The Ambiguity of Exoterism", p. 14.

Note 3: "*God became man that man might become God*": the essential teaching expressed by this patristic formula is common to many Church Fathers, including Irenaeus (c. 130-c. 200), according to whom "the Son of God became the Son of man so that man, by entering into communion with the Word and thus receiving divine sonship, might become a son of God" (*Against Heresies*, 3:19); and Athanasius (c. 296-373), who wrote, "The Son of God became man in order that we might become God" (*On the Incarnation*, 54:3).

79: Note 4: "Our Lord! *Do not impose upon us that which we have not the strength to bear*" (*Sūrah* "The Cow" [2]:286).

Note 6: *The "spirit" rather than the "letter"*: "The letter killeth, but the spirit giveth life" (2 Cor. 3:6).

80: *Imrulqais*, or Imru al-Qais bin Hujr al-Kindi (c. 526-c. 565), was a pre-Islamic Arabian poet.

Tarafa Ibn al-Abd was a sixth century Arabian poet.

Antara Ibn Shaddad al-Absi (525-608) was a pre-Islamic Arabian warrior and poet.

Hagar was the handmaiden of Abram's first wife, Sarai. Being barren, Sarai gave Hagar to Abram to bear a son, *Ishmael*, the patriarch of the Ishmaelites (see Gen. 16).

In the Muslim Paradise, the chosen "say only Peace, Peace" (illā qīlan salāman salāmā): "There hear they no vain speaking nor recrimination, (Naught) but the saying: Peace, (and again) Peace" (*Sūrah* "That Which Is Coming" [56]:26).

"And *God calleth to the abode of Peace*, and leadeth whom He will to a straight path" (*Sūrah* "Jonah" [10]:25).

Note 7: "*In His own image*": "And God said, Let us make man in our image, after our likeness" (Gen. 1:26).

The Latin phrase *credo quia absurdum est*, "I believe because it is absurd", comes from an apologetic work, *On the Flesh of Christ*, by Quintus Septimius Florens Tertullian (c. 160-c. 225), an early Church Father and ascetical writer.

Observations on Dialectical Antinomianism

83: The Latin *cogito ergo sum*, "I think therefore I am", is found in the French philosopher René Descartes' (1596-1650) *Principles of Philosophy* (1644).

Note 1: *Palamite theology* is the theology of Gregory Palamas (1296-1359), an Athonite monk and later Archbishop of Thessalonica, best known for his defense of the psycho-somatic contemplative techniques employed by the Hesychast Fathers.

84: "*God forgives whom He will and punishes whom He will*" (*Sūrah* "The Cow" [2]:284).

85: "*God doeth what He will*" (*Sūrah* "The Family of Imran" [3]:40, *passim*).

At the beginning of his *Mishkāt al-Anwār* ("The Niche for Lights"), al-*Ghazzali* (see editor's note for "The Ambiguity of Exoterism", p. 21, Note 14) speaks of certain "*mysteries not to be disclosed*" to the ignorant and sinners.

86: For *Junayd*, see editor's note for "The Notion of Eternity", p. 40.

87: For the Latin phrase *credo quia absurdum*, see editor's note for "Islam and Consciousness of the Absolute", p. 80, Note 7.

"Lo! This is naught but [false] *tales of the men of old* (asātīr al-awwalīn)" (*Sūrah* "The Believers" [23]:83).

"And God sent (unto them) Prophets as bearers of *good tidings* (bushrā) and as warners, and revealed therewith the Scripture with the truth" (*Sūrah* "The Cow" [2]:213 *passim*).

Note 2: The author's *La Soufisme, voile et quintessence* (Paris: Dervy-Livres, 1979) appeared in English as *Sufism: Veil and Quintessence* (Bloomington, Indiana: World Wisdom, 1981); a second edition, ed. James S. Cutsinger, was published by World Wisdom in 2006. The chapter "*Paradoxes d'un ésotérisme*" appears in English as "Paradoxes of an Esoterism".

88: For *Pascal's wager*, see editor's note for "The Decisive Intuition", p. 6.

Note 3: For *Apocatastasis*, see editor's note for "The Two Problems", p. 28.

89: Mansur al-Hallaj (858-922), the first Sufi martyr, was flayed and crucified by the exoteric authorities for his *theopathic exclamation, "I am the Truth"*.

Bayazid (Abu Yazid) al-Bastami (d. 874), known as the "sultan of the gnostics", made the *theopathic exclamation, "Glory be to me"*.

Note 6: Louis *Massignon* (1883-1962) was a French Islamicist, best known for his magisterial study *La Passion de Husayn Ibn Mansur al-Hallaj* (1975).

90: *The Koran specifies that in hell sufferings "shall not be lightened"*: "But as for those who disbelieve, for them is fire of hell; it taketh not complete effect upon them so that they can die, nor is its torment lightened for them" (*Sūrah* "The Creator" [35]:36 *passim*).

The Koran rejects the opinion of unbelievers that in the fire "their days will be numbered": "And they say: The fire (of punishment) will not touch save for a certain number of days. Say: Have ye received a covenant from God—truly God will not break His covenant—or tell ye concerning God that which ye know not? Nay, but whosoever hath done evil and his sin surroundeth him; such are rightful owners of the Fire; they will abide therein" (*Sūrah* "The Cow" [2]:80; cf. [3]:24).

Note 8: *The divine* Rahmah *"encompasseth everything"*: "My Mercy (*Rahmah*) encompasseth all things" (*Sūrah* "The Heights" [7]:156).

91: In the Abrahamic traditions *Gehenna* is the abode of hell.

Ancient *Gnostic terminology* distinguishes between three types of human beings: the *hylic* (*hylikos*) or *somatic* (*somatikos*), who is centered upon matter (*hyle*) or the body (*soma*); the *psychic* (*psychikos*), who is centered upon the soul (*psyche*); and the *pneumatic* (*pneumatikos*), who is centered upon the spirit (*pneuma*).

Note 9: "*One thing needful*": "One thing is needful: and Mary hath chosen that good part, which shall not be taken from her" (Luke 10:42).

92: While wintering at Gordium in 333 B.C., *Alexander* the Great (356-323 B.C.) cut the *Gordian knot* with a single sword-stroke.

Abd Allah *Ibn Abbas* (c. 618-c. 688) was a cousin of the Prophet, revered by Muslims for his knowledge and expertise in Koranic exegesis and the *Sunnah*.

Note 10: *Teresa of Avila* (1515-82) was a Spanish Carmelite nun and mystic who wrote extensively on the stages of the spiritual life and the levels of prayer.

Diversity of Paths

95: Sahl al-*Tustari* (c. 818-c. 896) was an early Sufi mystic and commentator on the Koran.

Note 1: *Louis Massignon's* (see editor's note for "Observations on Dialectical Antinominanism", p. 89, Note 6) *Essai sur les origines du lexique technique de la mystique musulmane*, or "Essay on the Origins of the Technical Vocabulary of Islamic Mysticism", was first published in 1922.

The French traditionalist *Jean-Louis Michon* (1924-2013) was the author of *Le soufi marocain Ahmad Ibn 'Ajība et son Mi'rāj*, first published in 1973 and containing a lexicon of Sufic terminology by Ibn Ajiba.

Henry *Corbin* (1903-78), a French theologian and philosopher, was Professor of Islamic Studies at the Sorbonne.

96: *The "Remembrance of God"* (dhikru 'Llāh), *of which the Koran says that it is "greater" than the prescribed prayer, or that it is the "greatest thing of all"*: "Recite that which hath been inspired in thee of the Scripture, and establish prescribed prayer (*salāt*). Lo! prescribed prayer preserveth from lewdness and iniquity, but verily remembrance of God is greater [or: the greatest thing of all] (*wa ladhikru 'Llāhi akbar*)" (*Sūrah* "The Spider" [29]:45). See also "Transcendence and Immanence in the Spiritual Economy of Islam", p. 110, author's Note 3.

Note 1: For *Shiism*, see editor's note for "The Ambiguity of Exoterism", p. 21, Note 14.

The Latin *Spiritus autem ubi vult spirat* means "The wind [Spirit] bloweth where it listeth" (John 3:8).

97: For the "*pneumatic*", see editor's note for "Observations on Dialectical Antinomianism", p. 91.

98: For *Apocatastasis*, see editor's note for "The Two Problems", p. 28.

Abu al-Qasim al-*Qushayri* (986-1072) was a Persian Sufi master, commentator on the Koran, and author of the *Risālah*, or "Epistle (to the Sufis)", a manual on the stages of the spiritual path.

Ibn al-Arif (1088-1141) was an Andalusian Sufi master, best known for his writings on the science of the virtues.

100: For *Ibn Arabi*, see editor's note for "The Ambiguity of Exoterism", p. 15, Note 2.

101: *Al-Khidr*, "the Green One", is a mysterious immortal who guides solitary initiates with an esoteric teaching that transcends the Law. He is described in the Koran as "one of Our slaves, unto whom We had given mercy from Us, and had taught him knowledge from Our presence"; when Moses asks him, "May I follow thee, to the end that thou mayst teach me right conduct of that which thou has been taught?", he responds, "Lo! thou canst not bear with me. How canst thou bear with that whereof thou canst not compass any knowledge?" (*Sūrah* "The Cave" [18]:66-69).

102: Note 4: The *Fusūs al-Hikam*, or "Bezels of Wisdom", one of *Ibn Arabi's* most renowned works, consists of a series of mystical reflections on the wisdom embodied in the lives and characters of twenty-seven prophets, including a *chapter on the "Muhammadan Wisdom"*.

Note 5: *Meister Eckhart* (see editor's note for "The Ambiguity of Exoterism", p. 15, Note 4) *expressed the in principle sacramental character of the gifts of nature by which we live* in remarking that "if someone were as well prepared for ordinary nourishment as he is for the holy sacrament [the Eucharist], he would receive God in this nourishment just as fully as in the sacrament itself" (quoted in *Christianity/Islam: Perspectives on Esoteric Ecumenism: A New Translation with Selected Letters*, p. 21).

104: Note 7: *Hasan ash-Shadhili* (1196-1258) was a Moroccan Sufi master and founder of the Shadhili Order.

Editor's Notes

Transcendence and Immanence in the Spiritual Economy of Islam

105: Note 1: For "*true man and true God*", see editor's note for "The Ambiguity of Exoterism", p. 14.

106: "The *letter killeth*, but the spirit giveth life" (2 Cor. 3:6).

108: For *Hasan ash-Shadhili*, see editor's note for "Diversity of Paths", p. 104, Note 7.

Jalal al-Din *Rumi* (1207-73), a Persian Sufi mystic and poet, was the founder of the Mevlevi order of "Whirling Dervishes", known for its use of *music and dance* in spiritual concerts dedicated to the remembrance of God.

David preferred music and dance inspired by God and offered to Him: "And David and all the house of Israel played before the Lord on all manner of instruments made of fir wood, even on harps, and on psalteries, and on timbrels, and on cornets, and on cymbals. . . . And David danced before the Lord with all his might. . . . So David and all the house of Israel brought up the ark of the Lord with shouting, and with the sound of the trumpet" (2 Sam. 6:5, 14-15).

Note 2: For *Le Soufisme: voile et quintessence*, see editor's note for "Observations on Dialectical Antinomianism", p. 87, Note 2.

109: For the *theopathic expressions* of al-*Hallaj* and *Abu Yazid* al-Bastami, see editor's note for "Observations on Dialectical Antinomianism", p. 89.

110: The *formula* "*God is greater* (Allāhu akbar)" (see *Sūrah* "The Spider" [29]:45) opens the canonical prayer and marks the change from one ritual position to another during prayer.

"*And verily the remembrance of God is greater* (wa la-dhikru 'Llāhi akbar)" (*Sūrah* "The Spider" [29]:45).

Dhikru 'Llāh *is one of the names of the Prophet, who in the Koran is presented as* "*a fair example for him who* looketh unto God and the Last Day, and *invoketh God much*" (*Sūrah* "The Clans" [33]:21).

"*Who hath seen me, hath seen God* (*Truth or Reality*: man rāʾanī faqad rāʾa 'l-Ḥaqq)" (*hadīth*).

Note 5: For *Shiism* and *Sunnism*, see editor's note for "The Ambiguity of Exoterism", p. 21, Note 14.

The Question of Perspectives in Muslim Spirituality

114: *Thomist sensualism*: Thomas Aquinas (see editor's note for "The Notion of Eternity", p. 34) followed Aristotle in teaching that "the principle of knowledge is in the senses" (*Summa Theologica*, Part 1, Quest. 84, Art. 6).

115: *"The beginning of wisdom is the fear of God"* (Ps. 111:10, Prov. 9:10; cf. Prov. 1:7).

116: Removing *"the rust from the mirror of the heart"*: "There is a means of polishing all things whereby rust may be removed; that which polishes the heart is the remembrance of God" (*hadīth*).

Rabiah Adawiyah (c. 713-801) was an early Sufi mystic and poet who articulated the perspective of divine love.

For Mansur al-*Hallaj*, see editor's note for "Observations on Dialectical Antinomianism", p. 89.

Muhammad ibn Abd Allah *ibn Masarra* (883-931) was an early Andalusian mystic and Neoplatonic philosopher.

Muhammad ibn al-Hasan al-*Niffari* (d. c. 970) was one of the earliest Sufi writers and the author of *The Book of Spiritual Stations* and *The Book of Spiritual Addresses*, works well known for the density and obscurity of their style.

For *Ibn Arabi*, see editor's note for "The Ambiguity of Exoterism", p. 15, Note 2.

117: *"Seek knowledge, be it in China"* (*hadīth*).

For *Plato*, see editor's note for "The Complexity of Dogmatism", p. 43.

Aristotle (384-322 B.C.) was an ancient Greek philosopher whose works had a profound influence on the intellectual tradition of the three Semitic monotheisms.

The *Neoplatonist* works of philosophers such as Plotinus (c. 205-70), Iamblichus (c. 245-c. 325), and Proclus (412-85) exerted a powerful influence on the mystical traditions of Judaism, Christianity, and Islam.

Henotheism was a term popularized by the Indologist Max Müller (see editor's note for "Foreword", p. xi) to denote the worship of a single God while accepting the possible existence of other deities.

119: For *Ghazzali*, see editor's note for "The Ambiguity of Exoterism", p. 21, Note 14.

Note 7: Abd al-Karim al-*Jili* (c. 1365-c. 1412) systematized the teachings of Ibn Arabi, notably in his most important work, *The Universal Man*, which is concerned with both cosmological and metaphysical questions.

120: For *Shiites*, see editor's note for "The Ambiguity of Exoterism", p. 21, Note 14.

The Mystery of the Prophetic Substance

121: *"By their fruits ye shall know them"* (Matt. 7:16).

For *Qushayri*, see editor's note for "Diversity of Paths", p. 98.

For *Ibn al-Arif*, see editor's note for "Diversity of Paths", p. 98.

122: *Shaykh al-Alawi* (1869-1934), a famous Algerian Sufi shaykh, was Frithjof Schuon's spiritual master.

124: *The four archangels* in Islam are Gabriel (Arabic: Jibrail), Michael (Mikhail), Raphael (Israfil), and Azrael (Izrail).

For the *Kaaba*, see editor's note for "The Ambiguity of Exoterism", p. 21.

126: Note 7: *Stella Maris*, Latin for "Star of the Sea", is one of the traditional titles of the Blessed Virgin Mary.

128: *The Koran specifies that it is necessary to remember God* "*much*" (dhikran kathīran): "O ye who believe! Remember God with much remembrance" (*Sūrah* "The Joint Forces" [33]:41).

"Pray *without ceasing*" (1 Thess. 5:17).

Note 9: *Stella Matutina*, Latin for "*Morning Star*", is a traditional epithet of the Blessed Virgin Mary.

129: *The fiat of the Virgin Mary . . . at the Annunciation*: "And Mary said, Behold the handmaid of the Lord; let it be done (*fiat*) unto me according to thy word" (Luke 1:38).

"*I am black, but beautiful*" (Song of Sol. 1:5).

"And verily thou [Muhammad] art of a *supereminent nature*" (khuluq ʿazīm)

(*Sūrah* "The Pen" [68]:4).

131: "*For the man subject to doubt there is no salvation either in this world or in the next*" (*Bhagavad Gītā*, 4:40).

133: "*Suffer the little children to come unto Me*" (Luke 18:16, Matt. 19:14).

The first law is to love God with all our faculties and the second—which is "like unto it"—is to love our neighbor as ourself: "Thou shalt love the Lord thy God with all thy heart, and with all thy soul, and with all thy mind. This is the first and great commandment. And the second is like unto it: Thou shalt love thy neighbor as thyself. On these two commandments hang all the law and the prophets" (Matt. 22:37-40 *passim*).

134: Praying before a statue of the Blessed Virgin Mary nursing (*lactatio*) the Child Jesus, Bernard of Clairvaux (see editor's note for "Christian Divergences", p. 54) continually besought her to "show that you are a mother"; the statue miraculously came alive, and the Virgin pressed her breast, causing a stream of milk to come forth and wet the lips of Bernard, dry from singing her praises.

Aisha (d. 678), the daughter of Abu Bakr and youngest of the wives of Muhammad, is quoted as the source for many *hadīth*, especially those concerning the Prophet's personal life.

Note 13: *The Koran speaks of rivers in the plural for each of the four substances* [water, milk, wine, and honey]: "A similitude of the Garden which those who keep their duty (to God) are promised: Therein are rivers of water unpolluted, and rivers of milk whereof the flavor changeth not, and rivers of wine delicious to the drinkers, and rivers of clear run honey" (*Sūrah* "Muhammad" [47]:15).

136: "Verily *God is beautiful and He loves beauty*" (*hadīth*).

137: "O Mary Lo! *God* has chosen thee *and purified* thee; He has *chosen* thee *above all women*" (*Sūrah* "Family of Imran" [3]:42).

Note 16: *Sita*, an incarnation of the goddess Lakshmi, was abducted by the demon king Ravana and taken from India to the island of Lanka, where she was eventually rescued by her husband, Rama, the seventh *avatāra* of the Hindu god Vishnu; after rescuing her, however, Rama began to doubt her fidelity and ordered her banished to the forest and killed; spared by the executioner, she was finally able to convince Rama of her devotion, though her own heart was now broken.

Note 17: For *Shiism*, see editor's note for "The Ambiguity of Exoterism", p. 21, Note 14.

138: For Meister *Eckhart*, see editor's note for "The Ambiguity of Exoterism", p. 15, Note 4.

"Folly" in the eyes of the world: "If any man among you seemeth to be wise in this world, let him become a fool, that he may be wise. For the wisdom of this world is foolishness with God" (1 Cor. 3:18-19).

140: Note 22: The Roman Catholic dogma of the *immaculate conception* states that, from the first moment of her conception, the Virgin Mary was free from all stain of original sin.

141: "For this *Melchizedek, king of Salem*, priest of the most high God . . . to whom also Abraham gave a tenth part of all; first being by interpretation King of righteousness, and after that also King of Salem, which is, King of peace; without father, without mother, without descent, having neither beginning of days, nor end of life; but made like unto the Son of God; abideth a priest continually" (Heb. 7:1-3).

For *Al-Khidr*, see editor's note for "Diversity of Paths", p. 101.

Selections from Letters and Other Previously Unpublished Writings

145: Selection 1: Letter of May 18, 1981.

Selection 2: "The Book of Keys", No. 765, "The *Risālah* of Sayyidatna Maryam".

146: Selection 3: Letter of June 30, 1982.

Selection 4: Letter of January 17, 1989.

For *religio perennis*, see editor's note for "Foreword", p. xii.

Selection 5: "The Book of Keys", No. 964, "Truth and Heart".

147: Selection 6: Letter of September 18, 1979.

René *Guénon* (1886-1951) was a French metaphysician and prolific scholar of religions, one of the formative authorities of the perennialist school, and a frequent contributor to the journal *Études Traditionnelles* ("Traditional Studies").

148: *Shankara* (788-820) was one of the most influential sages in the history of India and the pre-eminent exponent of *Advaita Vedānta*, the Hindu perspective of "non-dualism".

"There is no right superior to that of the truth" is a traditional Hindu maxim attributed to the Maharajahs of Benares.

Selection 7: Letter of December 12, 1981.

For *Ghazzali*, see editor's note for "The Ambiguity of Exoterism", p. 21, Note 14.

For *Ashari*, see editor's note for "The Decisive Intuition", p. 5, Note 1.

For *Ibn Arabi*, see editor's note for "The Ambiguity of Exoterism", p. 15, Note 2.

149: For *Mazdean dualism*, see editor's note for "The Decisive Intuition", p. 5, Note 4.

"God leads into error whom He will" (*Sūrah* "Abraham" [14]:4).

"God created man in His own image, in the image of God created He him" (Gen. 1:27).

He *"taught him the names"* of things and of creatures: "And Adam gave names to all cattle, and to the fowl of the air, and to every beast of the field" (Gen. 2:20); "And He (God) taught Adam all the names, then showed them to the angels, saying: Inform Me of the names of these, if ye are truthful" (*Sūrah* "The Cow" [2]:31).

150: *"He is God, there is none other except him; He knoweth the hidden and the manifest; He is the Ever-Compassionate and the Ever-Merciful"* (*Sūrah* "The Gathering" [59]:22).

Selection 8: Letter of August 8, 1989.

For *Qushayri*, see editor's note for "Diversity of Paths", p. 98.

For *Ibn al-Arif*, see editor's note for "Diversity of Paths", p. 98.

Selection 9: "The Book of Keys", No. 746, "Islam and *Fitrah*".

151: Selection 10: "Supplementary Reflections on the Protestant Question", unpublished, June 1983.

For Martin *Luther*, see editor's note for "Christian Divergences", p. 51.

For *Amida Buddhism*, see editor's note for "The Complexity of Dogmatism", p. 46, Note 4.

152: Girolamo *Savonarola* (1452-98), a Dominican friar, reformer, and apocalyptic preacher, was known for his condemnations of corruption among the clergy and specifically for his denunciation of Pope Alexander VI and his dissolute court.

Abrégé de Théologie dogmatique et morale, or "Summary of Dogmatic Theology and Morals", *by Father* Joachim *Berthier* (1848-1924), an Italian Dominican, theologian, and author, was first published in 1892.

153: *The chapter "Divergences chrétiennes"*, from the author's *Approches du Phénomène Religieux* (Paris: Le Courrier du Livre, 1984), appears in the current volume as "Christian Divergences".

GLOSSARY OF FOREIGN TERMS AND PHRASES

'Abd (Arabic): "servant" or "slave"; as used in Islam, the servant or worshiper of God in His aspect of *Rabb* or "Lord".

Ab intra (Latin): literally, "from within"; proceeding from something intrinsic or internal.

A contrario (Latin): literally, "from the opposite"; a form of argument in which a certain position is established or strengthened by highlighting the deficiencies of what opposes it.

Ad majorem Dei gloriam (Latin): "to the greater glory of God".

Advaita (Sanskrit): "non-dualist" interpretation of the *Vedānta*; Hindu doctrine according to which the seeming multiplicity of things is regarded as the product of ignorance, the only true reality being *Brahma*, the One, the Absolute, the Infinite, which is the unchanging ground of appearance.

A fortiori (Latin): literally, "from greater reason"; used when drawing a conclusion that is inferred to be even stronger than the one already put forward.

Anamnesis (Greek): literally, a "lifting up of the mind"; recollection or remembrance, as in the Platonic doctrine that all knowledge is a recalling of truths latent in the soul.

Ānanda (Sanskrit): "bliss, beatitude, joy"; one of the three essential aspects of *Apara-Brahma*, together with *Sat*, "being", and *Chit*, "consciousness".

Apara-Brahma (Sanskrit): the "non-supreme" or penultimate *Brahma*, also called *Brahma saguna*; in Schuon's teaching, the "relative Absolute".

Apocatastasis (Greek): "restitution, restoration"; among certain Christian theologians, including Clement of Alexandria, Origen, and Gregory of Nyssa, the doctrine that all creatures will finally be saved.

A posteriori (Latin): literally, "from after"; subsequently; proceeding from effect to cause or from experience to principle.

A priori (Latin): literally, "from before"; in the first instance; proceeding from cause to effect or from principle to experience.

Ātmā or *Ātman* (Sanskrit): the real or true "Self", underlying the ego and its manifestations; in the perspective of *Advaita Vedānta*, identical with *Brahma*.

Ave (Latin): "Hail"; referring to the Angelical Salutation, or "Hail Mary" (*Ave Maria*) (cf. Luke 1:28).

Barakah (Arabic): "blessing", grace; in Islam, a spiritual influence or energy emanating originally from God, but often attached to sacred objects and spiritual persons.

Barzakh (Arabic): as used in the Koran, a "barrier" or "separation" between paradise and hell, or this life and the next, or the two seas (fresh and salt); in the interpretation of Sufism, an "isthmus" connecting different planes of reality.

Bhakti or *bhakti-mārga* (Sanskrit): the spiritual "path" (*mārga*) of "love" (*bhakti*) and devotion; see *jnāna* and *karma*.

Bodhisattva (Sanskrit, Pali): literally, "enlightenment-being"; in *Mahāyāna* Buddhism, one who postpones his own final enlightenment and entry into *Nirvāna* in order to aid all other sentient beings in their quest for Buddha-hood.

Brahmā (Sanskrit): God in the aspect of Creator, the first divine "person" of the *Trimūrti*; to be distinguished from *Brahma*, the Supreme Reality.

Brahma or *Brahman* (Sanskrit): the Supreme Reality, the Absolute.

Brahma nirguna (Sanskrit): *Brahma* considered as transcending all "qualities", attributes, or predicates; God as He is in Himself; also called *Para-Brahma*.

Brahma saguna (Sanskrit): *Brahma* "qualified" by attributes and predicates; God insofar as He can be known by man; also called *Apara-Brahma*.

Chit (Sanskrit): "consciousness"; one of the three essential aspects of *Apara-Brahma*, together with *Sat*, "being", and *Ānanda*, "bliss, beatitude, joy".

Cogito ergo sum (Latin): "I think therefore I am."

Conditio sine qua non (Latin): an indispensable or essential condition.

Credo quia absurdum (Latin): "I believe because it is absurd".

Darshana (Sanskrit): a spiritual "perspective", point of view, or school of thought; also the "viewing" of a holy person, object, or place, together with the resulting blessing or merit.

De facto (Latin): literally, "from the fact"; denoting something that is such "in fact", if not necessarily "by right".

De jure (Latin): literally, "by right"; an expression often used in contradistinction with *de facto*.

Deus ex machina (Latin): literally, "god from the machine"; in Greek tragedy, the use of a machine to bring actors playing gods onto the stage during the play's denouement; by extension, an artificial or improbable device used to resolve the difficulties of a situation.

Dharma (Sanskrit): in Hinduism, the underlying "law" or "order" of the cosmos as expressed in sacred rites and in actions appropriate to various social relationships and human vocations; in Buddhism, the practice and realization of Truth.

Dhikr (Arabic): "remembrance" of God, based upon the repeated invocation of His Name; central to Sufi practice, where the remembrance is often supported by the single word *Allāh*.

Dhyāni-Bodhisattva (Sanskrit): literally, "enlightenment-being of meditation"; a *Bodhisattva*, such as Kshitigarbha (Jizo in Japanese), who appears to the eye of contemplative vision but is not accessible in a historical form.

Distinguo (Latin): literally, "I mark or set off, differentiate", often used in the dialectic of the medieval scholastics; any philosophical distinction.

Dominus tecum (Latin): literally, "the Lord is with thee"; part of the Angelical Salutation, or "Hail Mary" (*Ave Maria*) (cf. Luke 1:28).

Ex cathedra (Latin): literally, "from the throne"; in Roman Catholicism, authoritative teaching issued by the pope and regarded as infallible.

Ex opere operato (Latin): literally, "from the work performed"; Christian teaching that divine grace is mediated through the sacraments by virtue of the corresponding rites themselves and independently of the merits or intentions of those by whom the rites are performed; in contrast to *ex opere operantis*, "from the work of the one working".

Fard (Arabic, pl. *afrād*): "alone"; in Sufism, one who realizes the truth on his own and without membership in a *tarīqah*, or even without belonging to a revealed religion, receiving illumination directly from God.

Fātihah (Arabic): the "opening" *sūrah*, or chapter, of the Koran, recited in the daily prayers of all Muslims and consisting of the words: "In the Name of God, the Beneficent, the Merciful. Praise to God, Lord of the Worlds, the Beneficent, the Merciful. Owner of the Day of Judgment, Thee (alone) we worship; Thee (alone) we ask for help. Show us the straight path, the path of those whom Thou hast favored, not (the path) of those who earn Thine anger nor of those who go astray."

Fiat (Latin): "let it be done" (cf. Gen. 1:3, Luke 1:38).

Filioque (Latin): "and (from) the Son"; a term added to the Nicene Creed by the Western Church to express the "double procession" of the Holy Spirit from the Father "and the Son"; rejected by the Eastern Orthodox Church.

Gratia plena (Latin): literally, "full of grace"; part of the Angelical Salutation, or "Hail Mary" (*Ave Maria*) (cf. Luke 1:28, 42).

Grosso modo (Italian): "roughly speaking".

Hadīth (Arabic, plural *ahādīth*): "saying, narrative"; an account of the words or deeds of the Prophet Muhammad, transmitted through a traditional chain of known intermediaries.

Homo faber (Latin): literally, "man the artisan"; man as creator or producer.

Homo religiosus (Latin): literally, "religious man"; the inherently religious nature of the human species.

Homo sapiens (Latin): literally, "wise man"; the human species.

Hyperdulia (Latin): reverence paid to the Blessed Virgin; distinguished from *dulia*, the respect or homage shown to saints.

Hypostasis (Greek, plural *hypostases*): literally, "substance"; the transcendent form of a metaphysical reality, understood to be eternally distinct from all other such forms; in Christian theology, a technical term for one of the three Persons of the Trinity.

In divinis (Latin): literally, "in or among divine things"; within the divine Principle; the plural form is used insofar as the Principle comprises both *Para-Brahma*, Beyond-Being or the Absolute, and *Apara-Brahma*, Being or the relative Absolute.

In persona Christi (Latin): "in the person of Christ"; used in reference to the sacramental words and actions of the consecrating priest in a Christian liturgy.

Īshvara (Sanskrit): literally, "possessing power", hence master; God under-stood as a personal being, as Creator and Lord; manifest in the *Trimūrti* as *Brahmā*, *Vishnu*, and *Shiva*.

Japa-Yoga (Sanskrit): method of "union" or "unification" (*yoga*) based upon the "repetition" (*japa*) of a *mantra* or sacred formula, often containing one of the Names of God.

Jīvan-mukta (Sanskrit): one who is "liberated" while still in this "life"; a person who has attained a state of spiritual perfection or self-realization before death; in contrast to *videha-mukta*, one who is liberated at the moment of death.

Jnāna or *jnāna-mārga* (Sanskrit): the spiritual "path" (*mārga*) of "knowledge" (*jnāna*) and intellection; see *bhakti* and *karma*.

Karma, *karma-mārga*, *karma-yoga* (Sanskrit): the spiritual "path" (*mārga*) or method of "union" (*yoga*) based upon right "action, work" (*karma*); see *bhakti* and *jnāna*.

Latria (Latinized form of the Greek *latreia*): literally, "servitude, service"; the worshipful obedience owed only to God; to be distinguished from *dulia*, the respect shown to saints, and *hyperdulia*, the reverence paid to the Blessed Virgin.

Magnificat (Latin): literally, "doth magnify"; the song of praise sung by the Blessed Virgin Mary (Luke 1:46-55) when her cousin Elizabeth had greeted her as the mother of the Lord, so named from the opening word in the Vul-gate: *Magnificat anima mea Dominum*, "My soul doth magnify the Lord."

Mahabbah (Arabic): "love"; in Sufism, the spiritual way based upon love and devotion, analogous to the Hindu *bhakti-mārga*; see *makhafah* and *ma'rifah*.

Mahāyāna (Sanskrit): "great vehicle"; a form of Buddhism, including such traditions as Zen and *Jōdo-Shinshū*, regarded by its followers as the fullest or most adequate expression of the Buddha's teaching; distinguished by the idea that *Nirvāna* is not other than *samsāra* truly seen as it is.

Makhafah (Arabic): "fear"; in Sufism, the spiritual way based upon fear and works, analogous to the Hindu *karma-mārga*; see *mahabbah* and *ma'rifah*.

Mantra (Sanskrit): literally, "instrument of thought"; a word or phrase of divine origin, often including a Name of God, repeated by those initiated into its proper use as a means of salvation or liberation; see *japa-yoga*.

187

Maqām (Arabic, pl. *maqāmāt*): "place", "station"; in Sufism, the permanent spiritual degree or station reached by a practitioner of the path; contrasted with a passing spiritual state (*ḥāl*).

Maʿrifah (Arabic): "knowledge"; in Sufism, the spiritual way based upon knowledge or *gnosis*, analogous to the Hindu *jnāna-mārga*; see *mahabbah* and *makhafah*.

Materia prima (Latin): "first or prime matter"; in Platonic cosmology, the undifferentiated and primordial substance serving as a "receptacle" for the shaping force of divine forms or ideas; universal potentiality.

Māyā (Sanskrit): universal illusion, relativity, appearance; in *Advaita Vedānta*, the veiling or concealment of *Brahma* in the form or under the appearance of a lower, relative reality; also, as "productive power", the unveiling or manifestation of *Ātmā* as "divine art" or theophany. *Māyā* is neither real nor unreal, and ranges from the Supreme Lord to the "last blade of grass".

Mihrāb (Arabic): a prayer niche in the wall of a mosque indicating the direction of Mecca.

Muftī (Arabic): in Islam, a judge or legal authority empowered to make decisions of religious import.

Mutatis mutandis (Latin): literally, "those things having been changed which need to be changed".

Nembutsu (Japanese): "remembrance or mindfulness of the Buddha", based upon the repeated invocation of his Name; same as *buddhānusmriti* in Sanskrit and *nien-fo* in Chinese.

Nirvāna (Sanskrit): literally, "blowing out"; in Indian traditions, especially Buddhism, the extinction of suffering and the resulting, supremely blissful state of liberation from egoism and attachment.

Pandit (Sanskrit): a learned Hindu scholar of Vedic scripture, religious law, and ritual.

Para-Brahma (Sanskrit): the "supreme" or ultimate *Brahma*, also called *Brahma nirguna*; the Absolute as such; see *apara-Brahma*.

Paramātmā (Sanskrit): the "supreme" or ultimate Self; see *Ātmā*.

Pneuma (Greek): "wind, breath, spirit"; in Christian theology, either the third Person of the Trinity or the highest of the three parts or aspects of the human self (cf. 1 Thess. 5:23).

Pneumatikos (Greek): a person in whom the element spirit (*pneuma*) predominates over the soul and the body (cf. 1 Thess. 5:23, 1 Cor. 2:14-15).

Prakriti (Sanskrit): literally, "making first" (see *Materia prima*); the fundamental, "feminine" substance or material cause of all things; see *Purusha*.

Pratyeka-Buddha (Sanskrit): "independent Buddha"; in Buddhism, one who attains enlightenment without a teacher and who makes no attempt to instruct disciples.

Purusha (Sanskrit): "man"; the informing or shaping principle of creation; the "masculine" demiurge or fashioner of the universe; see *Prakriti*.

Qādi (Arabic): a Muslim judge appointed on the basis of his knowledge of Islamic law (*sharī'ah*).

Qiblah (Arabic): in Islam, the direction of prayer towards Mecca.

Quod absit (Latin): literally, "which thing, let it be absent"; a wish or a command used by the medieval Scholastics to call attention to an idea that is absurdly inconsistent with accepted principles.

Rahmah (Arabic): "compassion, mercy"; in Islam, one of the Names of God, who is supreme Compassion, Mercy, and Clemency.

Rahmān, Rahīm (Arabic): "clement", "merciful"; found in Islam in the invocatory formula *bismi 'Llāhi 'r-Rahmāni 'r-Rahīm*: "In the Name of God, the Clement, the Merciful", *Rahmān* being the compassion of God insofar as it envelops all things, and *Rahīm* being the beneficence of God insofar as it is directed toward men of good will.

Rajas (Sanskrit): in Hinduism, one of the three *guna*s, or qualities, of *Prakriti*, of which all things are woven; the quality of expansiveness, manifest in the material world as force or movement and in the soul as ambition, initiative, and restlessness; see *sattva* and *tamas*.

Rasūl (Arabic): "messenger", "envoy"; in Islam, one whom God sends with a message for a particular people.

Religio (Latin): "religion", often in reference to its exoteric dimension.

Religio perennis (Latin): "perennial religion".

Religionswissenschaft (German): "the science of religions".

Rosa Mystica (Latin): "Mystical Rose"; traditional epithet of the Blessed Virgin Mary, as found in the Litany of Loreto.

Sat (Sanskrit): "being"; one of the three essential aspects of *Apara-Brahma*, together with *Chit*, "consciousness", and *Ānanda*, "bliss, beatitude, joy".

Sat-Chit-Ānanda or *saccidānanda* (Sanskrit): "being-consciousness-bliss"; the three essential aspects of *Apara-Brahma*, that is, *Brahma* insofar as it can be grasped in human experience.

Sattva (Sanskrit): in Hinduism, one of the three *gunas*, or qualities, of *Prakriti*, of which all things are woven; the quality of luminosity, manifest in the material world as buoyancy or lightness and in the soul as intelligence and virtue; see *rajas* and *tamas*.

Sedes Sapientiae (Latin): "Throne of Wisdom"; traditional epithet of the Blessed Virgin Mary, who is the "seat" upon which her incarnate Son is enthroned.

Shahādah (Arabic): the fundamental "profession" or "testimony" of faith in Islam, consisting of the words *lā ilāha illā 'Llāh, Muhammadan Rasūlu 'Llāh*: "There is no god but God; Muhammad is the messenger of God."

Shakti (Sanskrit): creative "power" or radiant "energy"; in Hinduism, expressed tantrically as the consort or feminine complement of Shiva.

Sharīʿah (Arabic): "path"; Islamic law, as derived from the Koran and the *hadīth* as well as from traditional principles of interpretation by the various schools of jurisprudence; the legal prescriptions of the religion; Muslim exoterism.

Shūnyamūrti (Sanskrit): "the form or manifestation of the void"; traditional epithet of the Buddha, in whom is "incarnate" *shūnyatā*, ultimate "emptiness", that is, the final absence of all definite being or selfhood.

Sophia (Greek): "wisdom"; in Jewish and Christian tradition, the Wisdom of God, often conceived as feminine (cf. Prov. 8).

Sophia Perennis (Latin): "perennial wisdom"; the eternal, non-formal Truth at the heart of all orthodox religious traditions.

Spiritus autem ubi vult spirat (Latin): "the wind bloweth where it listeth" (cf. John 3:8).

Stella Maris (Latin): "Star of the Sea"; traditional epithet of the Blessed Virgin Mary.

Stella Matutina (Latin): "Morning Star"; traditional epithet of the Blessed Virgin Mary.

Sunnah (Arabic): "custom, way of acting"; in Islam, the norm established by the Prophet Muhammad, including his actions and sayings (see *hadīth*) and serving as a precedent and standard for the behavior of Muslims.

Sūrah (Arabic): one of the one hundred fourteen divisions, or chapters, of the Koran.

Tale quale (Latin): "of such a kind as, as such".

Talmud (Hebrew): "learning, study"; in Judaism, a body of writings and traditional commentaries based on the oral law given to Moses on Sinai; the foundation of Jewish civil and religious law, second in authority only to the *Torah*.

Tamas (Sanskrit): in Hinduism, one of the three *guna*s, or qualities, of *Prakriti*, of which all things are woven; the quality of darkness or heaviness, manifest in the material world as inertia or rigidity and in the soul as sloth, stupidity, and vice; see *rajas* and *sattva*.

Tarīqah (Arabic): "path"; in exoteric Islam, a virtual synonym for *Sharīah*, equivalent to the "straight path" mentioned in the *Fātihah*; in Sufism, the mystical path leading from observance of the *Sharīah* to self-realization in God; also a Sufi brotherhood.

Tasawwuf (Arabic): a term of disputed etymology, though perhaps from *sūf* for "wool", after the garment worn by many early Sufis; traditional Muslim word for Sufism.

'Ulamā (Arabic, singular *'alīm*): "those who know, scholars"; in Islam, those who are learned in matters of law and theology; traditional authorities for all aspects of Muslim life.

Ungrund (German): the Abyss; Beyond-Being.

Upāya (Sanskrit): "means, expedient, method"; in Buddhist tradition, the adaptation of spiritual teaching to a form suited to the level of one's audience.

Vacare Deo (Latin): literally, "to be empty for God"; to be at leisure for or available to God; in the Christian monastic and contemplative tradition, to set aside time from work for meditation and prayer.

Vedānta (Sanskrit): "end or culmination of the Vedas"; one of the major schools of traditional Hindu philosophy, based in part on the Upanishads, esoteric treatises found at the conclusion of the Vedic scriptures; see *advaita*.

Vincit Omnia Veritas (Latin): "Truth conquers all".

Yin-Yang (Chinese): in Chinese tradition, two opposite but complementary forces or qualities, from whose interpenetration the universe and all its diverse forms emerge; *yin* corresponds to the feminine, the yielding, the moon, liquidity; *yang* corresponds to the masculine, the resisting, the sun, solidity.

Yoga (Sanskrit): literally, "yoking, union"; in Indian traditions, any meditative and ascetic technique designed to bring the soul and body into a state of concentration.

For a glossary of all key foreign words used in books published by
World Wisdom, including metaphysical terms in English, consult:
www.DictionaryofSpiritualTerms.org.
This on-line Dictionary of Spiritual Terms provides extensive
definitions, examples, and related terms in other languages.

INDEX

BIOGRAPHICAL NOTES

FRITHJOF SCHUON

Born in Basle, Switzerland in 1907, Frithjof Schuon was the twentieth century's pre-eminent spokesman for the perennialist school of comparative religious thought.

The leitmotif of Schuon's work was foreshadowed in an encounter during his youth with a marabout who had accompanied some members of his Senegalese village to Basle for the purpose of demonstrating their African culture. When Schuon talked with him, the venerable old man drew a circle with radii on the ground and explained: "God is the center; all paths lead to Him." Until his later years Schuon traveled widely, from India and the Middle East to America, experiencing traditional cultures and establishing lifelong friendships with Hindu, Buddhist, Christian, Muslim, and American Indian spiritual leaders.

A philosopher in the tradition of Plato, Shankara, and Eckhart, Schuon was a gifted artist and poet as well as the author of over twenty books on religion, metaphysics, sacred art, and the spiritual path. Describing his first book, *The Transcendent Unity of Religions*, T. S. Eliot wrote, "I have met with no more impressive work in the comparative study of Oriental and Occidental religion", and world-renowned religion scholar Huston Smith said of Schuon, "The man is a living wonder; intellectually apropos religion, equally in depth and breadth, the paragon of our time". Schuon's books have been translated into over a dozen languages and are respected by academic and religious authorities alike.

More than a scholar and writer, Schuon was a spiritual guide for seekers from a wide variety of religions and backgrounds throughout the world. He died in 1998.

HARRY OLDMEADOW was, until his recent retirement, the Coordinator of Philosophy and Religious Studies at La Trobe University Bendigo. A widely respected author on the perennialist school, his publications include *Traditionalism: Religion in the Light of the Perennial Philosophy* (2000) and *Frithjof Schuon and the Perennial Philosophy* (2010). He has edited several anthologies for World Wisdom, the most recent being *Crossing Religious Frontiers* (2010), and has contributed to such journals as *Sophia* and *Sacred Web*. In addition to his studies of perennialism, he has written extensively on the modern encounter of Eastern and Western traditions in works such as *Journeys East: 20th Century Western Encounters with Eastern Religious Traditions* (2004) and *A Christian Pilgrim in India: The Spiritual Journey of Swami Abhishiktananda* (2008).